A PAULA A LA GIORNO DE
SUA QUARENTISSIMA COMPLIANNO.
SEPT 4. 1995.
22 MONTICELLO CREST

Dear Paula,
With love, gratitude
and prayers — for you to enjoy
and grow wisdom throughout
the next 40+ Priski Margaret

Jerry Mann

Buon Compleanno. Paula.

EMILIO ZIO Cesare

40? BIG DEAL!
Marco Madden

WERONKA
Happy 40th
Thanks for your
friendship & guidance

+ Kiron.
love + fishes
Karen

Paula: After 4 decades you
have become one of the
world's most gorgeous creatures.
I just hope I see you a couple
of decades from now.
Uncle Jim
Aunt Catherine

DON'T WORRY, IT DOES GET
BETTER.
Hayley Claudia
Giacomo

To Paula
My Senior, with all
due respect; Happy
Birthday. Love Ho
You and your youth.

LOVE,
Matt

Paula,
deAr
cousin,
Love
Always,
John
Mark

Love Chris
and Eve
and Madeleine

Paula,
Perhaps life is a spring
And Now...
Time to unwind

Xo
Dana.

Buon Compleanno
cara cugina
speriamo mille
da questi giorni.
amore Shawn
Jerry

THE
ITALIAN
GOURMET

Zia Fortunata

Happy Birthday Paula
"We Love You!"
Uncle
Chester & Aunt
Shirley

TO PAULA.
WHETHER MID LIFE OR
ANY OTHER CRISIS
THINK POSITIVE —
"LITTLE BIRDIE IN THE SKY
DROPPED SOME WHITEWASH IN MY EYE
I DIDN'T SWEAR, I DIDN'T CRY
I'M JUST GLAD COWS DON'T FLY"
DAD.

Happy 40th Paula
not as bad as anticipated
heh!
Love
Mom

Happy 40th Chula Vista
and a Chula Vista
to you!
Love Claude

THE
ITALIAN
GOURMET

GIORGIO MISTRETTA

AUTHENTIC INGREDIENTS AND
TRADITIONAL RECIPES FROM
THE KITCHENS OF ITALY

RAINCOAST BOOKS
VANCOUVER

Published in Canada by
Raincoast Book Distribution Ltd
112 East 3rd Avenue
Vancouver, BC V5T IC8

Canadian Cataloguing in Publication Data

Mistretta, Giorgio.
  The Italian gourmet

  (the Gourmet series)
  Includes index.
  ISBN 0-920417-13-2

  1. Cookery, Italian. I. Title. II. Series.
TX723.M58 1992   641.5945   C92-091259-1

Produced by Weldon Russell Pty Ltd
107 Union Street
North Sydney, NSW 2060 Australia

Publisher: Elaine Russell
Managing editor: Dawn Titmus
Senior editor: Ariana Klepac
Editorial assistant: Margaret Whiskin
Translator: Barbara McGilvray
US cooking consultant: Mardee Haidin Regan
Copy editor: Gill Hewett
Design concept: Judy Hungerford
Designers: Judy Hungerford, Kim Webber
Illustrators: Kathie Smith, Jan Smith
Food photographers: Carlo Cantini, Rowan Fotheringham,
  Andre Martin, Gian Luigi Scarfiotti
Food stylists: Lucy Andrews, Carolyn Fienberg, Fausto Monti
Proofreader: Jill Wayment
Indexer: Garry Cousins
Production: Jane Hazell

Typeset by Adtype , North Sydney, Australia
Produced by Mandarin Offset, Hong Kong
Printed in Hong Kong

A KEVIN WELDON PRODUCTION

Front cover: photographer Rowan Fotheringham, food stylist Suzie Smith

Back cover: Trenette alle Cozze e Zafferano (left, recipe page 42); Farfalle all'Astice (right, recipe page 43)

Endpapers: mandarins, photograph John Callanan

Opp. title page: photograph Ray Joyce

Title page: Fiori di Zucca Farciti alla Ricotta (left, recipe page 174); Zucchini a Scapece (right, recipe page 175)

Opp. contents: balsamic vinegars

Acquacotta (left, recipe page 77); Garmugia Lucchese (right, recipe page 77)

CONTENTS

INTRODUCTION

INTRODUCTION

ITALY IS A COUNTRY FAMED THROUGHOUT THE WORLD NOT ONLY FOR ITS HISTORY, ITS ART TREASURES AND ITS IMMENSE ARCHEOLOGICAL heritage, but also for its cuisine. Yet in spite of appearances, Italian cuisine in the usual sense of the term is a relatively recent phenomenon. Up to the beginning of the 1950s in fact, there was no such thing as "the Italian table," for the country's food traditions were subject to almost the same political and administrative divisions as its history. In other words, travelers would have been able to recognize which region they were in simply from the type of food they found: *agnolotti* and cheese fondue meant Piedmont and the Valle d'Aosta; if the risotto came to the table with saffron in it, there could be no doubt they were in Milan, but if that same risotto came without the saffron and contained frogs' legs, it meant they had reached Pavia; finally, a soft white risotto with butter and Parmesan would suggest the city of Parma. The same goes for the rest of Italy: the fragrance of basil in Liguria, of wild fennel in Sicily, the tomato sauce of Naples, and so on.

¶ The reasons for such clear gastronomic divisions are to be found in the produce typical of each individual area and in the deep diversity of usages and customs between one region and another. For a better understanding of this

Previous pages: The fashionable cafés of Piazza San Marco in Venice are the perfect location to sample Italy's superb coffee. JOHN CALLANAN

Opposite: In the Italian coffee bar customers drink their espresso, cappuccino or macchiato standing at the bar. The bars usually sell panini (sandwiches) and other snacks, too. PISTOLESI/ACTION PRESS

concept, it should be remembered that when the unified Italy was born in 1861, only 600,000 Italians out of a total population of 25 million could speak the national language. The others spoke only the dialect of their particular region. The same kind of difference was noticeable in the various regional cooking styles. The use of pasta, customary in the south, was practically unknown in the north: a Piedmontese recipe book published in Turin around 1850 gave instructions for cooking macaroni (which everyone knows is ready to eat after 8–10 minutes of boiling) together with a chicken, and serving it only when the chicken was ready. In Lombardy, Piedmont and the Veneto, for example, the most prominent foods in the daily diet were rice and corn; the corn could be ground into flour to make that "poor" dish known as polenta, which was capable of absorbing and enhancing the flavors of richer ingredients.

¶ These cooking and eating habits, jealously guarded for centuries within the bounds of ancestral traditions, are all at the base of modern Italian cuisine. Time and the evolution of Italian taste towards lighter foods, plus the genuine triumph of the so-called Mediterranean diet, whose secrets of success are found in the products of the Italian soil, have enabled intelligent cooks and restaurants to take ancient dishes and revise and modify them, presenting them in new ways without radically changing their flavor.

¶ While the recipes gathered in this volume take into account the great Italian regional traditions, for the most part they belong to the new and decidedly modern direction being taken by Italian cuisine — using fewer animal fats and more careful cooking methods, and abandoning almost entirely the heavy sauces of the old days. What we are presenting is today's Italian cuisine as it is offered by the country's most talented chefs at its most advanced restaurants.

❧ A trip around Italy can be the source of some extraordinary and unexpected experiences in putting together a comprehensive and reliable panorama of Italian gastronomy today. A few gastronomic islands deserve a place of honor in an imaginary "tour by the palate." The first, beginning in the north and moving south, is in Piedmont, around the town of Alba, more or less halfway between Turin and the border with Liguria. This is the Langhe, distinctive for its hills covered in chestnut and walnut forests interrupted by steep cliffs, and for its gently undulating expanses of vines. It is not a very large area; a comprehensive tour would cover no more than about 60 miles (100 km), but they are the richest 60 miles in Italy, as far as food and drink are concerned.

❧ Truffles and Barolo wine are the first two items that come to mind, but if we are speaking of wine we should add Barbaresco, Nebbiolo, Barbera and Dolcetto, and in the case of food, *agnolotti* and *tagliolini pasta*, *porcini* and *ovoli* mushrooms, game, *torrone* and a hundred other things.

❧ A basic feature of Langhe cuisine is the wealth of antipasto dishes. Pasta is preceded by a taste of at least ten different things: anchovies with herbs, cold veal with anchovy sauce, liver pâté, soused zucchinis (courgettes) and eggs, bell peppers (capsicums) coated with *bagna cauda* (a sauce made with anchovies, oil and garlic), raw and cooked salamis, mini-sausages, tiny fresh cheeses, and so the list goes on.

❧ *Agnolotti* and *tagliolini* are classic pasta courses and are followed by an assortment of roast or stewed meats. Curiously enough, at the conclusion of the meal there are no cakes or tarts, as in the rest of Italy, only cream or chocolate puddings or a mixture of fruit and sweet flavors such as baked peaches with amaretto.

❧ Heading south, no gastronome can bypass Parma. No other Italian city is so closely bound to its eating traditions; indeed, much of Parma's present wealth has been built on its gastronomic resources. The city is most renowned for two products: its ham and its sublime cheese,

Parmesan. Oddly enough, the one product is a direct consequence of the other. Whey, a by-product of cheesemaking is also an important food for pigs. In the nearby hills of Langhirano countless legs of pork are hung, duly treated with salt and spices, and are caressed during the required seasoning period by the steady breeze from the Apennines.

❧ At lunch in Parma, when the overture of *prosciutto* or *culatello* (cured loin of pork) is over, there is an embarrassment of choice for the next course. Will it be *anolini*, *tortelli* or *bomba*? The decision is a difficult one. The *bomba* is a baked rice mold enriched with a sumptuous pigeon sauce. *Tortelli*, a kind of herb-stuffed ravioli, constitute a delicious signal to herald the arrival of good weather. Never did a ritual dish fit so well with the convivial spirit of a city than when these *tortelli* are eaten on the night of June 23 each year. Staying up until dawn is obligatory, in order to touch the "St John's dew" in the fields for good luck.

❧ *Tortelli* are very easily made: young beet (beetroot) greens are cut straight from the garden, blanched, sautéed in butter, minced, mixed with ricotta, Parmesan and egg and enclosed in morsels of egg pasta. They are boiled in water and then dressed with butter and Parmesan.

❧ With *anolini* the story is more complex. The true natives of Parma are very jealous of this wonderful filled pasta of theirs. And rightly so. Unlike all the other Italian filled pastas that contain some meat, an *anolino* contains just the merest hint, an allusion, the idea of a filling, which results in an exhilarating lightness, a delicate, subtle taste that is impossible to duplicate. Just the thought that there is no meat within, only the cooking essence of a superbly rich beef stew together with Parmesan cheese that has been aged for at least two years, conveys some idea of the elegance of this dish. The classic *anolino* is eaten swimming in its cooking stock.

❧ After a small fish course the attention turns to a delicious meat course. From the tradition of family cuisine comes *stracotto di manzo* (braised beef). The braised beef that gave up its cooking juices for the *anolini* filling now serves as a main course. Of wealthier origin (for not everyone could afford such an abundance of meat) is the

Lemons form an integral part of Italian cuisine, and are used in savory as well as sweet dishes. JOHN CALLANAN

bollito misto (mixed boiled meats). This is found right along the Po Valley area from Piedmont to the Veneto, but in Parma it takes on a personality of its own, thanks to a special combination of ingredients. To achieve perfection, the large tray of boiled meats must include calf's head, stuffed capon, tongue, beef, breast of veal, the fresh pork sausages known as *cotechino* and *zampone* (this one packed into a pig's leg), pork spareribs, pig's trotters and cooked ham.

❡ From Parma and the Emilia region we cross the Apennines to Florence. One feature of Tuscan eating is immediately obvious: there is virtually no dried pasta. The components of a typical regional menu might include *ribollita* (a Florentine soup of white beans, vegetables, olive oil, bread and cheese), tripe, risotto black with cuttlefish ink, rabbit, pigeon, steak — dishes of worker or peasant origin (except the last one) that distinguish Florentine cuisine today.

❡ Florence was indisputably the cradle of a great aristocratic cuisine flourishing at court and in the palaces of the nobility, but it was also the first city to bring together into a guild all the workers in the various food sectors. The butchers', bakers', oil-mill workers', vintners' and grocers' branches of the guild always ensured that supplies were strictly controlled according to very precise regulations. This led to the creation of a gastronomy that over time has lost its class-based distinctions and come to be completely identified with the city and the Tuscan region.

❡ Today all over Tuscany you will find connoisseurs ready to recommend the *ribollita* at this restaurant, the *pappa al pomodoro* (tomato soup) at that one, and so on. Tuscan cooking is a truly frugal cuisine that has scaled the heights of popularity simply because it is so basic. The background to every dish is the superb oil from the olive trees that alternate on the Tuscan hills with expanses of vines and neatly cultivated fields. Consequently, Tuscan cooks have a sort of natural talent for frying, and you can easily confirm this by ordering a mixed fry of rabbit and artichoke, for example, or brains and zucchini (courgette) flowers.

❡ Two other regions blessed with special culinary features are found in the extreme south: Apulia to the east, Sicily to the west. Apulia, the heel of the boot, is a vast reservoir of culinary riches that the rest of Italy draws from. At least nine out of every ten fruit-sellers in Milan are from this region. Every evening thousands of trucks set out from the Apulian countryside along the Adriatic freeway, and by dawn the produce picked the previous day is being unloaded in the northern markets. With a very fertile soil and favorable climate, Apulia produces everything: durum wheat, tomatoes, table grapes, artichokes, radicchio, bell peppers (capsicums), onions, lettuce, fennel and a magnificent, strong-flavored olive oil.

❡ With this as a starting point, plus a sea teeming with fish, and free pastures for sheep and cattle resulting in a production of fresh dairy foods that is unique in Europe, Apulian cooking becomes a simple matter, relying on the harmonious blending of the complex range of local tastes and flavors.

❡ Lunch in Apulia begins with cheeses: mozzarellas large and small, *burrini* (little spheres of cheese wrapped around a nut of butter), miniature *caciotte* (little round buffalo-milk cheeses), and especially that unique miracle among cheeses, *burrata di Andria* — a delicate, creamy-textured cheese surrounded by a coating of soft mild cheese. It continues with a pasta of your choice, lasagne (still called here by the Latin name, *lagane*), *orecchiette* or "little ears," macaroni of all shapes and sizes, all with a variety of sauces. The two most traditional sauces are turnip tops sautéed with garlic and oil, and the rich, highly flavored cooking juices from *involtini* (meat rolls), known in this region as *brasciole*.

❡ Apulian cooking is similar to the cuisine of the wider Mediterranean world, which is understandable, for this region stretches out eastward into the ocean and has always been a natural landing place for ships coming from Egypt and Asia Minor. Puréed fava (broad) beans, for example, which are found also in Sicily, are Egyptian in origin, and the numerous dishes made with chickpeas and assorted meat and vegetable mixtures, either baked in the oven or stewed, recall similar Middle Eastern and North African dishes.

❡ The extraordinary cuisine of Sicily is even richer in its contacts with the rest of the Mediterranean. "If there is fragrance issuing from a house, it means incense is sold there, or else the cook is Sicilian," wrote Cratinus of Athens in the

Much of Italy's fruit and vegetable produce is grown in Apulia, the fertile "heel" of Italy. WALTER LEONARDI/APL

fifth century. Everyone — from the Phoenicians to the Normans, from the Arabs to the Greeks, from the Byzantines to the Bourbons, and finally the Piedmontese — left something behind to contribute.

¶ The dominant motif everywhere is pasta, interpreted in a thousand ways. Sicily is the site of pasta's paternity. The Arab geographer Idrisi, who lived at the court of Ruggero II in the first half of the twelfth century, described the production of vermicelli on the plains of Trabia, not far from Palermo, where shiploads of it were leaving "to supply not only the countries of Calabria, but also those of the Muslim and Christian worlds."

¶ Outstanding among Sicilian pasta dishes are the *bucatini con le sarde* of Palermo, with the flavors of wild fennel, fresh sardines, pine nuts, almonds, golden raisins, anchovies and saffron; the *spaghetti alla Norma* of Catania, and above all *timballo di maccheroni*, a dish of very ancient origin. Mohammed Ibn Timnah, Emir of Catania, described it thus: a loaf of bread halved, stuffed with a chicken that has been browned in oil and herbs, cooked slowly in stock, boned and chopped up small, and mixed with almonds, pistachio nuts, capers, parsley, egg and lemon. In the modern version the bread is replaced by a sweet shortcrust pastry, while macaroni and sausage, sweetbreads, tomatoes, onions and other ingredients are added to enrich the already sumptuous filling.

¶ The triumphant finish to any Sicilian lunch is the local confectionery, rising to the level of the sublime: little marzipan fruits created in the cloistered convents of Palermo; cassata, *cannoli* filled with ricotta and candied fruits; soft honey and sesame-seed nougat still bearing the Arab name *cubbaita*. Their color, fragrance and taste bear the legacy of a centuries-old art carried all over the world by Sicilian pastry chefs. And it was a native of Catania, Procopius of the Knives, who first served gelato in his Café Procope, destined to become a historic meeting place in Paris during the Enlightenment. The recipe for gelato remains unaltered, and the world has greeted it with the admiration and respect that is warranted by inimitable craftsmanship.

ANTIPASTI

A N T I P A S T I

TRADITIONALLY, ITALIAN *ANTIPASTO* — THE TERM CORRESPONDS TO THE FRENCH *HORS D'OEUVRE* AND THE ENGLISH "APPETIZER" — is not part of the family's main daily meal, which is generally very simple and limited to a first course of soup or pasta, a main dish of meat or, more rarely, fish with a vegetable accompaniment, and fresh fruit and coffee to finish. On the other hand, one cannot imagine a formal Italian dinner beginning without an *antipasto*.

¶ The most famous of all Italian *antipasto* dishes is undoubtedly *prosciutto*, often served alone, accompanied by melon or figs when these are in season, but also presented on large trays together with an assortment of sliced meats *(salumi)*.

¶ The leader of the field in this area is Piedmont. A formal Piedmontese dinner will include no less than ten or fifteen different *antipasti*, often more. As well as *prosciutto*, various types of salami and *coppa*, there will be hard-cooked eggs stuffed and coated with mayonnaise; stuffed bell peppers (capsicums); morsels of pâté; a salad of raw meat,

Previous pages: This shop window displays several of the cured meats commonly served as affettato *(sliced meats), a popular antipasto dish. The meats shown include* prosciutto *(cured ham)* speck *(smoked ham),* coppa *and* pancetta *(cured pork) and* salame felino *(salami from Felino).* CRALLE/ACTION PRESS

Opposite: Italians use a total of 130,000 tons (tonnes) of olives annually for cooking. In addition to their use in olive oil, olives are served as an antipasto and used as an ingredient in many dishes such as puttanesca *pasta sauce.* AUSTRALIAN PICTURE LIBRARY/OLYMPIA

ground (minced) and mixed with oil and herbs; and raw meat sliced wafer-thin and served with slivers of Parmesan cheese or with fresh *porcini* or *ovoli* mushrooms and, in fall, with white truffles.

¶ Other regions are not far behind: in Liguria the stuffed vegetables are famous — zucchini (courgettes), eggplants (aubergines), onions, tomatoes, bell peppers (capsicums) — with fillings made from the vegetable pulp mixed with Parmesan, breadcrumbs, garlic and marjoram. In Tuscany dinner begins with the classic *bruschetta*, a slice of unsalted homemade bread toasted on the broiler (grill), spread with garlic and covered with olive oil, tomato slices and basil leaves. In Lombardy a classic *antipasto* is made with small slices of boiled sturgeon with a little olive oil and some liver pâté. In Emilia, probably as a legacy of the large Hebrew settlements established in this region, there are various interpretations of the theme of unleavened bread. The *piadina* of Romagna, a flat circle of dough cooked on a hotplate and eaten with ham or fresh cheese, is served both as an *antipasto* and as a mid-afternoon snack in the country. The same is true of the *chizze* of Reggio Emilia, consisting of two small thin sheets of pastry filled with Parmesan cheese and fried; and of the Modene *tigelle*, like *chizze* but with salt pork not cheese.

¶ Modern Italian gastronomy has been much infuenced by an emphasis on taste which has led to an increase in the range of foods available. This abundance of choice is reflected in today's Italian *antipasti*.

BOTTARGA E PATATE

FISH ROE WITH POTATOES

The term bottarga *refers to pressed and dried fish eggs. Sliced very thin, it is always served as an antipasto, accompanied by slices of tomato or potato. Bottarga is produced mainly in Sardinia, and to a lesser degree along the Ligurian coast and in Sicily.*

2 or 3 medium potatoes
3 oz (90 g) bottarga *(mullet or tuna roe)*
olive oil

SERVES 4

¶ Cook the potatoes in their skins in plenty of lightly salted boiling water. When they are cooked, peel and cut into fairly thick slices.

Arrange the slices in the center of a serving plate. Place a few slivers of *bottarga* on top and drizzle a thin stream of olive oil over. Serve at once.

BOTTARGA

This is the ovarian sac of fish, which is extracted whole from the female as soon as she is caught. There are two types: the more common is tuna, but the eggs of the gray mullet that are found in abundance in the brackish waters of Oristano are more highly prized. The eggs are salted and placed under weights to compress and dry them; then they are hung in the shade to dry in the sea breeze. The ageing process takes four or five months.

Bottarga e Patate

Top left: Ascolane olives; top right: Italian olives; bottom left: Gaeta olives; bottom right: Sicilian olives

OLIVES

The entire Mediterranean reserves a sacred place for the olive. In southern Italy, as in Greece, offering a guest bread and olives is considered the most significant of all welcoming rituals. Apart from its appearance in many legends (according to Hebrew tradition, it was one of the three trees that sprouted from seeds placed in Adam's mouth after his death — the other two were a cedar and a cypress), the olive tree has always captured the imagination because of its longevity. The specimen that still stands today in the Garden of Gethsemane in Jerusalem, believed to be 3,000 years old, is well known; but in Italy there is one known as *l'ulivo della strega* (the witch's olive tree) in Grosseto, that is said to be 3,500 years old.

In addition to the production of oil, olives are also used in cooking (in Liguria, Tuscany and the south they are part of many dishes using smoked cod, rabbit or stewed lamb) and as a tasty accompaniment for drinks or as part of a plate of antipasti.

Consumption of table olives is widespread in Italy, and constantly increasing. Of a total of over 300,000 tons (about 300,000 tonnes) of olives produced annually in Europe, Italians eat almost half.

Generally preserved in brine or oil, the olives most commonly used for preserving are the small dark-colored Ligurian *taggiasca*; the large attractive bright green ones from Apulia or Ascoli Piceno (in the Marches region); Gaeta olives, which are black; the black or green varieties flavored with bay leaf, chili pepper or other additions according to the region that produces them; and *olive conciate*, crushed and pickled with onions, fennel, celery, oregano, thyme, chili pepper and other ingredients.

One way to preserve olives is to soak them in water for 10 days, changing the water every two days, then drain the olives. Prepare brine for preserving the olives by bringing to a boil sufficient water to cover them, to which salt has been added — 3 oz (90 g) salt are needed for 4 cups (1 qt/1 l) of water — then remove from the heat.

When the water is cool pour it over the olives, cover the container and store in a dark place. After 20 days the olives will be ready to use.

CROSTINI DI ALICI

ANCHOVY TOAST

All along the coast from the Tyrrhenian to the Ionian and the Adriatic Sea, small anchovies are marinated in lemon juice or vinegar and offered along with many other antipasto dishes. This dish is a typical example from the Abruzzi/Molise coast between Pescara and Vasto, where the presence of chili pepper among the ingredients is very important.

9 oz (280 g) fresh anchovy or sardine fillets
1 cup (8 fl oz/250 ml) wine vinegar
1 garlic clove, minced
1 tablespoon dried oregano
⅓ cup (3 fl oz/90 ml) extra-virgin olive oil
salt
ground chili pepper (to taste)
4 slices coarse-textured bread

SERVES 4

❡ Marinate the anchovies in a deep dish in just enough vinegar to cover for about 10 minutes. (Canned anchovies may be used, but rinse well under running water, then dry and bypass the vinegar step.) Drain thoroughly. Put them on a plate and sprinkle with the garlic, oregano, olive oil, salt and chili pepper.
❡ Toast the bread slices, place on a serving plate and arrange the prepared anchovies on each slice while still hot. Serve at once.

GUAZZETTO DI FRUTTI DI MARE SU FETTUNTA

SEAFOOD STEW ON GARLIC TOAST

This recipe brings together two Tuscan traditions: the fisherman-style seafood stew and the bruschetta or crostini of the farm kitchen.

8 small squid
8 mussels
13 oz (410 g) small clams
2 teaspoons butter
1 tablespoon olive oil
1 tablespoon chopped shallot
1 cup (8 fl oz/250 ml) dry white wine
½ cup (4 fl oz/125 ml) heavy (double) cream
2 cups (16 fl oz/500 ml) fish stock
½ teaspoon saffron threads or ¼ teaspoon ground
   saffron
salt and white pepper
32 medium shrimp (prawns), shelled and deveined
1 red bell pepper (capsicum), cut into small dice
1 tablespoon chopped flat-leafed parsley
8 slices coarse-textured bread, each 1 × 3 in
   (2.5 × 7.5 cm), toasted and rubbed with garlic
additional olive oil, for the toast

SERVES 4

❡ Clean the squid and make a cross-shaped cut in the mantle of each one for three-quarters of its length. This has the effect of opening them up like flowers during cooking.
❡ Steam the mussels until they open. Remove the meat, reserving their liquid and discarding the shells. Strain the reserved liquid. Prepare the clams in the same manner as the mussels.
❡ In a large skillet, combine the butter and olive oil. Add the shallot and sauté until golden. Add the mussel liquid, wine, cream, fish stock, saffron, and salt and pepper to taste. Mix well and cook for a few minutes.
❡ Add the squid, mussels, clams, shrimp, bell pepper and parsley to the skillet, and cook for 2 or 3 more minutes on low heat, stirring a couple of times as it cooks.
❡ Drizzle a thin stream of olive oil over the slices of toast. Place 2 slices on each plate, cover with the seafood stew, and serve.

SFOGI IN SAOR

SOUSED SOLE

This is an elegant version of the classic, uniquely Venetian sarde in saor, soused sardines. The substitution of small sole in place of sardines creates a lighter antipasto dish which has a more delicate flavor than the traditional version.

all-purpose (plain) flour, for dusting
2 lb (1 kg) small whole sole, cleaned
vegetable oil, for deep-frying
2 lb (1 kg) onions
2 cups (16 fl oz/500 ml) olive oil
1 cup (8 fl oz/250 ml) white wine vinegar
2 cups (16 fl oz/500 ml) dry white wine
½ cup (3 oz/90 g) golden raisins (sultanas)
½ cup (2 oz/60 g) pine nuts
2 bay leaves
pinch of white peppercorns
pinch of salt

SERVES 4–6

Clockwise from top: Crostini di Alici, Sfogi in Saor, Guazzetto di Frutti di Mare su Fettunta

❧ Lightly flour the fish. Deep-fry the fish in hot oil for 3 to 4 minutes or until golden.

❧ In a medium saucepan, combine the onions and olive oil and cook until the onions are lightly browned. Add the vinegar, wine, raisins, pine nuts, bay leaves, peppercorns and salt. Stir thoroughly and cook for 15 minutes.

❧ Layer the fried sole in a deep dish, alternating with layers of the sauce. Set aside to rest for several hours before serving.

PROSCIUTTO

The word *prosciutto* comes from the Latin *proexucatus*, meaning deprived of all liquid. This type of ham is a pride of Italian gastronomy and has very ancient origins.

To emphasize the difference between the air-dried ham and the one — cooked and at times smoked — more readily available throughout the world, the Italian language defines them as *prosciutto* crudo ("raw ham") and *prosciutto cotto* ("cooked ham"). However, it has become customary to simply call the more popular air-dried variety, *prosciutto*, and to add the clarifying word *cotto* only when requesting the cooked type.

Prosciutto is the leg of the pig that has been treated with a mixture of salt and spices and left to age in well-aired surroundings. The average maturing time varies from 14 to 16 months, reaching 18 months and even more for hams of the very highest quality.

SAN DANIELE AND PARMA PROSCIUTTO

Air-dried hams are produced in just about every Italian region but the two main types are from Parma and San Daniele. The best examples of both types are highly prized by experts and gourmets, who dispute which of the two *prosciutti* is superior.

Both take their names from the places where they are made.

Parma *prosciutto* is processed and aged in the Sub-Apennines around the city of Parma, and especially in the town of Langhirano.

San Daniele *prosciutto* is produced at San Daniele in Friuli, not far from Udine, near the foothills of the Carnic Alps, and differs from Parma *prosciutto* in both shape and processing.

Before ageing, the ham is placed under a weight which flattens it and forces out most of the moisture. Another difference is that in San Daniele *prosciutto* the whole of the pig's leg is processed, including the shin and trotter, whereas in the production of Parma *prosciutto* the thigh is cut off where it joins the shin. Both types, however, are distinguished by their fine fragrance and wonderfully sweet flavor. Some experts consider San Daniele slightly more delicate, and some say this is due to the frequent summer storms that lash the San Daniele area, constantly alternating the air between very dry and relatively humid, and giving the meat a kind of gentle hydrothermic massage that accentuates even further its particular characteristics.

A good *prosciutto* must be light pink in color, and the most prized examples (aged for 18 to 24 months) tend toward a deeper though still soft pink, with a hint of orange in the case of San Daniele.

Ham-making is an age-old art in Italy. Precise information regarding San Daniele ham is found in a fifteenth-century manuscript by Maestro Martino, the cook to the Patriarch of Aquileia. The production of the most highly prized hams is protected by regula-

tions set down by co-operatives formed to safeguard the typical features of the product. In Parma, for example, legs weighing less than 22 pounds (10 kg) may not be used.

The final word on the superiority of San Daniele *prosciutto* over Parma *prosciutto*, or vice versa, has not yet been written, and probably never will!

What can be said is that a few paper-thin slices of either one (freshly cut and preserving a fine rim of fat) enjoyed with fresh figs — or with slices of a sweet honeydew melon or cantaloupe (rockmelon) — are certainly one of life's pleasant luxuries!

TUSCAN AND BOAR PROSCIUTTO

In Tuscany and in Umbria (Norcia in particular) hams of a different type are produced. Here, the legs come from leaner pigs which often have been crossed with boars and the result is the distinctly "saltier" taste of *prosciutto toscano*.

The boar ham or *prosciutto di cinghiale* is in widespread use in Tuscan households in particular, thanks to the plentiful colonies of boar found in the woods of this region, and also due to the presence of proper small-scale breeding farms where the boars are reared in the wild state within special enclosures. The ham they produce has a much more distinctive flavor

and the leg is not skinned but retains its characteristic rind thick with bristles.

BRESAOLA AND CULATELLO

Bresaola, typical of the Valtellina area at the northern end of Lake Como, is beef that has been cured with salt and spices and aged in a special net. It is eaten in thin slices with olive oil, lemon juice and pepper. This dish is called *carpaccio di bresaola*.

Another member of the *prosciutto* family is *culatello*. This is considered the finest and most prestigious of all Italian *salumi*. Produced in a limited area around Parma including the towns of Zebello, San Secondo and Polesine Parmense on the Po River plains, this *prosciutto* is made from the best part of the rump.

The leg is rubbed with salt and spices while still warm (in other words, immediately after the pig is slaughtered), wrapped in pieces of salt pork, tied up tightly in the pig's

bladder, and placed in a well-ventilated cellar to mature.

In contrast to *prosciutto*, which needs the fresh breeze from the hills, *culatello* is aged in flatlands that are subject to mists. After a year the ham is wrapped in a cloth dampened with white wine for several days. After that, the skin and fat are completely removed and the ham is served cut into wafer-thin slices.

Finally there are the much rarer hams made from the haunches of goats, chamois or deer in the Alpine areas of the Valle d'Aosta and the Valtellina to the north of Turin and Milan. They are called *violini di Chiavenna*, which reflects the way they are held under the chin, like a violin, when being sliced.

1. prosciutto di San Daniele;
2. prosciutto di cinghiale;
3. prosciutto toscano;
4. prosciutto di Parma;
5. bresaola; 6. culatello

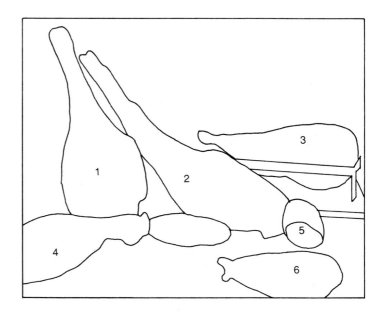

OLIVE RIPIENE ALL'ASCOLANA

ASCOLI-STYLE STUFFED OLIVES

This dish comes from Ascoli Piceno in the Marches, a region largely characterized by the cultivation of olives; The big, flavorful olives produced in the area are preserved in brine, then pitted and stuffed with a filling similar to the one used for ravioli and tortellini, *after which they are crumbed and deep-fried.*

4 oz (125 g) salt pork, finely ground (minced)
3 tablespoons olive oil
3 oz (90 g) lean beef, ground (minced)
5 oz (155 g) lean pork, ground (minced)
2 tablespoons tomato juice
4 chicken livers
⅔ cup (3 oz/90 g) stale bread without crust
1 cup (8 fl oz/250 ml) meat stock
3 eggs
⅓ cup (50 g) freshly grated Parmesan cheese
pinch of freshly grated nutmeg
¼ teaspoon ground cinnamon
salt and freshly ground pepper
60 extra-large green olives, pitted
1 cup (4 oz/125 g) all-purpose (plain) flour
⅔ cup (3 oz/90 g) dry breadcrumbs
vegetable oil, for deep-frying
2 lemons

SERVES 6

❡ In a large skillet, combine the salt pork with the olive oil and fry gently for about 20 seconds. Add the beef and pork and cook until they begin to brown. Add the tomato juice diluted with 1 tablespoon of warm water, reduce the heat to moderate and cook for about 20 minutes, or until the meat is cooked through. If the preparation becomes dry add a small quantity of warm water. Add the chicken livers and cook for 5 minutes.
❡ Remove the meat and liver from the pan and chop the liver finely. Transfer to a bowl and mix in the cooking juices. Soak the bread in the stock. Squeeze thoroughly. Add the bread and 1 beaten egg to the bowl containing the meat. Stir in the Parmesan and flavor with the nutmeg, cinnamon, and salt and pepper to taste. Mix the stuffing mixture well. Fill each olive with some of the stuffing.
❡ Dip each olive in the flour. Break the remaining 2 eggs into a bowl and beat with a fork. Immerse the olives in the egg, then take them out and dip them in the breadcrumbs. Deep-fry the olives in piping hot oil then drain on paper towels and serve hot, garnished with the lemon.

INSALATA DI MARE

SEAFOOD SALAD

This is a refined version of a popular Mediterranean-style dish traditionally containing garlic, onion, capers and anchovies. By adding only olive oil, however, the marriage of the unmistakable flavor of the artichoke with the delicate seafood tastes is enhanced.

salt
4 red mullet fillets
4 sole fillets
1 John Dory fillet
8 small squid, cleaned
8 large shrimp (king prawns), shelled and deveined
6 oz (185 g) small octopus (sea strawberries), cut up
2 young artichokes, trimmed and with chokes removed
¼ cup (2 fl oz/60 ml) extra-virgin olive oil

SERVES 4

❡ Place 5 cups (1¼ qt/1.25 l) of water in a large saucepan. Add a pinch of salt and bring water to a boil. Place a strainer over the water and, working in batches as necessary, steam the fish fillets, squid, shrimp and octopus in the covered saucepan until just cooked through (about 5 minutes). Drain.
❡ Cut the uncooked artichokes into very thin slices and arrange them on 4 plates. Add to each plate, in the order given, a mullet fillet, a sole fillet, 2 squid, 2 shrimp, a portion of octopus and a slice of John Dory fillet. Scatter a little salt on top and sprinkle with olive oil. Serve warm.

Top: Olive Ripiene all'Ascolana; bottom: Insalata di Mare

CHEESE SERVED AS ANTIPASTI

In general only fresh cheeses feature in Italian antipasto selections. In Piedmont, and to a lesser extent in Lombardy, a single variety is offered, a cylindrical goat's cheese about 1½ inches (4 centimeters) long and more or less the same in diameter called *tomino*, which is eaten with olive oil and pepper. From central Italy down to the south the variety is much greater, and sometimes the fresh cheeses are embellished in the kitchen. Such is the case with mozzarella, which may be presented at the table whole or in various shapes such as *bocconcini* (small and spherical) and *trecce* (plaited), or

as the classic *mozzarella in carrozza*, slices sandwiched between two pieces of bread, dipped in beaten egg and bread-crumbs and then fried and *mozzarella di bufala*. It also features in fillings for various types of *panzerotti*, wafers of fresh pasta cut into circles and then folded into half-moons over a filling that also includes tomato; these are then fried or baked in the oven.

For the real triumph in Italian fresh cheeses we must go to Apulia and Campania where there are genuine specialties that cannot be reproduced. The buffalo-milk mozzarella produced in the Cilento area south of

Naples is famous; so are the *caciotte*, little round cheeses from the farms of Apulia, and the *burrini*, little spheres of cheese wrapped around a nut of pure butter. The queen of all dairy products in the region is the *burrata di Andria*. About the same size as a mozzarella, its exterior is simply a coating of soft, mild cheese that surrounds another delicate, creamy textured cheese that has barely curdled. The flavor is superb, and it is a great pity this cheese cannot be exported. In fact, it must be eaten within 24 hours of being made. After that it begins to harden and loses its characteristic fragrance.

It is served as a starter for restaurant lunches throughout most of Apulia, but especially in the country areas around Foggia and Bari.

Pecorino, produced in every region of central and southern Italy, is made from ewe's milk (some cheeses are also made from goat's milk — *formaggia di capra*). The best-known varieties of Pecorino are *Pecorino romano* (from Rome), *Pecorino toscano* (from Tuscany) and *Pecorino sardo* (from Sardinia).

Pecorino romano is hard after long ageing (known as *stagionato*) and can also be used for grating over many local dishes. *Pecorino sardo* can be eaten two weeks after being made. It is a very tasty cheese, slightly salty and piquant. Some of the Pecorino cheeses from Sardinia are also smoked. *Pecorino toscano* is also ripe after two weeks when the inside is very creamy; it is then the most delicate of all the varieties.

1. Sardinian Pecorino; 2. mozzarella; 3. caciotta; 4. Roman and Tuscan Pecorino; 5. mozzarella made from buffalo's milk; 6. matured Pecorino; 7. goat's cheese; 8. mozzarella plaited cheese

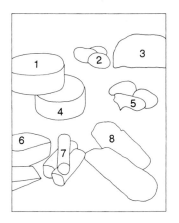

FAGIOLI CON GAMBERETTI E BOTTARGA

WHITE BEANS WITH SHRIMP AND BOTTARGA

This dish comes from the Tuscan coastal area between Viareggio and Livorno, where beans are cultivated and there is an active shrimp (prawn) industry. Once typical family fare, it then moved into the restaurant kitchen and today, partly because of its typically Mediterranean features, its success has spread throughout Italy.

2½ cups (8 oz/250 g) cooked small white (navy) beans
5 oz (155 g) shrimp (prawns), cooked and shelled
1 ripe tomato, finely chopped

¼ cup (1 oz/30 g) grated bottarga *(pressed dried roe of tuna)*
extra-virgin olive oil
salt
SERVES 4

❡ Combine all the ingredients in a salad bowl. Take care in checking for salt, as the *bottarga* will contribute to the saltiness of the mixture. Serve warm or cold.
Note: For a richer dish, the shrimp may be replaced by crayfish or langoustines (about 2 lb/1 kg total weight). Some tender salad greens may also be added.

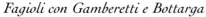

Fagioli con Gamberetti e Bottarga

Lombata d'Agnello "Tre Marie"

LOMBATA D'AGNELLO "TRE MARIE"

"THREE MARIAS" COLD LOIN OF LAMB

This dish can be served either cold, in paper-thin slices, or as a main course, presented hot and in larger portions. It is an example of the mountain fare typical of central Italy, where pastoral traditions and a rich peasant culture still survive.

2½ lb (1.2 kg) loin of milk-fed lamb,
   trimmed and boned
salt and freshly ground pepper
10 pistachio nuts, shelled
about 13 oz (410 g) pork tenderloin (fillet)
½ cup (4 fl oz/125 ml) extra-virgin olive oil
1 onion, finely chopped
1 carrot, finely chopped
2 cups (6 oz/185 g) cooked white (navy) beans
3 oz (90 g) small arugula (rocket lettuce) leaves

SERVES 8

¶ Preheat the oven to 425°F (220°C). Discard the lamb kidney. Flatten out the loin of lamb, skin side down, and season with salt and pepper.
¶ Insert the pistachio nuts here and there in the pork fillet; season with salt. Lay the pork on top of the lamb. Carefully roll the lamb around the pork.
¶ Salt the outside of the roll, tie it at regular intervals with kitchen string, brush well with olive oil and place in a baking dish with the onion and carrot mixed together.
¶ Put the dish in the oven and roast for 15 minutes. Reduce the heat to 350°F (170°C) and roast for about 1 hour, turning the meat from time to time. Meat is done when the juices run clear. Remove the roast from the oven and allow to cool.
¶ Dress the beans and arugula leaves with oil, salt and pepper.
¶ Cut the meat into thin slices and serve, garnished with the salad.

SALAMI

The term *salumi* is used in Italy for an extensive range of animal products, mostly obtained from the flesh of the pig but also sometimes from cattle, produced by salting and ageing in cool, well-ventilated surroundings. The large family of *salumi* is divided into three. The first includes salami, for which the meat is ground (minced) and mixed with spices and flavorings; the second covers other products in a casing where specific parts of the animal are left whole; and the third includes the so-called *salumi da cuocere*, pork products to be cooked.

There are numerous salamis, and the production (which the industry controls) is substantial. Salamis are composed of two parts ground lean meat to one part ground fat, although in some instances the fat is not ground but inserted as long, thin rectangular or square strips. The tradition of homemade salami still survives, with every farming family raising its own pig for domestic use, and this custom has produced a diversity of salami types that vary according to taste, tradition and local requirements. In the south, for example, where

the climate is warmer, hot chilies are added to the salami mixture for the dual purpose of enhancing the taste and preventing the development of harmful bacteria.

The most common Italian salamis take their names from the places where they are produced. Varzi in the Apennines, between Lombardy and Emilia, has two famous salamis, a traditional version and the small ones known as *cacciatori*. These firm salami got their name, meaning "hunters," because they were considered an ideal source of energy — easy

to carry and not perishable — by game lovers on hunting expeditions.

Felino, in the Parma hills, produces a well-known salami with elongated white patches. Similar to these two, in its rather coarse texture and obvious larding, is the one produced at Fabriano (in the Marches) where the celebrated *ciauscolo*, a very soft-textured salami for spreading on bread, is also produced. Quite different is the very finely textured Milan-style salami. Garlic and pepper are generally among the ingredients, but in the *finocchiona* of Tuscany the dominant flavor is provided by the fennel seeds liberally distributed through the meat.

The origins of Bologna's famous mortadella can be traced back to the second half of the fourteenth century and its name reflects the fact that the necessary ingredients were initially pounded in a mortar. To produce mortadella the meat is firstly reduced to a paste, then powdered milk and whole strips of pork fat are added before the mixture is flavored with spices, lightly smoked and stuffed into natural or manufactured gut.

The flavor of many varieties is enriched with the inclusion of whole black peppercorns, and the visual appeal of others is enhanced by the addition of green olives (stuffed with red bell pepper/capsicum) or green pistachio nuts. Nearly all good mortadellas have in common the long cylindrical shape (with a diameter of about 8 in/20 cm), the smooth texture, and a subtle flavoring of white wine and coriander.

Mortadella is the cheapest of the salamis and for this reason, as well as for its very fine texture and the fact that other ingredients are added to the pork meat to prepare it, it is considered a product in its own right, and a very popular one at that. By far the national bestseller of all kinds of *salumi*, mortadella is commonly

enjoyed — freshly sliced and full of fragrance — as part of a plate of *antipasto all'Italiana* (appetizer) or as a snack, as a filling for a *panino* (bread roll) or inside a slice of warm *pizza bianca* (a white pizza topped only with a sprinkling of olive oil and a few grains of coarse pepper).

A second group of *salumi* includes those made from meat that is processed in whole pieces rather than ground. Using the finest parts of the meat, the *coppa* of Piacenza and the *capocollo* from the south are both made from the end section of the fillet, running from the rump to the neck of the animal.

Soppressata must be considered a Tuscan specialty. The correct procedure for its preparation requires the competent blending — in galantine — of some of the soft parts of the pork's head with *lingua salmistrata* (specially treated and marinated morsels of tongue), and then seasoning with pepper, spices and pistachio nuts, before being encased in pigskin.

Particular parts of the shoulder or belly are used in Trentino and Alto Adige to make what could be described as a luxurious, rectangular-shaped, smoked ham called *"speck."* The manufacturers have their own secret formulas of spices and flavorings to be added to the brine in which the meat is left for some time. Usually these include bay leaf, nutmeg, juniper berries, cinnamon

and coriander, among others. The most delicate stage is the cold smoking for 10 days at a temperature no higher than 68°F (20°C), using pine and juniper wood. *Speck* is finally ready for eating after 20 weeks.

Another group of *salumi* is typified by three specialties from the Emilia region: the classical *cotechino*, the *zampone di Modena* (stuffed pig's trotters) and the not-so-well-known *salame da sugo*. Cotechino and zampone are both brought to the table after a lengthy boiling in water, and are normally served with a purée of potatoes, beans, spinach or sauerkraut.

In Rome — and in many other parts of Italy — it is imperative that these cooked *salumi* be served with lentils as an integral part of the sumptuous New Year's Eve dinner. There is an old belief that directly links the future prosperity of the diners with the quantity of lentils they consume at that special occasion!

For *salame da sugo*, made only in Ferrara, the best parts of the pig are ground (minced), mixed with spices and red wine and placed in the animal's bladder. After hanging for a year the sausage is suspended in the center of a large pan of water and boiled for at least 4 hours, then it is carried to the table where a cross is cut in the top of it. The filling is extracted through this opening and spooned onto a bed of potato purée. This very rich and tasty dish holds center stage at Christmas dinner in Ferrara.

1. *soppressata;* 2. *cacciatorini;*
3. *finocchiona toscana;*
4. *salame toscano;*
5. *soppressa veneta;* 6. *salame milano;* 7. *mortadella bologna;* 8. *pancetta;*
9. *salami caserecci;*
10. *salame milano aperto;*
11. *salame calabrese con peperoncino*

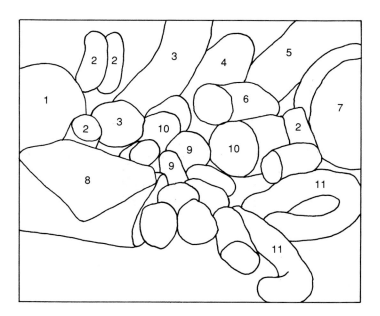

MELANZANE E LAVARELLO AFFUMICATO

EGGPLANT AND SMOKED FISH

The lavarello *is a fish typical of the Italian lakes, particularly Lake Maggiore. It is eaten fresh, smoked or sun-dried. In this dish the contrasting flavors of northern and southern Italy come together, as the fish is served alongside eggplant (aubergine) prepared according to a classic Sicilian recipe.*

1 medium eggplant (aubergine)
1¼ cups (10 fl oz/310 ml) extra-virgin olive oil
2 garlic cloves
2 bay leaves
4 smoked lavarello *or smoked trout, filleted*
For the mayonnaise:
1 egg yolk
¼ teaspoon salt
1 cup (8 fl oz/250 ml) extra-virgin olive oil
juice of 1 lemon or 1 tablespoon white wine vinegar
1 tablespoon chopped chives

SERVES 4

❡ Cut the eggplant into very small dice, leaving the skin on. In a saucepan or skillet, combine the olive oil, garlic and bay leaves. Set over high heat and bring to a boil. Add the diced eggplant and cook for 2 minutes. Remove from the heat, cover the pan and set aside in a warm place for 15 minutes.
❡ Meanwhile, make the mayonnaise. Place the egg yolk, salt, and a quarter of the olive oil in a blender. Turn it on and add the rest of the oil in a slow thin stream. Then add the lemon juice and mix in the chives. Taste, add extra salt, if necessary, and refrigerate.
❡ Arrange the smoked fish fillets on 4 individual plates. Mound some eggplant beside each, and add the mayonnaise. Serve with hot brown bread.

LAVARELLO IN CARPIONE

SWEET AND SOUR FISH

Carpione *applies to the method of preserving food in a more or less acidic marinating liquid that is enriched with vegetable flavors. Fish are traditionally fried and then immersed in the marinade. The following recipe belongs to the more modern school of Italian cooking. The fish is not fried but boiled, and no fats are used in the sauce, so that the dish is a light one.*

¾ cup (6 fl oz/180 ml) dry white wine
1⅔ cups (13 fl oz/410 ml) white wine vinegar
3 oz (90 g) onion, finely sliced
3 oz (90 g) carrot, cut into julienne strips
1 celery stalk, cut into julienne strips
1 leek, cleaned and finely chopped
2 oz (60 g) zucchini (courgettes), finely chopped
2 lb (1 kg) lavarello *or other small freshwater fish such as trout, tench, umber or perch*
1 teaspoon sugar

1 bay leaf
3 sage leaves
pinch of salt
pinch of peppercorns

SERVES 4

❡ In a large saucepan, bring the wine and vinegar to a boil. Place the onion, carrot, celery and leek into the pan and cook for 5–7 minutes, adding the zucchini for the last 2 minutes.

❡ Meanwhile, scale and fillet the fish. Roll up the fillets, skin-side out. Put the fillets in a skillet and pour the liquid and vegetables over them. Set over moderate heat and bring to a boil and cook for 1 minute, shaking the pan so the mixture does not stick to the bottom. Let the fish cool then add the sugar, bay leaf, sage leaves, and salt and peppercorns. Cover and refrigerate for 24 hours. Serve the fish garnished with its vegetable sauce.

Left: Melanzane e Lavarello Affumicato; right: Lavarello in Carpione

Left: Carpaccio Cipriani; right: Sformatini di Fagiolini Verdi e Tonno

CARPACCIO CIPRIANI

CIPRIANI'S SLICED BEEF

Created at Harry's Bar in Venice by Giuseppe Cipriani, carpaccio is one of the modern Italian dishes that has become famous throughout the world. Each cook varies the sauce according to personal preference. This version is from the Hotel Cipriani in Venice.

1 egg yolk
1 cup (8 fl oz/250 ml) olive oil
juice of 1 lemon or 1 tablespoon white wine vinegar
salt and freshly ground pepper
½ teaspoon dry mustard
3 tablespoons meat stock
a few drops Tabasco sauce
1 lb 10 oz (815 g) beef sirloin, of a good red color

SERVES 4–6

❡ Place the egg yolk in a blender with a quarter of the oil. Turn the blender on and add the rest of the oil in a slow thin stream. Flavor with lemon juice and salt and pepper. Dissolve the dry mustard in the stock and mix it into the mayonnaise, along with a few drops of Tabasco.
❡ Using an electric slicer, cut the beef into paper-thin slices. (It is impossible to cut the beef thin enough by hand.) Arrange the slices to completely cover each plate. In a thin stream, pour the mayonnaise over the beef in spirals, beginning at the center. Serve at once.

SFORMATINI DI FAGIOLINI VERDI E TONNO

GREEN BEAN AND TUNA MOLD

The simple green bean and tuna salad served in so many Italian homes is transformed by a new approach which enhances its esthetic appeal.

8 oz (250 g) young green beans
9 oz (280 g) canned tuna
3 tablespoons (1½ oz/45 g) butter
3 tablespoons olive oil
1 garlic clove
pinch of oregano
pinch of marjoram
pinch of chopped flat-leafed parsley
additional olive oil for serving

SERVES 4

❡ Cook the beans in boiling salted water until just al dente; drain. Arrange the beans on the bottom and sides of 4 small baking dishes (about 3 in/8 cm in diameter).
❡ Using a food processor or by hand, combine the tuna, butter, olive oil, garlic and herbs. Chop as finely as possible. Spoon the mixture into the dishes. Cover and refrigerate for at least 30 minutes.
❡ Invert each mold onto the center of a serving plate and drizzle olive oil over each before serving.

the range of soused seafoods. The taste of sardines, succulent sole or anchovies is enhanced by drenching them in a pickled blend made from salt and additives.

Freshwater trout, *trota verace*, is a perfect fish, with its delicate, sweet and firm flesh that lends itself to be cooked in most ways. Smoked trout, *trota affumicata*, is a sultry treatment, especially when accompanied by sauteéd onions, capers and lemon juice.

Sardines abound in the Italian seas. In the upper Adriatic, they are first dipped in flour and fried and then immersed in a white wine and vinegar marinade with onion, bay leaf and other flavorings. These are sardines *in saor*, a classic Venetian antipasto. When preserved in salt (*sardine sotto sale*), sardines retain the taste of their original home, the sea.

1. & 2. sardines preserved in salt; 3. scallops; 4. shrimps (prawns); 5. clams; 6. tuna in oil; 7. soused sardines; 8. mussels; 9. soused sole; 10. soused anchovies; 11. smoked trout; 12. seafood salad

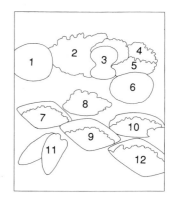

FISH SERVED AS ANTIPASTI

Anchovies, sardines, squid both large and small, crabs, prawns, shrimp (prawns), sea urchins, baby octopus and a variety of other shellfish can all be brought together into the one large family of Italian seafood antipasti. Live or absolutely fresh fish must be used if they are to be eaten raw, as in the case of shellfish (such as mussels, clams, venus shells, scallops, shrimps, sea urchins) or fresh anchovies, which are usually served cut open, boned and marinated briefly in lemon juice. Also included in this category are oysters, but in Italy oyster-farming is very limited, and most of the oysters served in restaurants come from France.

Tuna with its fleshy, tasty meat preserved in oil is a pleasant addition to any antipasti platter. It is popular in central and southern Italy, and is a specialty particularly in Sicilian cooking. Appearing in an array of recipes, it has been a feature of Italian cuisine since Roman times.

Another addition to this specialty platter is

ZUCCHINI IN FIORE

ZUCCHINI IN FLOWER

In the ancient Ligurian tradition of stuffed vegetables this dish is a novelty. A mousse of lobster is used in place of the classical filling of puréed vegetables, egg and Parmesan and the cooking takes place not in the oven but by steaming. The fanned zucchini (courgette) attached to its flower swollen with filling, both set against the red background of the sauce, is a most elegant sight.

2½ oz (75 g) raw lobster meat
2½ oz (75 g) fillet of sole
salt and freshly ground pepper
⅓ cup (3 fl oz/90 ml) heavy (double) cream
2 egg whites
8 small zucchini (courgettes) with flowers attached
homemade light tomato sauce, for serving

SERVES 4

❧ In a food processor, blend the lobster meat, sole, salt and pepper and cream until soft and smooth. Keep in the refrigerator until ready to cook.
❧ Beat the egg whites until stiff. Fold gently into the stuffing. Fill the flower of each zucchini with this mixture. For a decorative effect, carefully cut the zucchini in several slices lengthwise with a small, sharp knife, leaving the end attached to the flower so the slices can be fanned out.
❧ Steam the prepared zucchini for 6 minutes. Arrange two in the center of each plate on top of a pool of tomato sauce.

Zucchini in Fiore

VERDURE RIPIENE ALLA LIGURE

LIGURIAN STUFFED VEGETABLES

These vegetables are especially characteristic of the Ponente Riviera, between Genoa and the French border at Ventimiglia, where the greatest concentration of family-run market gardens is found and consequently much new-season produce is available. For many years, between the two world wars, a restaurant close to the Ponte San Luigi frontier was famous for offering a menu exclusively of stuffed vegetables, which brought the large international clientele of the Côte d'Azur flocking to its tables. The use of curdled milk is an example of the influence of Middle Eastern gastronomic traditions introduced through Saracen rule and sea trading. The top three vegetables listed must be very small — no more than 5–7 oz (155–220 g) each in weight.

8 miniature winter squash (pumpkins)
8 eggplants (aubergines)
8 onions
1 medium onion
olive oil
3 oz (90 g) stale bread without crust
2–3 tablespoons curdled milk or whole-milk yogurt
2 eggs
2 garlic cloves, minced
2 sprigs fresh marjoram
¾ cup (3 oz/90 g) freshly grated Parmesan cheese
salt
2 teaspoons dried oregano

SERVES 4

❧ Scoop out the flesh of the winter squash, eggplants and onions, and keep each one separate from the others, reserving the vegetable cases. Chop the medium onion finely then divide between the flesh of the three vegetables. Heat a little olive oil in a small skillet. Fry the pulp of each vegetable and its portion of onion in this for

Top: Verdure Ripiene alla Ligure; bottom: Pâté di Radicchio

a few minutes, one at a time, each time changing the oil. As each vegetable is cooked remove it to a separate bowl.

❡ Place the bread in a small bowl and add enough milk to thoroughly wet it, then squeeze the excess moisture from the bread.

❡ Beat the eggs in a bowl, add the garlic, marjoram, Parmesan, the bread and the curdled milk. Taste for salt. Divide the egg mixture among the three bowls of vegetables. Mix again, adding a little more bread steeped in milk if necessary to achieve the right consistency for the stuffing.

❡ Fill each vegetable case with its own stuffing, arrange them all in a baking dish brushed with olive oil, and sprinkle with oregano. Bake in a 350°F (180°C) oven for about 30 minutes or until a good crust has formed on the stuffed vegetables. Serve warm or cold.

PÂTÉ DI RADICCHIO

RADICCHIO PÂTÉ

Radicchio is usually served raw as a salad, or cooked on a grill, or sometimes in a risotto. But this typically Italian vegetable, characteristic of the region in the triangle between Treviso, Padua and Venice, lends itself to many other methods of preparation.

1 lb (500 g) radicchio
1 teaspoon powdered or 2 leaves unflavored gelatin
2–3 tablespoons water
2 tablespoons dry Marsala or dry sherry
2 tablespoons Cognac
3 tablespoons butter, melted
salt and freshly ground pepper
hot, buttered toast, for serving

SERVES 4

❡ Trim and wash the leaves of radicchio and dry them thoroughly, then blanch them for a few moments in boiling salted water. Pat dry on paper towels.

❡ Dissolve the gelatin in the water in a small saucepan over low heat, then add the Marsala and Cognac.

❡ In a food processor, combine the radicchio, gelatin, melted butter, salt and pepper. Blend until the mixture is smooth.

❡ Transfer to a sheet of foil and roll up into a cylinder. Refrigerate for 3 to 4 hours, until firm. Slice and serve with the toast.

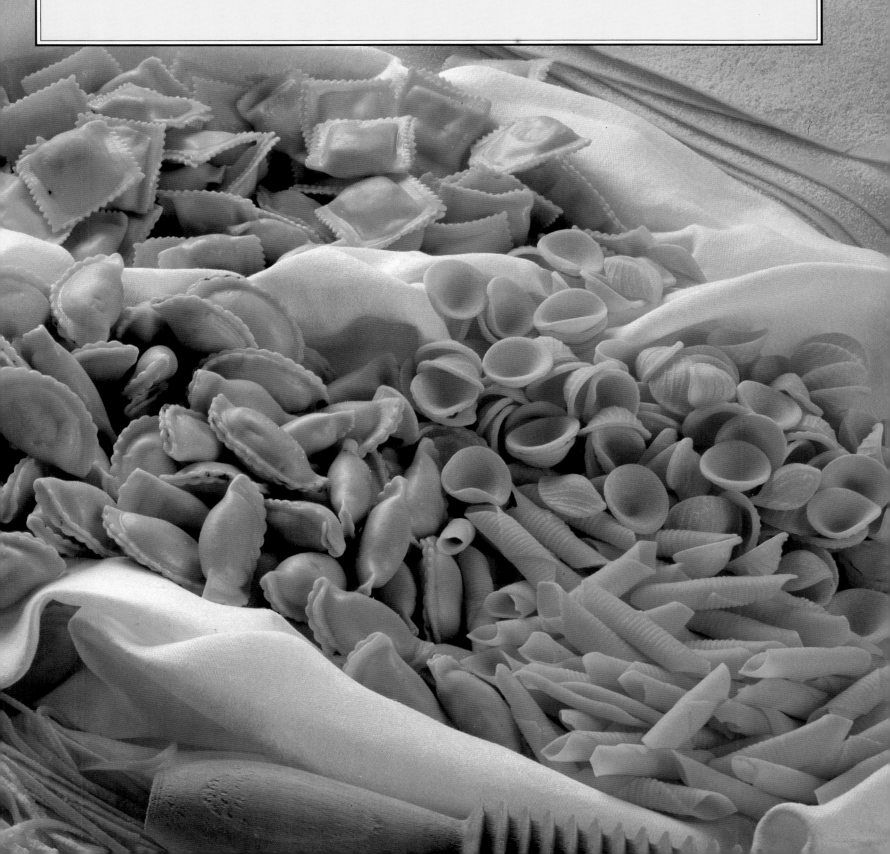

Pasta, Rice, Soups and Polenta

PASTA, RICE, SOUPS AND POLENTA

THERE IS NO DOUBT THAT PASTA IS THE EMBLEM OF ITALIAN COOKERY. ALONG THE WESTERN COAST, FROM Liguria down to Sicily, a climate suitable for drying and the wealth of durum wheat grown in the south are two factors favoring the production of dried pastas.

❡ On the eastern shores, from Apulia up to Romagna, a series of homemade pastas has evolved — *maccheroni alla chitarra*, *orecchiette*, *strascinati*, and *garganelli* — available both fresh and dried. Finally in the Po Valley, with a humid climate that prevents drying, we find the simplest form of pasta, the sheets from which *tagliolini*, tagliatelle, lasagne and the enormous range of filled pastas are derived.

❡ It is incorrectly thought that Marco Polo discovered spaghetti in China and brought it to Italy. Actually what Marco Polo describes in his book is a food made with flour from the breadfruit tree, which he saw not in China but on the island of Fanfur — Sumatra. Also, there is

plentiful evidence that pasta existed in Italy long before. In documents kept in the State Archives in Genoa, there is a will where a quantity of macaroni was referred to at least 50 years before Marco Polo's adventure. These same archives also contain a rental contract of 1316 drawn up for Maria Borgogno whose profession was pasta maker. Finally, the famous Etruscan Tomb of Reliefs in Cerveteri features in a stucco bas-relief pasta-making utensils — the table and the rolling pin for rolling out the pasta sheets, and the fluted wheel for cutting the edges.

❡ Even the names given to pasta have ancient origins. The term *tria* (from the Arabic *itriya*) still survives in the south of Italy, along with the Latin *lagane*, the root of the modern "lasagne." Then there are the French *nouilles*, the English "noodles" and the German *nudeln*, all of which come from the Latin term *nodellus*, used to describe the skeins of tagliatelle laid out to dry.

❡ Today's Italian pasta is either commercially produced, in which case it is dried, or it is fresh and made at home or in restaurants.

❡ The dried commercial form is made with durum wheat flour and water and the major production centers are the Ligurian Riviera, a few places in Tuscany near the cities of Pisa and Lucca, the city of Parma, and the regions of Apulia, Campania and Abruzzo. The homemade variety, made in sheets, uses common wheat which requires mixing with eggs. The addition of other substances gives different colors to pasta: boiled and chopped spinach mixed into the dough will give green pasta, carrots or tomatoes make it red, and so on.

Previous pages: The average Italian consumes more than 50 lb (25 kg) of pasta each year. Although pasta is made from a very basic dough, Italians have devised an astonishing array of shapes and forms, fresh, dried and stuffed. Each type of pasta complements a particular sauce. CARLO CANTINI

Opposite: Stuffed pasta can be filled with a variety of ingredients from beef and cabbage to mortadella, chicken or turkey. It is thought that stuffed pasta was invented to use up leftovers. AUSTRALIAN PICTURE LIBRARY/OLYMPIA/ WALTER LEONARDI

TORTIGLIONI AL TRITO DI ERBE AROMATICHE

SPIRAL PASTA WITH HERBS

This Sicilian first course, from the Palermo region, tempers the garlic's aggressiveness by cooking it in butter.

13 oz (410 g) tortiglioni *(large pasta spirals)*,
    rigatoni *or* fusilli
3½ oz (105 g) butter
6 garlic cloves, minced
1 cup (8 fl oz/250 ml) dry white wine
2–3 black peppercorns, crushed
ground chili pepper
finely chopped mint, basil and flat-leafed parsley,
    combined to make 1 cupful
salt and freshly ground pepper
½ cup (2 oz/60 g) freshly grated Pecorino cheese

SERVES 4

❡ In a large pot of boiling salted water, cook the pasta until just al dente; drain.
❡ Put the butter and garlic in a wide shallow terracotta casserole dish over medium heat and cook until the garlic begins to brown. Pour in the wine and cook until evaporated. Add the crushed black peppercorns.
❡ Add the pasta to the sauce mixture, stirring in the chili and herbs. Season with salt and pepper to taste.
❡ Sprinkle with the Pecorino cheese and serve.

FUSILLI ALLA SORRENTINA

SORRENTO-STYLE PASTA

Because the ingredients in this sauce are not actually cooked, it has a particularly fresh flavor.

1¼ lb (625 g) ripe tomatoes, peeled, seeded and chopped
3 oz (90 g) black Gaeta olives, pitted
⅔ cup (5 fl oz/155 ml) olive oil
1 garlic clove, minced
a little myrrh or dried sweet cicely seeds
1 teaspoon dried oregano
1 cup chopped basil
1¼ lb (625 g) fusilli *(spiral pasta)*
1¼ cups (5 oz/155 g) freshly grated Caciotta *cheese*

SERVES 4

❡ In a bowl, combine the tomatoes, olives, olive oil, garlic, myrrh, oregano and basil. Set aside for

Top: Fusilli alla Sorrentina; bottom: Tortiglioni al Trito di Erbe Aromatiche

at least 30 minutes, stirring from time to time to blend the flavors.
❡ Meanwhile cook the pasta in boiling salted water until al dente. Drain and transfer to a large serving dish. Add the sauce and the cheese. Mix well. Serve at once.

TRENETTE ALLE COZZE E ZAFFERANO

TRENETTE WITH MUSSELS AND SAFFRON

The term trenette, *used only in Liguria (in the rest of Italy this type of pasta is known as* bavette *or* linguine), *comes from the Arab word* itrja. *It provides confirmation of the theory that pasta-making came to Liguria from Sicily by sea, during coastal trading in medieval times.*

1 garlic clove, minced
1 sprig flat-leafed parsley, finely chopped
2 mint leaves, finely chopped
1 cup (8 fl oz/250 ml) extra-virgin olive oil
1 cup (3½ oz/105 g) cooked, shelled mussels
13 oz (410 g) trenette *(thin ribbon pasta)*
4 pinches of saffron threads

SERVES 4

❡ In a large skillet sauté the garlic, parsley and mint in the olive oil until golden.
❡ Add the mussels and cook for 2 or 3 minutes over medium heat. Set aside once the flavors are well mixed.

❡ Meanwhile, cook the *trenette* in plenty of boiling salted water until al dente. Drain the *trenette*; turn them into the skillet and stir carefully so that the pasta is coated with the mussel sauce.

❡ Serve, topping each serving with a pinch of saffron threads.

FARFALLE ALL'ASTICE

BUTTERFLY PASTA WITH LOBSTER

Sardinian waters are famous for their crustaceans and the most prized of all is the lobster. The greatest merit of this wonderfully easy recipe lies in the freshness of the lobster and the use of just a few basic ingredients. If preferred, remove the lobster flesh from the shell before cooking; this will shorten the cooking time.

2 garlic cloves, crushed
½ cup (4 fl oz/125 ml) extra-virgin olive oil
2 lobsters, about 1 lb (500 g) each
2 lb (1 kg) tomatoes, peeled and quartered
salt
13 oz (410 g) farfalle *(butterfly-shaped pasta)*
ground chili pepper to taste
2 tablespoons chopped flat-leafed parsley

SERVES 4

❡ In a large stewpan, brown the garlic in the olive oil. Cut the lobsters up, crushing the nippers; add to the oil and garlic. Cook, stirring often, for about 15 minutes. Add the tomatoes and cook for about 30 minutes. Taste for salt.

❡ Cook the *farfalle* in plenty of boiling salted water until al dente; drain. Divide the pasta among 4 plates. Top each serving with a few pieces of lobster and some sauce. Sprinkle with chili pepper and chopped parsley before serving.

Left: Trenette alle Cozze e Zafferano; right: Farfalle all'Astice

Left: Spaghetti all'Acciuga in Salsa d'Arancia; right: Tagliatelle con Fiori di Zucca e Scampi

SPAGHETTI ALL'ACCIUGA IN SALSA D'ARANCIA

SPAGHETTI WITH ORANGE AND ANCHOVY SAUCE

The use of the orange in cooking is not new. In Sicilian popular tradition oranges are often served as a salad with oil and salt, to accompany a main course. This dish from Calabria brings together anchovies and oranges in a most interesting way.

6½ oz (200 g) anchovies packed in salt
olive oil
1 garlic clove, minced
2 oranges, peeled, pith removed, and diced
½ cup (2 oz/60 g) breadcrumbs
½ cup (4 fl oz/125 ml) orange liqueur
salt
1 lb (500 g) spaghetti
1 bunch mint
SERVES 4–6

❦ Wash the anchovies well to remove all the salt, open them up and take out the backbones. Cut them into small pieces.
❦ Warm a skillet and add the oil and the garlic.
❦ Let the garlic fry gently for a moment and then add the anchovies and work them with a fork, using the tips of the prongs, to achieve a creamy consistency.
❦ Now add the oranges, add also the breadcrumbs and the orange liqueur, and taste, adding salt if necessary.

¶ Meanwhile cook the spaghetti in plenty of boiling salted water until al dente; drain. Dress with the sauce and serve sprinkled with mint.

TAGLIATELLE CON FIORI DI ZUCCA E SCAMPI

TAGLIATELLE WITH ZUCCHINI FLOWERS AND LARGE SHRIMP

This is one of the most modern and interesting examples of the Ligurian combination of vegetables with seafood.

1 shallot, finely chopped
2 tablespoons olive oil
3 tablespoons (1½ oz/45 g) butter
8 large shrimp (king prawns), peeled
12 zucchini (courgette) flowers, cut into thin strips
salt and freshly ground pepper
½ cup (4 fl oz/125 ml) heavy (double) cream
10 oz (315 g) tagliatelle

SERVES 4

¶ In a skillet, cook the shallot with the olive oil and butter. As soon as it browns add the shrimp and cook for 4 minutes.
¶ Add the zucchini flowers and toss. Taste for salt and pepper.
¶ Gently stir in the cream to finish, then turn off the heat.
¶ Cook the pasta in boiling salted water until al dente; drain. Dress with the prepared sauce and serve.

DRIED PASTA

The term *pasta secca*, dried pasta, refers to commercially produced pasta. To be of good quality, it must be made only from durum wheat flour kneaded with water. There are pastas produced outside Italy that do not observe this golden rule but are made with a mixture of durum and common wheat flours. These are second-rate pastas with a shorter cooking time and, more importantly, they do not hold their shape during cooking, coming to the plate as a limp mass that not only fails to bind with the sauce but is not pleasing to the palate. Thus the first rule in buying a package of pasta is to ascertain the quality by checking the ingredients on the label. Note that a pasta made with durum wheat flour alone will leave the cooking water almost completely clear, having shed only a minimal amount of starch into it, whereas water in which mixed-flour pasta has been boiled will be milky.

Another hint for recognizing good pasta is to check its surface. If the texture is perfectly smooth, this means it has been made with machines using nonstick plates; if the texture is rough, a bronze plate has been used. The latter is to be preferred because the pasta will amalgamate better with the sauce, which tends to slip off if the pasta is too smooth.

The most important thing to consider in making a pasta dish is the degree of "doneness": the pasta when cooked must be al dente — soft and yet definitely still firm, never slack. It is necessary to use one's judgment regarding doneness. Cooking times can vary and may depend on different factors: the quality of the water (it can be more or less hard and more or less rich in mineral salts); the altitude (at sea level water boils at 212°F /100°C, but at higher altitudes cooking will take longer); and the proportion of water to pasta. Use 1 quart (1 liter) of water for every 3 ounces (90 grams) pasta, regardless of whether it is short or long pasta. Put a large pot filled with water over high heat, add salt (5 quarts/5 liters of water need at least 2 tablespoons of salt) and wait for it to boil before adding the pasta.

Be wary of pasta in a restaurant that appears as soon as it is ordered. Many lazy and less-than-reputable cooks precook large quantities of pasta and simply put the required amount back into boiling water for a few seconds before sending it out to the unsuspecting diner.

A further problem in cooking good pasta is how to drain it. Always use a colander, of course, but the amount of water that must be left dripping from the pasta varies according to the thickness of the sauce being served with it. Take, for example, the most elementary form of serving pasta: with butter and Parmesan. In order to achieve a perfect blend the pasta must be minimally drained, perhaps by lifting it straight from the saucepan with pasta tongs. Then the Parmesan is added and given a preliminary stir to help it melt. The final addition is butter that has been left out of the refrigerator for at least an hour so it will melt easily.

Tagliatelle is the classic egg noodle which originated in the Emilio–Romagna region. It is made from a rich dough of flour and egg, which is then rolled out into thin transparent sheets. The sheets are cut into narrow strips and may be then arranged into variations including the nest form, *nidi di tagliatelle*. The classic dressing for tagliatelle is ragu, however it is also a marvelous vehicle for most meat and creamy sauces. Tagliatelle also go well in baked dishes.

Large tubular pasta with spiral ridges are known as *tortiglioni*. They are ideally suited to accompany a thick stew but are also common in baked pasta recipes.

Butterfly-shaped pasta, *farfalle*, are delicious, especially when married with delicate creamy sauces. They are easily made from homemade pasta which is achieved by cutting small squares and pinching them in the middle.

Perhaps the most versatile of all the pasta shapes is spaghetti which literally means "little strings." It is commonly made in two or three different thicknesses, including thin spaghetti or *spaghettini*. This is the most suitable for cooking with a large number of sauces. Expert chefs never drain spaghetti in a colander but lift it out with an oversize slotted spoon made of wicker. The best sauces for spaghetti are oil-based, as this allows it to remain slippery and separate. As for eating spaghetti — only the fork is acceptable. The true Italian can deftly twist and lift spaghetti, which is something that few people, unless born to it, have mastered. There is historical evidence that spaghetti existed in Sicily in the twelfth century and that it was one of the many skills of the Saracens.

Similar to thick spaghetti, but hollow, *bucatini* can be versatile and is sometimes used instead of spaghetti in many sauces.

Anellini da minestra, are pasta rings made especially for delicious Italian soups. This is true particularly in Northern Italy which has a large repertoire of thick nourishing soups, a necessity in cold climates. In central and southern Italy, soups are fresher and lighter, and pasta is generally not used.

Italian dishes may also include a mixture of the small pasta shapes including *sedanini*, *ditali*, *pennette*, *rigatoni*, and *conchiglie*. The shell pasta, *conchiglie* can be used in recipes which recommend *ditali* (see below) or *orecchiette* (the traditional pasta of the Apulia region). *Conchiglie* is well suited to vegetable sauces such as broccoli or zucchini (courgettes) or with cheese dressings.

Ditali is a small tube pasta which usually has ridges along its length. The ridges are designed to catch the succulent sauces that accompany it.

Pennette is a tubular pasta particularly suited to rich sauces. This type of pasta is either ridged or smooth and the ends are cut at an angle so that they look like quill pens. *Pennette* are one of the best shapes to use in the dish, *pasticci*.

Trenette genovesi are matchstick noodles made in Genoa. In fact, the *trenette*-shape pasta originated in the Ligurian area, of which Genoa is a part. Applied to Genoese cooking, it becomes a delicious combination of pasta generally cooked in olive oil with basil and garlic. Some gourmets say *trenette* are always dressed with pesto sauce and that actually it would be odd to eat *trenette* without it. Pesto sauce is traditionally made from Ligurian basil, olive oil, Pecorino and Parmesan cheeses.

1. nests of tagliatelle;
2. tortiglioni; 3. farfalle;
4. spaghetti; 5. bucatini;
6. anellini for soup;
7. trenette genovesi;
8. pennette; 9. mixture of small pasta shapes: sedanini, ditali, pennette, rigatoni, conchiglie

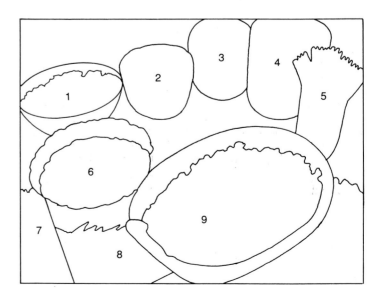

TRENETTE AL PESTO

PASTA WITH PESTO SAUCE

This is the prince of Genoese dishes. In Italian cuisine, pesto is considered the most important and the most famous of uncooked sauces. A true pesto, as the name indicates (it means ground or pounded), is made in a stone mortar with a boxwood pestle. With the development of food processors and blenders the tradition of the mortar is disappearing, especially in restaurants. If you wish to make the dish in the style of the Levantine Riviera (which runs between Genoa and the Cinque Terre with Camogli and Portofino in the middle), potatoes and green beans are served together with the pasta.

2 bunches basil
3 tablespoons pine nuts
2 garlic cloves
1 tablespoon freshly grated sharp Pecorino cheese
1 tablespoon freshly grated Parmesan cheese
2 cups (16 fl oz/500 ml) extra-virgin olive oil
salt
2 or 3 potatoes, cut into pieces (optional)
5 oz (155 g) green beans, trimmed (optional)
13 oz (410 g) trenette (thin ribbon pasta)
1 tablespoon (1½ oz/15 g) butter

SERVES 4

❡ Immerse the basil leaves in boiling water for 1 minute (this guarantees a lovely bright-green pesto that will not go dark). Wash and dry the leaves and shred them by hand. Put the basil in a mortar with the pine nuts and garlic and work until the mixture is reduced to a paste. Add the cheeses and oil a little at a time, still pounding, alternating the Pecorino and Parmesan and taking care that each addition is absorbed before adding more.
❡ As the mixture thickens add a little more oil, and at the end taste and add salt, if necessary. The resulting pesto is a creamy soft sauce. (If you prefer to use an electric mixer the order of procedure is the same. It only takes a few minutes, and the result can be quite satisfactory.)
❡ About 10 minutes before cooking the pasta, cook the potatoes in boiling salted water until tender. While the pasta is cooking, cook the green beans in boiling salted water until al dente.
❡ Cook the *trenette* in boiling salted water until al dente. Before draining the *trenette*, stir the butter and a little of the pasta's cooking water into the pesto sauce to dilute it and give it a creamier consistency.
❡ Drain the pasta and vegetables, dress with the pesto, and serve.

BUCATINI ALLA NORMA

PASTA, "NORMA" STYLE

This is a typical Sicilian dish made with bucatini *(hollow spaghetti) and featuring eggplants (aubergines) as the main ingredient. The name "Norma" derives from the Catanians' custom of using the title of the opera* Norma, *written by Vincenzo Bellini, who was a native of Catania, to describe anything they consider especially beautiful or good.*

2 medium eggplants (aubergines)
kosher (coarse) salt
oil, for deep frying
¼ cup (2 fl oz/60 ml) olive oil
2 garlic cloves, peeled and bruised
1 chili pepper, cut in half
1 lb (500 g) ripe tomatoes, peeled, seeded and coarsely chopped
a few small basil leaves
salt
13 oz (410 g) bucatini
¾ cup (3 oz/90 g) freshly grated, salted ricotta

SERVES 4

❡ Slice the eggplants, sprinkle the slices on both sides with kosher salt and place them on a sloping chopping board to drain for 2 or 3 hours to rid them of their bitter juices. Wash the slices under running water; then dry completely on paper towels.
❡ Deep-fry in hot oil until golden; place on paper towels to drain.
❡ Meanwhile, in a shallow terracotta pan or a saucepan, make the tomato sauce: Heat the olive oil, then add the garlic cloves and the chili pepper. Then cook on medium heat until the garlic begins to become golden brown; then remove them from th pan and discard.
❡ Add the tomatoes and the basil and season with salt. The tomato sauce will be ready in approximately 15 or 20 minutes. Discard the chili pepper once the sauce is thoroughly cooked.
❡ Cook the *bucatini* in a large pan in boiling salted water until al dente; drain.
❡ Layer the pasta in a large tureen adding a few slices of fried eggplant, a little of the sauce, and a coating of ricotta between the layers. Continue in this manner until all the ingredients are used. Serve.

Left: Trenette al Pesto; right: Bucatini alla Norma

CONCHIGLIE ALLE VERDURE

SHELL PASTA WITH VEGETABLE SAUCE

The elements of this vegetable ragù are as Mediterranean as you will find — a wonderful combination of flavors blended and fused with a minimum of olive oil.

1 onion, thinly sliced
1 eggplant (aubergine), diced
4 tomatoes, cut into wedges and seeded
1 garlic clove, crushed
½ cup (4 fl oz/125 ml) olive oil
salt
1 green or yellow bell pepper (capsicum), diced
1 teaspoon dried oregano
3 oz (90 g) green beans, boiled until al dente
9½ oz (300 g) medium pasta shells
¼ cup (1 oz/30 g) freshly grated Parmesan cheese
freshly ground pepper

SERVES 4

❡ In a large skillet, combine the onion, eggplant, tomatoes and garlic in half the oil, adding salt if required. Cook until softened.
❡ Sauté the bell pepper and oregano in the remaining oil until soft. Add the bell pepper mixture and the green beans to the tomato mixture and cook for 5 minutes.
❡ Meanwhile, cook the pasta in plenty of boiling salted water until al dente; drain. Transfer the pasta to a tureen. Add the vegetable sauce and the cheese; mix well. Serve with a grinding of black pepper.

Top: Conchiglie alle Verdure; bottom: Fettuccine ai Peperoni

FETTUCCINE AI PEPERONI

FETTUCCINE WITH BELL PEPPER SAUCE

This Neapolitan recipe is really the simple but inspired combination of a classic peperonata, a dish usually served to accompany a main course, with pasta. It is a demonstration, if one is needed, of how easily pasta can adapt to any kind of sauce.

1½ lb (750 g) red and yellow bell peppers (capsicums)
2 garlic cloves, minced
⅓ cup (3 fl oz/90 ml) olive oil
1 teaspoon capers, drained
6 black olives, pitted
2 tomatoes, peeled
salt and freshly ground pepper
9½ oz (300 g) fettuccine
½ cup (2 oz/60 g) freshly grated Parmesan cheese

SERVES 4

❡ Wash the bell peppers, remove the ribs and seeds, and cut into very thin strips. In a large skillet, gently fry the garlic in the oil. Before the garlic colors, add the bell peppers and cook until they are limp.
❡ Add the capers, olives and tomatoes and adjust the seasonings. Cook until all the ingredients combine into a well-blended sauce.
❡ Cook the *fettuccine* in plenty of boiling salted water until al dente; drain. Transfer the pasta to the skillet and stir rapidly; sprinkle the Parmesan on top and serve.

PENNE ALL'ARRABBIATA

PENNE WITH SPICY TOMATO SAUCE

This extremely common dish is offered in all Italian restaurants especially where the cooking style is Tuscan or Roman. The name salsa all'arrabbiata (enraged sauce) comes from the hot red pepper.

1 tablespoon bacon drippings (lard)
1 onion, finely chopped
2 garlic cloves, minced
3 oz (90 g) pancetta, diced
1¼ lb (625 g) ripe tomatoes, puréed
salt
½ teaspoon ground chili pepper
13 oz (410 g) penne
¾ cup (3 oz/90 g) freshly grated Pecorino cheese

SERVES 4

Left: Penne all'Arrabbiata; right: Linguine alla Caprese

❡ Melt the bacon drippings in a large shallow skillet. Add the onion and garlic and cook over moderate heat until soft, but do not brown. Add the *pancetta* and cook for 2 or 3 minutes. Add the tomatoes, salt and chili pepper. Cook for a few minutes on high heat, until the sauce is creamy.

❡ Cook the *penne* in plenty of boiling salted water until al dente; drain. Transfer to the pan of sauce, add half the Pecorino, and stir rapidly. Serve, with the remaining Pecorino served separately.

LINGUINE ALLA CAPRESE

LINGUINE CAPRI-STYLE

Right around the Italian coast one can find numerous pasta dishes with seafood sauces. This one is typical of Capri, and is perhaps the richest of them all.

13 oz (410 g) mussels, scrubbed
9 oz (280 g) clams, scrubbed
1 cup (8 fl oz/250 ml) extra-virgin olive oil
6 oz (185 g) small shrimp (prawns), raw
   (if heads are removed, use an extra
   3 oz/90 g shrimp, chopped)
6 oz (185 g) small squid, cleaned and cut into small strips
2 garlic cloves, chopped
1 cup (8 fl oz/250 ml) dry white wine
13 oz (410 g) ripe tomatoes, peeled, seeded and chopped

salt and freshly ground black pepper
13 oz (410 g) linguine
2 tablespoons finely chopped flat-leafed parsley

SERVES 4

❡ Place the mussels and clams in a large skillet over high heat along with 3 tablespoons of olive oil. The heat will cause them to open and lose the water contained in their shells. Remove the meat from the shells and set aside, reserving their liquid in the pan. Peel the shrimp and set aside. Add the crushed heads and shells to the skillet. Cook gently until the liquid is quite thick. Strain the mixture through a fine strainer and reserve the resulting juices; discard the solids.

❡ In a stewpan, combine the squid, the remaining oil and the garlic. Cook, moistening frequently with the wine, until all the wine has been added and evaporated. Add the tomatoes; adjust the seasonings. Add half the reserved cooking juices from the shellfish and cook over moderate heat for 20 minutes. If the mixture dries out, add more of the juices. Add the shrimp and cook for 10 minutes. Add the shelled mussels and clams, mix well and cook for 3 or 4 minutes, until blended thoroughly.

❡ Cook the pasta in plenty of boiling salted water until al dente; drain. Transfer the pasta to the pan containing the sauce. Mix well, sprinkle each serving with pepper and parsley, and serve.

Left: Lagane e Ceci; right: Vincisgrassi

LAGANE E CECI

FETTUCCINE WITH CHICKPEAS

Typical fare in the southern Campania, Basilicata and Apulia regions, this dish still appears regularly on tables although its origins go back more than a thousand years.

¾ cup (5 oz/155 g) chickpeas
2½ cups (10 oz/315 g) durum wheat flour
1 cup (8 fl oz/250 ml) water
salt and freshly ground pepper
1 garlic clove
⅔ cup (5 fl oz/155 ml) extra-virgin olive oil
3 oz (90 g) tomatoes, peeled, seeded and diced
1 cup chopped basil leaves

SERVES 4

❦ Wash the chickpeas well in salted water, then soak overnight in fresh water.

❦ Work the flour with the water and salt to make a firm, elastic dough. Roll out into a thin sheet, sprinkle with flour and allow to rest for a few minutes. Roll pasta up and cut into *fettuccine* about ⅜ in (1 cm) wide. Spread out on a pastry board to dry a little.

❦ Drain the chickpeas. Cook them, covered, in 2 qt (2 l) water over moderate heat for 1½ hours, or until they are quite soft. Drain off any excess water remaining.

❦ In a large skillet, gently fry the garlic clove in 3 tablespoons of olive oil; remove when it begins to color. Add the diced tomatoes, basil and salt and pepper to taste.

❦ Cook the *fettuccine* in plenty of boiling salted water until al dente; drain. Transfer to the saucepan with the chickpeas. Stir in the sauce. Serve in deep bowls, adding 1 tablespoon of olive oil to each serving.

VINCISGRASSI

ANCONA BAKED LASAGNE

Local history has it that this dish, characteristic of Ancona and fairly similar to the baked lasagne of Bologna or Romagna, was named Vincisgrassi in honor of Prince Alfred Candidus of Vindischgraetz, an Austrian nobleman who was sent from the Austrian Empire to the Marches region.

1 celery stalk, chopped
1 small carrot, chopped
1 onion, chopped
⅓ cup (3 fl oz/90 ml) extra-virgin olive oil
5 oz (155 g) ground (minced) veal
3 oz (90 g) sweetbreads, ground (minced)
3 oz (90 g) chicken giblets, diced
5 oz (155 g) tomatoes, peeled and coarsely chopped
salt and freshly ground pepper
10 oz (315 g) lasagne noodles
⅔ cup (2½ oz/80 g) freshly grated Parmesan cheese
For the béchamel sauce:
2 tablespoons (1 oz/30 g) butter
2 tablespoons all-purpose (plain) flour
1½ cups (12 fl oz/375 ml) milk, heated
salt and freshly ground pepper

SERVES 4

❡ In a large skillet, fry the celery, carrot and onion in the olive oil until the onion is golden. Add the veal and cook, stirring for about 10 minutes. Then stir in the sweetbreads, giblets, tomatoes and salt and pepper to taste. Cover the skillet and cook over moderate heat for approximately 1 hour.
❡ Brush a large, round baking dish with a little olive oil. Blanch the pasta and drain it while it is still very firm. Put a layer of pasta in the baking dish and cover it with some of the meat sauce and a little of the grated Parmesan. Top with another layer of the pasta, some more sauce and Parmesan and a third layer of the pasta. Continue in this way until you have 5 layers. The final layer must be of pasta.
❡ Make the béchamel sauce: In a saucepan, melt the butter until it begins to foam. Then stir in the flour and cook, stirring, for about 2 minutes, until the mixture bubbles, but do not let it brown. Add the milk, stirring continuously. Bring to a boil, then add salt and pepper to taste, cook, stirring, for a further 2 or 3 minutes. Remove the béchamel from the heat and pour over the pasta.
❡ Bake in a 350°F (170°C) oven for about 20 minutes.

MELANZANE CHARLESTON

EGGPLANT CHARLESTON

The Charleston is a restaurant in Palermo where this recipe was created in the 1960s, when the dish immediately became popular among certain aristocratic food circles all over the region. Eggplant has a place of honor in Sicilian cooking. Here it serves both as sauce and container for a very rich and attractive pasta.

4 medium–large eggplants (aubergines)
vegetable oil, for deep-frying
5 cups (1¼ qt/1.25 l) tomato sauce (purée)
1 cup fresh basil leaves
1¼ lb (625 g) fresh pasta dumplings (small gnocchi or shell pasta)
5 oz (155 g) fresh mozzarella, diced
1 cup (4 oz/125 g) freshly grated Parmesan cheese
salt and freshly ground pepper

SERVES 4

❡ Cut a slice from the side of each eggplant; scoop out the pulp and cut it into very small dice. Immerse the eggplant cases in abundant hot oil and fry them until golden. Drain and set aside. Fry the diced pulp until golden. Drain.
❡ In a skillet, combine the tomato, basil and fried eggplant pulp. When heated through turn off the heat.
❡ Boil the pasta dumplings until al dente; drain. Add to the sauce; stir in the mozzarella and the Parmesan. Mix well, season with salt and pepper to taste and spoon into the fried eggplant cases. Serve at once.

Melanzane Charleston

Fresh and Stuffed Pasta

STUFFED PASTA
It is impossible to say exactly when it was that a cook first had the idea of filling two pieces of pasta dough with a mixture of ingredients. Certainly the custom is an ancient one, and there are those who attribute the birth of ravioli, *tortelli* and *tortellini* and *tortellini verdi* (spinach *tortellini*), to housekeepers who, looking for ways to use up the leftovers from the meals of the nobility, thought it a good idea to grind (mince) everything and bind the mixture with egg, cheese and herbs.

That this theory has some foundation is demonstrated by the fact that filled pastas originated in the Po Valley where the tradition of the *sfoglia* or home-made pasta dough developed. That the house-keepers were right is shown by the success the many varieties of stuffed pasta have had in Italian gastronomy.

The process of preparing a pasta casing is identical to that described for homemade fresh pasta. The starting point is a thin *sfoglia all'uovo*, a sheet of egg pasta dough.

But when it comes to the filling, there are no restrictions placed on the imagination of the cook. The essential thing is that the filling should always be firm but fairly soft, and should not get too moist during cooking nor yet remain a little solid mass separate from the pasta surrounding it. The degree of density is easily adjusted by adding breadcrumbs, which may be either dry or soaked in milk and squeezed.

Nearly all Italian stuffed pastas are cooked in boiling salted water, drained and then dressed with the chosen sauce or with butter and Parmesan. In a few instances they are baked in the oven, like the lasagna of Ferrara, but then the pasta has been cooked in water first. Ravioli, *tortellini*, *tortelli*, *orecchiette* and *garganelli* are immersed in water already at its maximum boil, stirred very carefully to avoid breaking them up, and removed with a slotted spoon as they rise to the surface. Since it is not possible to sauce them all at once and stir them again, they are usually put into each diner's bowl in layers and sprinkled one layer at a time with sauce and whatever other condiments are used, including the cheese. A finishing touch of sauce and cheese is added at the end.

Tortelloni are large stuffed pasta filled with ricotta and spinach, or with ricotta, parsley and Parmesan. They are a modern innovation to cut down on the time needed for preparation. A variation on these are *capellacci ferraresi* which are pasta hats from Ferrara filled with pumpkin. *Tortelloni* is made in a variety of sizes. Nowadays housewives make it by a machine, either electric or hand-cranked, or buy them ready made in specialist pasta shops.

FRESH PASTA
The art of making pasta at home still survives today in Emilia Romagna. Here, in the old days, a woman who was to be married had to demonstrate her pasta-making

skills to her future mother-in-law before the wedding could take place. The pasta dough had to be golden and rolled out so thinly that you could see the hand that was lifting it. Although such demonstrations are no longer required, being a good *sfoglina* (good at making pasta dough) is still seen as a source of pride and a worthy goal. All major restaurants in the region have a section of the kitchen reserved for the *sfogline*, whose only task is to make the fresh pasta every morning. In the family home, too, although rolling-out is increasingly entrusted to a manual or electric roller machine, the kneading is still done by hand because the quality of the pasta depends more than anything else on the sensitivity of the person working the dough, who can gauge by touch the progress of amalgamation of the ingredients.

The basic method of making pasta consists of blending common wheat flour, which may be either pure white or whole wheat (whole-meal), with eggs and sometimes water or other liquids. A tablespoon of oil makes a smoother dough, a tablespoon of wine, particularly if it is spiced wine, will give it a unique flavor, while a handful of cooked, chopped spinach will turn it green and one or two tablespoons of tomato paste will make it red.

The ratio of ingredients is generally one egg to every 3 ounces (90 grams) of flour, but this is not always maintained. Some people use more eggs, others use fewer and compensate with water, and there are those who use only egg yolks. The important thing to remember is that the proportions are relative and depend on the quality of the flour, the climate, and the humidity in the air. The final result must be a firm, compact dough, and this will be achieved according to the capacity of the flour to absorb liquid, not by carefully measuring the ingredients. Indeed, in Emilia people never talk about making "a kilo of pasta," but rather about preparing "a 10-egg pasta dough." Regardless of quantity, the same method is always used.

Heap the flour onto a pastry board, *"a fontana"* (in the form of a fountain), with a well in the center. Put the eggs in the center of the well and add a little table salt and any other ingredients. Start quickly, incorporating the flour into the liquid ingredients with your fingers, until the mixture forms a single mass. At this point you need to work the dough vigorously with the palm of your hand, adding more flour if the dough is too soft.

When the dough is ready, it must rest for at least 30 minutes before being rolled out by hand or put through the rolling machine.

Having obtained a flat sheet of pasta dough, you proceed to making the final product. Rolling up the sheet and slicing the roll into strips will give you *pappardelle*, lasagne, spinach lasagne, and tagliatelle or *tagliolini*, depending on the width. Genoese lasagne or *piccagge* is usually cut square. Cutting it into little rectangles and pinching them in the center produces *farfalle*, or, by using specially shaped cutters, you can make various shapes, particularly the small ones to be used in soups.

Nowadays there are manual and electric machines equipped with spiral presses and draw-plates which make it possible to prepare *bucatini*, *rigatoni*, *penne*, *conchiglie* and similar types of pasta at home as well.

Cooking times for fresh pasta are shorter than for dried. The suggestions made earlier regarding the quantity of water to use are also valid here. Remember though, that pasta made at home with common wheat flour is more fragile. Pouring it quickly into a colander to drain may break it, with the result that it looks a little unattractive. It is a good idea, therefore, to drain fresh pasta when it is cooked using a slotted spoon or wire skimmer.

One last piece of advice: while cooked dried pasta may be put into a pan with its sauce for a final cooking, as will be seen from some of the recipes in this book, the same must never happen with fresh pasta, for its magic point of perfection would then be irretrievably lost.

Pasta is everyday food, yet any Italian knows that the cooking and serving of it calls for great love and care. Parmesan is never added indiscriminantly in Italy, as it is often elsewhere. In some dishes the pasta is drained before it is quite cooked and then it is either baked or put into the pan in which the sauce is cooking.

1. tortellini; 2. spinach tortellini; 3. narrow lasagna strips and spinach lasagna; 4. Genoese lasagna (also known as piccagge); 5. ravioli or agnolotti filled with meat; 6. tortelli; 7. Apulian orecchiette; 8. Roman garganelli; 9. tagliatelle; 10. cappellacci; 11. tortelloni

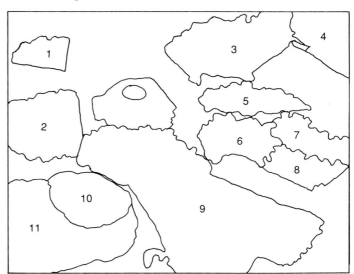

FARFALLE CON PROSCIUTTO, PISELLI E ERBE DI CAMPO

BUTTERFLY PASTA WITH HAM, PEAS AND WILD HERBS

Although there are a number of ready-packed commercial butterfly pastas on the market, many families — especially in Emilia — keep up the custom of making these pasta shapes at home.

For the pasta:
3¼ cups (13 oz/410 g) all-purpose (plain) flour
9 eggs
3½ oz (105 g) cooked, chopped spinach
For the sauce:
3½ oz (105 g) prosciutto, *cut into thin strips*
3½ oz (105 g) butter
3½ oz (105 g) shelled green peas
1 cup mixed chopped herbs: basil, mint, marjoram,
    chicory, thyme, rosemary
¾ cup (3 oz/90 g) freshly grated Parmesan cheese

SERVES 4

❡ Make the pasta: Work the flour with the eggs to form a dough. Halve the dough, add the spinach to one half and work it in. Roll out each half into a thin sheet.
❡ Cut each sheet into rectangles 1½ × ¾ in (4 × 2 cm) using a fluted pastry wheel.
Pinch the middle of each rectangle to form a butterfly shape.
❡ Make the sauce: In a large skillet, brown the *prosciutto* in half the butter. Add the peas and herbs and cook until tender.
❡ Meanwhile, cook the pasta in plenty of boiling salted water; drain. Turn the pasta into the skillet and toss with the sauce and the remaining butter. Sprinkle with the grated Parmesan and serve.

ORECCHIETTE CON CAVOLI E PANCETTA

LITTLE EARS WITH CAULIFLOWER AND BACON

Here is a truly great dish from Apulia. Just as the Pied-montese make gnocchi *from the potatoes they grow in abundance, the south of Italy prepares a similar dish using the raw material that is easiest to come by — durum wheat flour. Unlike potato gnocchi, orecchiette are left to dry for a day after shaping.*

2 cups (10 oz/315 g) fine-ground semolina
    (continental flour)
1 cauliflower, trimmed and cut into medium florets

salt
1 cup (8 fl oz/250 ml) extra-virgin olive oil
2 garlic cloves, peeled and bruised
freshly ground pepper
½ cup (1 oz/30 g) fresh breadcrumbs, browned in oil
½ cup (2 oz/60 g) freshly grated Pecorino cheese
1½ oz (45 g) fresh pancetta, minced

SERVES 4

❡ Heap the semolina on a pastry board and make a well in the center. Gradually add water

Left: Farfalle con Prosciutto, Piselli e Erbe di Campo; right: Orecchiette con Cavoli e Pancetta

and knead to a thick, smooth dough. Cover and set aside to rest for 30 minutes, covered with a damp cloth.

❦ Pinch off a piece of dough about the size of a hazelnut and mold it with your hands into a cylinder shape. Cut each cylinder into disks less than ⅜ in (1 cm) thick. Using the tip of a finger, press each disk down on the board with a forward motion to create the characteristic little concave dumplings called *orecchiette*. Spread them out to dry for 1 hour before cooking.

❦ Cook the cauliflower florets in plenty of boiling salted water for 10 minutes, add the *orecchiette* and cook for a few more minutes.

❦ Meanwhile, in a skillet, cook the garlic in the olive oil until golden. Discard the garlic. Add the *pancetta* and fry gently.

❦ Drain the *orecchiette* and cauliflower. (The *orecchiette* are cooked when they rise to the surface of the water.) Transfer to the skillet; season with black pepper. Add the breadcrumbs and Pecorino. Mix well and serve.

Top: Gnocchi di Carciofi al Timo; bottom: Gnocchi alla Bava

GNOCCHI DI CARCIOFI AL TIMO

ARTICHOKE GNOCCHI WITH THYME

This recipe uses ingredients typical of the countryside around Rome. The delicate taste of the artichoke is enhanced by a touch of thyme, with the other ingredients ranked together in second place in deference to the star of the dish.

3½ cups (13 oz/410 g) all-purpose (plain) flour
4 artichoke hearts, minced
2 eggs, beaten
9 oz (280 g) bread without crusts, cubed
1 cup (8 fl oz/250 ml) dry white wine
¾ cup (3 oz/90 g) freshly grated Parmesan cheese plus
   additional cheese, for serving
salt
3 tablespoons (1½ oz/45 g) butter
1 sprig thyme

SERVES 4

❦ Heap the flour on a pastry board and make a well in the center. Add the artichoke hearts, eggs, bread, wine, Parmesan and a pinch of salt. Knead vigorously; set aside to rest for about 30 minutes, covered with a damp cloth.
❦ Knead the dough and shape into a thin cylinder. Cut the dough into ¾ in (2 cm) lengths.
❦ Cook the *gnocchi* in plenty of boiling salted water; drain. In a skillet heat the butter with the thyme sprig. Sauté the *gnocchi* quickly. Sprinkle with a little Parmesan and serve.

GNOCCHI ALLA BAVA

GNOCCHI WITH CHEESE AND CREAM SAUCE

This rich, traditional Piedmontese family dish calls for the use of a cheese that melts easily. The original recipe specifies Fontina, a cheese typical of the Valle d'Aosta with its own characteristic flavor, but other cheeses are also used. Potato gnocchi made according to this recipe may also be served with other sauces.

2 lb (1 kg) floury potatoes, well scrubbed
about 1¾ cups (6½ oz/200 g) all-purpose (plain) flour
5 oz (155 g) Fontina cheese, sliced paper-thin
2½ oz (75 g) butter
salt

SERVES 4

❦ Put the potatoes into a saucepan of cold salted water and bring to a boil. Cook until they are quite soft. Drain and quickly peel. While still hot put through a potato ricer or sieve held over a pastry board. Gradually work in the flour with your hands to make a soft, smooth dough. Continue kneading until the dough no longer sticks to your hands — only then is it ready.
❦ Break off pieces of dough and roll out on the board with the palm of your hand, to make long sticks as thick as your little finger. Cut into ¾ in (2 cm) lengths and arrange them on the board. Sprinkle with flour to prevent them sticking together. One by one press each piece lightly against the tines of a fork or the surface of a grater, while at the same time pushing downward. This gives them their characteristic shape.
❦ When all the *gnocchi* are formed, cook in boiling water until they come to the surface; drain. Preheat the oven to 475°F (260°C). Arrange the *gnocchi* in layers in a buttered baking dish, placing the cheese between the layers. Dot the surface with the butter. Bake for 3 to 4 minutes. Serve immediately.

GARGANELLI AL VINO ROSSO, SCALOGNO E ZUCCHINI

PASTA WITH RED WINE, SHALLOTS AND ZUCCHINI SAUCE

The Emilia–Romagna region, with Bologna as its capital, is divided into two parts which differ noticeably in inhabitants and in gastronomic traditions. Garganelli are perhaps the most typical example of a first course served in Romagna.

For the pasta:
3¼ cups (13 oz/410 g) all-purpose (plain) flour
4 eggs
For the sauce:
2 small zucchini (courgettes)
salt
2½ oz (75 g) butter
2 shallots, chopped
½ cup (4 fl oz/125 ml) juices from a roast or beef stock
¾ cup (6 fl oz/185 ml) dry red wine
⅓ cup (1½ oz/45 g) freshly grated Parmesan cheese

SERVES 4

❡ Work the flour with the eggs to form a dough and roll out into a thin sheet. Cut the pasta into 2 in (5 cm) squares; roll each square around a pencil-shaped stick and then roll it over the comb (a rectangular wooden frame about 8×4 in [20 × 10 cm] with fine wooden strips across it positioned very close together). This gives the classic ridged macaroni. If you do not have a pasta comb you can roll the pasta over a cylindrical grater.

❡ Finely slice the zucchini, salt them and let them sweat for at least 30 minutes and then dry them. Melt 3 tablespoons of the butter in a saucepan. Add half the shallots, the meat juices and wine; stir and cook over low heat. In a skillet, gently fry the remaining shallots and the zucchini for a few seconds in the remaining butter.

❡ Cook the *garganelli* for about 5 minutes and drain them when al dente. Add to the shallot and wine sauce and add the Parmesan. Serve, garnished with the zucchini and shallots.

Garganelli al Vino Rosso, Scalogno e Zucchini

RAVIOLI DI CASTAGNE IN SALSA BIANCA

CHESTNUT RAVIOLI IN MASCARPONE SAUCE

The key to the originality of this ancient Umbrian dish lies in its simple reliance on basic country ingredients.

6 oz (185 g) chestnuts in their shells
6 oz (185 g) ricotta
pinch of salt
pinch of freshly grated nutmeg
pinch of ground rosemary
3¼ cups (13 oz/410 g) all-purpose (plain) flour
4 eggs
6 oz (185 g) mascarpone
3 sage leaves

SERVES 4

❡ Make a cut in the shells of the chestnuts with a sharp knife and cook them in water for 45 minutes. Drain and remove the shell and internal skin.
❡ In a blender or food processor combine the chestnuts, ricotta, salt, nutmeg and rosemary. Blend until smooth.
❡ Make the pasta dough with the flour and eggs. Roll it out and cut into 4 in (10 cm) wide strips and place ½ teaspoons of filling at 2 in (5 cm) intervals along one side of each strip, folding each strip lengthwise back over the filling, pressing well around the filling. Cut the ravioli with a ravioli wheel or fluted pastry wheel. Cook them in plenty of boiling salted water for 5 to 7 minutes, until they rise to the surface, then drain.
❡ Meanwhile, make the sauce: Put the mascarpone in the top of a double boiler with the sage leaves and beat with a wooden spoon until it becomes a fairly liquid cream. Serve the ravioli with the mascarpone sauce.

RAVIOLI DI SPIGOLA IN SALSA DI ARSELLE

SEA BASS RAVIOLI WITH CLAM SAUCE

Only recently has fish been used in Italian stuffed pastas, beginning on the Tyrrhenian coast between Genoa and Leghorn and from there taking off all over Italy. Today you can find magnificent fish ravioli even in cities nowhere near the sea.

For the filling:
10 oz (315 g) skinless sea bass fillets
2 oz (60 g) escarole
½ cup (4 fl oz/125 ml) olive oil
3 tablespoons dry white wine
3 tablespoons fish stock
1 teaspoon chopped flat-leafed parsley
1 tablespoon extra-virgin olive oil
salt and freshly ground pepper

For the pasta:
1⅔ cup (6½ oz/200 g) all-purpose (plain) flour
6 egg yolks, beaten together
1 tablespoon olive oil
1 tablespoon milk
pinch of salt
1 egg yolk, beaten, for brushing the dough

For the sauce:
½ cup (4 fl oz/125 ml) olive oil
1 garlic clove
1½ lb (750 g) baby clams, scrubbed
3 tablespoons dry white wine
1 large tomato, peeled, seeded and chopped
salt and freshly ground pepper
1 teaspoon chopped flat-leafed parsley

SERVES 4

❡ Make the pasta: Heap the flour on a board and make a well in the center. Add the egg yolks, oil, milk and salt. Work into a smooth dough. Roll into a ball and set aside, covered with a damp cloth.
❡ Make the filling: In a skillet, combine the fish fillets, escarole, oil, wine and fish stock. Cook, covered, over moderate heat for 6 or 7 minutes. Remove from the heat; drain off excess liquid. Finely chop the fish and escarole. Transfer to a small bowl, add the parsley and olive oil. Adjust the seasonings.
❡ Make the ravioli: Roll out the dough into 2 thin sheets, 12 in (30 cm) square, and brush with the beaten egg yolk. Place the filling on the first sheet in ½ teaspoon amounts, 2 in (5 cm) apart. Top with the second sheet, press down gently around each mound of filling, then use a ravioli wheel or fluted pastry wheel to cut 2 in (5 cm) square ravioli.
❡ Make the sauce: In a large skillet, heat the olive oil and garlic. Cook until lightly browned. Add the clams, cover and cook over high heat for 5 minutes. Set aside to cool, discarding any that do not open. Remove the clams from their shells; strain and reserve the cooking liquid.
❡ In a large, shallow skillet, combine the clams and white wine and cook until the wine evaporates completely. Add the tomatoes and the reserved cooking liquid. Adjust the seasonings. Stir in the parsley and cook for 5 minutes.
❡ Cook the ravioli in plenty of boiling, salted water until they rise to the surface, then drain. Dress with the hot sauce and serve.

Top: Ravioli di Castagne in Salsa Bianca; bottom: Ravioli di Spigola in Salsa di Arselle

Tagliatelle con i Funghi

TAGLIATELLE CON I FUNGHI

TAGLIATELLE WITH MUSHROOMS

While it is especially common in Liguria, Piedmont and Emilia, where most of the porcini mushrooms are gathered, this recipe in fact is part of traditional Italian cuisine.

2⅔ cups (9½ oz/305 g) all-purpose (plain) flour
2 whole eggs plus 2 egg yolks, beaten together
½ cup (4 fl oz/125 ml) olive oil
salt
1 tablespoon (½ oz/15 g) butter
1 garlic clove, peeled and bruised
6½ oz (200 g) porcini (boletus) mushrooms,
    thinly sliced
1 sprig flat-leafed parsley, chopped
freshly ground pepper

SERVES 4

❡ Heap the flour on a pastry board and make a well in the center. Add the beaten eggs and yolks, 2 tablespoons of the olive oil and a pinch of salt. Work the mixture into a soft, smooth dough and roll out into a very thin sheet. Roll up the sheet and with a sharp knife cut into tagliatelle not more than ¼ in (5 mm) in width. Lay the pasta out on the board sprinkled with flour to dry for 1 hour before cooking.
❡ In a skillet combine the remaining oil, the butter and garlic. Cook until the garlic colors; discard the garlic. Add the *porcini* and cook until browned. Taste for salt.

❡ Cook the tagliatelle in boiling, salted water until al dente; drain. Add to the skillet along with the parsley. Sauté for 30 seconds. Season with pepper just before serving.

RAVIOLI AL PROFUMO DI MAGGIORANA

MARJORAM-FLAVORED RAVIOLI

The ravioli, stuffed with ricotta and spinach, have a very light flavor, while the sauce that accompanies them has faint echoes of Genoese pesto (though it lacks the fundamental garlic).

For the pasta:
3¼ cups (13 oz /410 g) all-purpose (plain) flour
4 eggs, beaten together
½ cup (4 fl oz/125 ml) water
2 tablespoons olive oil
pinch of salt
1 egg, beaten, for brushing the dough
For the filling:
9 oz (280 g) ricotta
5 oz (155 g) cooked spinach
2 eggs
½ cup (2 oz/60 g) freshly grated Parmesan cheese
pinch of freshly grated nutmeg
salt and freshly ground pepper
For the sauce:
¾ cup (3 oz/90 g) pine nuts
¼ cup (2 fl oz/60 ml) extra-virgin olive oil
8 oz (250 g) marjoram leaves
6 oz (185 g) basil leaves
3½ oz (105 g) butter
salt

SERVES 4

❡ Make the pasta: Heap the flour on a board and make a well in the center. Add the eggs, water, olive oil and salt. Work into a smooth dough. Roll into a ball and set aside, covered with a damp cloth.
❡ Meanwhile, make the filling: Put the ricotta and spinach through a food mill, adding the eggs, Parmesan, nutmeg, salt and pepper. Mix well.
❡ Make the ravioli: Roll out the dough into 2 thin sheets, 12 in (30 cm) square, and brush with the beaten egg. Place the filling on the first sheet in ½ teaspoon amounts, 2 in (5 cm) apart. Top with the second sheet, press down gently around each mound of filling, then use a ravioli wheel or fluted pastry wheel to cut 2 in (5 cm) square ravioli.
❡ Make the sauce: In a blender or food processor, combine the pine nuts, 1 tablespoon of the olive

oil, the marjoram and basil; blend until smooth. Transfer to a large, shallow skillet. Add the butter, the remaining olive oil and salt to taste and cook until well mixed.

❡ Cook the ravioli in plenty of boiling, salted water until they rise to the surface, then drain. Add the ravioli to the sauce, stir to coat them and blend the flavors, then serve.

RAVIOLI AI CARCIOFI

ARTICHOKE RAVIOLI

These ravioli from Liguria celebrate the wealth of wonderful vegetables in the region, using the famous Albenga artichokes in place of the more traditional meat fillings.

For the pasta:
3¼ cups (13 oz/410 g) all-purpose (plain) flour
3 whole eggs plus 2 egg yolks, beaten together
pinch of salt
1 egg, beaten, for brushing the dough
For the filling:
8 small Italian artichokes
1 small leek, washed well and thinly sliced
3 tablespoons (1½ oz/45 g) butter, melted
salt and freshly ground pepper
2 tablespoons olive oil

2 whole eggs plus 1 egg yolk, beaten together
¾ cup (3 oz/90 g) freshly grated Parmesan cheese
For the sauce:
3 tablespoons (1½ oz/45 g) butter
pinch of thyme leaves

SERVES 4

❡ Make the pasta: Work the flour with the eggs and the salt. Roll the dough into a ball. Let it rest, covered with a damp cloth.

❡ Meanwhile, make the filling: Wash and trim the artichokes. Cut each artichoke into 4 wedges. In a skillet, combine the artichokes, leek, half the butter and salt and pepper to taste. Cook slowly for about 15 minutes, then purée the mixture in a blender or food processor. Stir in the olive oil, eggs and Parmesan.

❡ Make the ravioli: Roll out the dough into 2 thin sheets, 12 in (30 cm) square, and brush with beaten egg. Place the filling on the first sheet in ½ teaspoon amounts, 2 in (5 cm) apart. Top with the second sheet and press down gently around each mound of filling. Use a ravioli wheel or fluted pastry wheel to cut 2 in (5 cm) square ravioli. Cook them in plenty of boiling salted water until they rise to the surface, then drain. Serve dressed with melted butter flavored with the thyme.

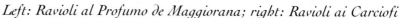

Left: Ravioli al Profumo de Maggiorana; right: Ravioli ai Carciofi

CASUNZIEI DI PATATE

POTATO CASUNZIEI

This complex dish requires three separate preparation procedures; it also calls for an appropriate explanation. Casunziei come from the poorest of peasant origins, yet here they are elevated to the status of haute cuisine. The animal fats once plentiful in the sauce have come down to a film of butter for greasing the pan in which the filling is cooked. Apart from this, extra-virgin olive oil reigns supreme. And the presentation of the dish, cleverly put together to make the most of its colors, transforms a coarse mountain food into a model of elegance.

For the stuffing:
8 oz (250 g) potatoes, peeled and cut into julienne strips
1 tablespoon (½ oz/15 g) butter
½ onion, chopped
2 oz (60 g) mascarpone cheese
2 oz (60 g) ricotta
4 teaspoons freshly grated Parmesan cheese
1 egg yolk
pinch of freshly grated nutmeg
2 tablespoons extra-virgin olive oil
salt and freshly ground pepper
For the pasta:
2⅔ cups (9½ oz/300 g) all-purpose (plain) flour
2 whole eggs plus 2 egg yolks, beaten together
1 tablespoon extra-virgin olive oil
For the sauce:
½ onion, chopped
2 fl oz (60 ml) extra-virgin olive oil
2 potatoes, peeled and diced
1½ oz (45 g) smoked ricotta, sliced paper-thin

SERVES 4

❡ Make the stuffing: In a large skillet, fry the potatoes in the butter until just beginning to brown. Add the onion and cook for 5 minutes, until soft. Set aside to cool briefly. Stir in the mascarpone, ricotta, Parmesan and egg yolk; season with the nutmeg, olive oil and salt and pepper. Stir well. Set aside.
❡ Make the pasta: Make a dough with the flour, eggs and olive oil. Roll out into a thin sheet; cut into 2¾ in (7 cm) circles. Place a little stuffing in the center of each circle and fold the dough over into a half-moon shape. Seal each one with a little water and press closed with your fingers.
❡ Prepare the sauce: In a large skillet, soften the onion in 1 tablespoon of the olive oil. Add the potatoes, cover with water and cook for 30 minutes over moderate heat. Put this mixture through a food mill and stir in the remaining oil.

The sauce will have a velvety texture. Set aside and keep warm.
❡ Boil the *casunziei* in salted water for 3 to 4 minutes; drain.
❡ Pour some of the sauce onto each plate. Arrange the *casunziei* on top, in a fan shape. Finish each serving with a wafer-thin slice of smoked ricotta.

AGNOLOTTI AI FORMAGGI

AGNOLOTTI FILLED WITH CHEESES

The wide variety of cheeses produced in every Italian region has fostered the creation of recipes that feature one or more dairy products as major ingredients. Here, the dish comes from the valleys around Lake Maggiore and the local cow's milk cheeses are combined with ricotta and fresh goat's cheese.

Left: Casunziei di Patate; right: Agnolotti ai Formaggi

For the pasta:

4⅓ cups (1 lb/500 g) all-purpose (plain) flour

2 whole eggs plus 2 yolks, beaten together

1 tablespoon olive oil

pinch of salt

For the filling:

1 small onion, chopped

1 tablespoon (½ oz/15 g) butter

3 tablespoons ricotta

3 tablespoons finely diced valley cheeses, such as
Fontina and Montasio

2 tablespoons fresh goat's cheese

1 tablespoon marjoram leaves

2 pinches thyme leaves

salt and freshly ground pepper

pinch of freshly grated nutmeg

For the sauce:

3 oz (90 g) fresh porcini (boletus) mushrooms, stalks
removed, thinly sliced

3 oz (90 g) melted butter

SERVES 6

❧ First make the pasta: Make a dough from the flour, eggs, olive oil and salt. Roll out into a sheet.

❧ Make the filling: In a small skillet, sauté the onion in the butter. Stir in the ricotta, the valley cheeses, the goat's cheese, the marjoram and thyme. When the ingredients are completely mixed, add a small amount of the salt, pepper and nutmeg.

❧ Make the *agnolotti*: Roll out the dough into 2 thin sheets, 12 in (30 cm) square. Place the filling on the first sheet in ½ teaspoon amounts, 2 in (5 cm) apart. Top with the second sheet, press down gently around each mound of filling, then use a ravioli wheel or fluted pastry wheel to cut 2 in (5 cm) square *agnolotti*. Cook them in plenty of boiling, salted water for 5 to 7 minutes, until they rise to the surface, then drain. Serve covered with the raw mushrooms and melted butter.

ANOLINI ALLA PARMIGIANA

PARMA-STYLE ANOLINI

Similar in shape to tortellini *but completely different in substance,* anolini *are a source of gastronomic pride in Parma. Originally reserved for special occasions when poor families could afford to have meat, wisely only the cooking juices mixed with breadcrumbs were used for the pasta stuffing, leaving the meat itself to serve as the main course. The traditional recipe states that the meat should cook for 3 days, but for today's busy families this time is considerably reduced.*

For the capon and beef stock:
½ capon, about 3 lb (1.5 kg)
2 lb (1 kg) beef brisket
20 cups (5 qt/5 l) water
2 onions, each stuck with 2 cloves
2 carrots
2 celery stalks
2 tablespoons salt
For the filling:
2 cups (16 fl oz/500 ml) meat stock
1 tablespoon homemade tomato sauce
1 lb (500 g) beef round steak
2 oz (60 g) pancetta, cubed
3 or 4 garlic cloves, sliced
3 tablespoons (1½ oz/45 g) butter
½ cup (4 fl oz/125 ml) olive oil
1 onion, minced
salt and pepper
3 cups (24 fl oz/750 ml) dry red wine
1 celery stalk, sliced
1 carrot, sliced
3 whole cloves
6 tablespoons dried breadcrumbs, toasted
1½ cups (6 oz/185 g) freshly grated Parmesan cheese
pinch of freshly ground nutmeg
2 eggs, beaten
For the pasta:
4⅓ cups (1 lb/500 g) all-purpose (plain) flour
2 whole eggs plus 3 egg yolks, beaten together
1 tablespoon olive oil
salt

SERVES 6

❡ Make the capon and beef stock: In a large saucepan place the capon, beef, water, onions, carrots, celery and salt. Bring to a boil and simmer, covered, for 2 hours. Remove the meat. Strain the liquid and set aside for cooking the *anolini*.
❡ Make the filling: Heat the stock with the tomato sauce; keep warm.

❡ Make small cuts in the meat and insert the *pancetta* cubes and sliced garlic. In a large wide pan, terracotta if possible, melt the butter with the olive oil. Add the onion and cook until softened. Add the meat, sprinkle with salt and pepper, and cook until browned on all sides. Pour in the wine, and then enough stock to completely cover the meat. Add the celery, carrot and cloves. Cover, reduce the heat and cook very slowly for 3 to 4 hours, or until the meat is cooked and the juices well reduced and rich tasting.
❡ Remove the meat. Strain the cooking liquid into a bowl. Add the breadcrumbs, Parmesan, nutmeg and the eggs. Add more cheese, if necessary, to give a soft but compact texture to the stuffing.
❡ Make the pasta: Heap the flour on a board and make a well in the center. Add the beaten eggs, oil and a pinch of salt. Knead the dough; roll out into a very thin sheet. Cut into 2 in (5 cm) circles, place ½ teaspoon filling in the center of each circle. Fold the pasta over the filling and press the edges together to seal well.
❡ Cook the *anolini* for 5 to 7 minutes in the capon and beef stock, immersing them when the liquid reaches a rolling boil. They are cooked when they rise to the surface of the stock. Serve with the stock and the remaining grated Parmesan as a side dish.

TORTELLINI CON RIPIENO E RAGÙ DI ASPARAGI

ASPARAGUS TORTELLINI WITH ASPARAGUS SAUCE

This is a most elegant modern version of a traditional dish, and recognition is due to Pina Bellini, the exceptional Milanese cook who created it. The idea of substantially altering such a classic dish by giving it a refined asparagus filling is a winner, both for its originality and for its simplicity.

For the filling:
6 oz (185 g) asparagus tips
3 oz (90 g) ricotta
½ cup (2 oz/60 g) freshly grated Parmesan cheese
3 tablespoons heavy (double) cream
salt and freshly ground pepper
For the pasta:
2½ cups (10 oz/310 g) all-purpose (plain) flour
2 eggs
3 tablespoons dry white wine
pinch of salt

For the sauce:
11 oz (345 g) asparagus tips
3 tablespoons (1½ oz/45 g) butter

SERVES 4

❧ Make the filling: Cook the asparagus tips in boiling, salted water until tender but still slightly crunchy; drain. Push the asparagus through a sieve and mix with the ricotta, Parmesan, cream, and salt and pepper to taste.

❧ Make the pasta: Knead the flour with the eggs, white wine and salt until it is smooth and elastic.

❧ Make the *tortellini*: Roll the dough out into 2 thin sheets of equal size. Place the filling on the first sheet in ½ teaspoon amounts, 2 in (5 cm) apart. Top with the second sheet and press down gently around each mound of filling. Use a 2 in (5 cm) diameter cookie-cutter or glass to cut out the *tortellini*, then roll each one round the end of the index finger and press the ends together.

❧ Make the sauce: Cook the asparagus tips in boiling, salted water until al dente. Reserve 3 tips per person for decoration and cut the rest into rounds. Melt the butter in a pan over barely simmering water. Add the asparagus rounds and cook, leaving them only long enough to barely soften.

❧ Cook the *tortellini* in plenty of boiling, salted water for 5 to 7 minutes, until they rise to the surface, then drain. Serve, topped with Parmesan and the hot sauce. Garnish with the reserved asparagus tips.

Left: Anolini alla Parmigiana; right: Tortellini con Ripieno e Ragù di Asparagi

RAVIOLI FRITTI

FRIED RAVIOLI

The ingredients for this pasta filling are similar to those used in some savory baked tarts made in Liguria.

For the filling:
²⁄₃ cup (4 oz/125 g) fresh, or ¹⁄₃ cup (2 oz/60 g) dried
    cannellini *(white) beans*
2 lb (1 kg) peeled pumpkin, coarsely chopped
¹⁄₃ cup (2 oz/60 g) long-grain rice, cooked
2 eggs, beaten
¹⁄₂ cup (2 oz/60 g) freshly grated Parmesan cheese
¹⁄₄ cup (1 oz/30 g) freshly grated Pecorino cheese
1 garlic clove
¹⁄₂ cup chopped flat-leafed parsley
¹⁄₂ cup chopped marjoram
salt and freshly ground pepper
4 tablespoons extra-virgin olive oil
For the pasta:
4¹⁄₃ cups (1 lb/500 g) all-purpose (plain) flour
pinch of salt
olive oil, for frying
SERVES 4

¶ Make the filling: Cook the *cannellini* beans in boiling, salted water for 35 minutes, or until tender. If using dried beans, soak them for 12 hours in cold water, before cooking for 45 minutes, or until tender. Drain.
¶ Preheat the oven to 350°F (180°C). Bake the pumpkin for 30 minutes, or until tender. Cool. When thoroughly dry, combine the pumpkin, rice and beans. Stir in the eggs, cheeses, garlic and herbs. Season to taste, add the olive oil and mix.
¶ Make the pasta: Work the flour and salt with enough water to make a very soft dough. Let it

Ravioli Fritti

rest for at least 30 minutes, covered with a damp cloth.
¶ Roll out the pasta until ¹⁄₁₆ in (1 mm) thick. Cut it into 4 in (10 cm) squares. Place 1 tablespoon of the filling in the center of each square. Fold the dough over diagonally to form large triangles.
¶ Fry the ravioli in very hot oil. Remove with a skimmer when golden brown. Serve at once.

RISO AL SALTO

TOSSED RICE CAKES

This delicate Milanese dish is underestimated by most people but it is a noble dish, prepared in modern Milanese cuisine in the following way.

2¹⁄₂ cups (12 oz/375 g) Carnaroli or Arborio (Italian
    long-grain) rice
1 small onion, finely chopped
5 tablespoons (2¹⁄₂ oz/75 g) butter
¹⁄₂ cup (2 oz/60 g) freshly grated Parmesan cheese
¹⁄₂ cup (4 fl oz/125 ml) dry white wine
6 cups (1¹⁄₂ qt/1.5 l) meat stock, heated to a boil (see
    introduction to Risotto alla Milanese page 70)
pinch of saffron
freshly ground pepper
SERVES 4 (MAKES 4 RICE CAKES)

¶ In a high-sided stewpan (tinned copper, if possible), fry the onion in 2 tablespoons (1 oz/30 g) butter over medium heat until golden. Add the rice, stirring with a wooden spoon until it has absorbed the butter completely. Pour in the wine and stir until it has evaporated. Add the stock, a ladleful at a time, stirring often so that the rice does not stick to the bottom of the pan. The heat should be moderately high only. Add the saffron after 6 minutes. After 7 or 8 minutes remove the risotto from the heat and stir in the remaining butter and the Parmesan and quickly spread the rice out on a platter so that it cools quickly to ensure that it does not overcook.
¶ Make the rice cakes: Lightly butter a 10 in (25 cm) cast-iron or nonstick skillet and set over moderate heat. Place about 3 tablespoons of the rice in the center, press into an even pancake to cover the base of the pan and cook until golden and crispy. The skilled cook will be able to turn the rice cake over by tossing it in the pan, but it can also be turned by sliding it onto a plate and putting it back to cook the other side. Keep the cooked ones warm until all are done, then serve immediately, seasoned with pepper. (See photograph page 74.)

and Friuli regions. Spelt, a type of wheat widely used in Roman times, is still grown in a few places in Lunigiana, an area bordering Tuscany and Liguria, and in Umbria. It is used with vegetables in several soups.

Some legumes, particularly *borlotti* and some varieties of white bean, are also especially suited to soup-making. But by far the most frequently seen legumes on Italian tables are chickpeas, fava beans and green peas. Lentils make a ritual appearance at New Year's Eve dinner served with *zampone* or boiled *cotechino* sausage.

In Italy the best lentils are grown at Castelluccio in Umbria, on the Fucino River plain east of Rome, and at Altamura in Apulia. Both lentils and chickpeas are used in the dried form and soaked in cold water for at least 12 hours before cooking. And some beans such as cannellini, are commonly eaten in salads.

GRAINS AND LEGUMES

The first definite traces of the cultivation of grains were discovered in France and go back as far as 10,000 years. Grains are certainly the world's oldest form of nourishment. Their importance was such that Demeter, the Greek goddess of the earth and of fertility, was depicted with hair made from golden ears of corn.

Included with this group, by extension, are the legumes (pulses) — the different varieties of peas and beans, such as

chickpeas, peas, lentils, lima (butter) beans, and fava (broad) beans, which also have grains, but contained in pods rather than ears. For almost as long, legumes, which are rich in protein, have provided nourishing food, especially for poorer families. There are a number of particularly Italian varieties, such as *borlotti* and cannellini.

At least seven of the known forms of cereal grains occupy an important place in Italian

cooking: "common" wheat, semolina, durum wheat, rice, buckwheat, barley and spelt. The first three, ground into flour, are used mainly in the making of bread and pasta; the others are used directly in the preparation of dishes. In Valtellina, north of Lake Como, ground buckwheat is used to make a strong, dark polenta which features in a number of local dishes. Barley features in some major soups of the Alto Adige

1. cannellini beans; 2. red lentils; 3. spelt; 4. borlotti beans; 5. green lentils; 6. chickpeas; 7. lima (butter) beans; 8. fava (broad) beans; 9. peas; 10. brown lentils

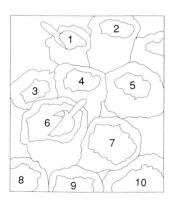

Left: Risotto alla Milanese; right: Risotto alla Certosina

RISOTTO ALLA MILANESE

MILANESE RISOTTO

There is a popular legend that says this risotto was created during the building of the Milan Cathedral, when one of the workmen had the idea of adding a pinch of the saffron, used to make the gold for the windows, to a normal risotto and having it served at his wedding feast. The true story is probably simpler: rice and saffron reached Milan in the wake of the Spaniards during the fifteenth century, and this risotto could in fact be the poor cook's version of the far richer paella of the conquerors. A good-quality stock is essential to the success of the dish. It must be made from beef, veal and chicken immersed in cold water with an onion stuck with a few cloves, a celery stalk and a carrot. When ready, it is strained and put back on the heat next to the rice as it cooks.

about 20 saffron threads
about 8 cups (2 qt/2 l) meat stock, heated to a boil
3½ oz (105 g) butter
1 small onion, finely chopped

2½ cups (13 oz/410 g) Carnaroli or Arborio (Italian long-grain) rice
1 cup (8 fl oz/250 ml) dry white wine
salt
⅔ cup (2½ oz/80 g) freshly grated Parmesan cheese
SERVES *4*

¶ Dissolve the saffron in 1 cup (8 fl oz/250 ml) of boiling stock. Meanwhile, in a high-sided stewpan, which should be made of tinned copper, if possible, fry the onion in half the butter over medium heat until golden. Add the rice, stirring with a wooden spoon until it has absorbed the butter completely. Pour in the wine and continue stirring until it has evaporated. Begin adding the stock, a ladleful at a time, stirring often so that the rice does not stick to the bottom of the pan. The heat should be moderately high only. Add a little salt and cook for about 10 minutes.
¶ Add the saffron and continue cooking, adding more stock. Taste from time to time, and when the rice is still fairly firm (al dente), turn off the heat.

RISOTTO ALLA CERTOSINA

CARTHUSIAN RISOTTO

As its title suggests, this recipe belongs to the monastic tradition and is an admirable example of a major meatless dish as required by the rules governing the lives of the monks who created it. This risotto brings together the products of the soil and the sea in the area of Pavia, and is linked to the Carthusian monastery of Pavia.

1 lb (500 g) freshwater crayfish (yabbie)
1 celery stalk
1 small onion
1 carrot
1 bay leaf
½ cup (4 fl oz/125 ml) olive oil
1 garlic clove
1 oz (30 g) dried mushrooms, soaked for 30 minutes,
    drained and chopped
½ cup (4 fl oz/125 ml) dry white wine
1 tablespoon tomato paste
1 cup (3 oz/90 g) fresh or frozen green peas, cooked
salt and freshly ground pepper
2½ cups (13 oz/410 g) Carnaroli or Arborio
    (Italian long-grain) rice
6 cups (1½ qt/1.5 l) vegetable stock
2 tablespoons chopped flat-leafed parsley

SERVES 4

Mix in the cheese and the remaining butter. Set aside, covered, for 3 or 4 minutes before serving. Remember that rice continues to cook and absorb liquid for as long as it is hot. Thus, when the heat is turned off, the mixture should still be moist.

SAFFRON

The Italians first became acquainted with saffron when the Arabs introduced it into Sicily, and then later when the Spaniards, who had inherited this spice from the Arab world and used it chiefly for paella alla valenciana, *came to rule in Milan. The Sicilians still produce a special bread and a cheese known as* piacintinu *(literally "which pleases"), both containing saffron. The best saffron for Italian cooking (it is used not only in* risotto alla milanese *but also in* brodetto, *a fish soup from the Marches region, and in other recipes) is the one found in the crocuses grown on the Navelli tablelands near l'Aquila. Because powdered saffron might not be pure, it is always best to buy the whole crocus pistils or threads.*

❡ Place the crayfish, celery stalk, onion, carrot and bay leaf in a large saucepan and cover with water. Bring the water to a boil over high heat and then cook for about 8 to 10 minutes.
❡ Remove the crayfish and break off the tails; set aside.
❡ Crush the crayfish heads and bodies; strain the liquid. Strain the cooking liquid; add to the crayfish juices.
❡ In a stewpan or casserole, combine the oil and garlic. Sauté until the garlic begins to color; discard the garlic. Add the mushrooms and cook briefly; pour in the wine and cook until it has evaporated. Stir in the tomato paste, peas and the reserved crayfish tails, then the crayfish cooking juices. Cook slowly over low heat for 10 minutes. Season to taste.
❡ In a saucepan, combine the rice with the vegetable stock and cook over moderate heat for 14 to 16 minutes, until the rice has completely absorbed the stock and is al dente.
❡ Mix the crayfish mixture in with the cooked rice and serve sprinkled with parsley. No cheese is necessary.

RISOTTO CON LE RANE IN FIORE DI ZUCCHINO

RISOTTO WITH ZUCCHINI FLOWERS STUFFED WITH FROGS' LEGS

This is a classic dish from the country around Pavia, where on spring evenings the many rice paddy-fields yield rich frog catches. The most traditional version has only the rice, frogs' legs and flavorings. In this modern recipe, the dish is further developed and enriched with the delicate taste of zucchini (courgette) flowers.

For the stuffed zucchini (courgette) flowers:
10 oz (315 g) frogs' legs, boned
¼ onion, chopped
1 cup (8 fl oz/250 ml) oil
2¼ cups (11 oz/345 g) Carnaroli or Arborio (Italian long-grain) rice
3½ cups (28 fl oz/875 ml) frog stock (made by boiling up frog trimmings with celery, carrot and onion), or chicken stock, heated to a boil
salt
3 tablespoons freshly grated Parmesan cheese
1 egg, beaten
1 large sprig flat-leafed parsley, chopped
1 strip of lemon zest (rind)
8 zucchini (courgette) flowers
For the frogs' legs:
24 frogs' legs
1 tablespoon (½ oz/15 g) butter
½ garlic clove
1 tablespoon chopped flat-leafed parsley
3 tablespoons dry white wine

SERVES 4

❡ In a large skillet, gently fry the 10 oz (315 g) frogs' legs and onion in half the oil. When the onion is translucent add the rice, stirring with a wooden spoon until it has absorbed the butter completely. Add the boiling stock, a ladleful at a time, stirring to assist absorption; add salt to taste. When the rice is al dente (after about 14 minutes) remove from the heat and beat in the Parmesan mixed with the egg, parsley and lemon zest. Spread out on a platter and leave to cool.
❡ Fill the zucchini flowers with the risotto, brown them in a skillet with the remaining oil.
❡ In a stewpan, over moderate heat, cook the 24 frogs' legs in the butter with the garlic, parsley and white wine for 5 minutes, stirring. Remove the garlic when it browns.
❡ Serve 2 zucchini flowers for each person in the center of the plate surrounded by the frogs' legs arranged in the shape of a crown.

RISOTTO "PRIMAVERA"

RISOTTO WITH SPRING VEGETABLES

This is one of the dishes that has made Harry's Bar in Venice famous throughout the world. It is also an example of the endless combinations made possible by the versatility of rice. The name suggests a dish rich in the vegetables that are first to appear in the markets when the good weather arrives, but the recipe works equally well with other vegetables, depending on what is available.

½ onion, chopped
3 tablespoons (1½ oz/45 g) butter
1⅓ cups (6½ oz/200 g) Carnaroli or Arborio (Italian long-grain) rice
2 cups (16 fl oz/500 ml) meat stock, heated to a boil
3 oz (90 g) thin asparagus, cooked and sliced
3 oz (90 g) zucchini (courgettes), cooked and sliced
2 oz (60 g) shelled green peas, cooked
2 oz (60 g) button mushrooms (champignons), sliced
1 red or green bell pepper (capsicum), roasted, peeled and chopped
¼ cup (1 oz/30 g) tomatoes, peeled and seeded
½ cup (2 oz/60 g) freshly grated Parmesan cheese

SERVES 4

❡ In a saucepan gently fry the onion in 1 tablespoon (½ oz/15 g) of the butter over very low heat. When the onion is golden, add the rice, stirring with a wooden spoon until it has absorbed the butter completely. Add the stock, a ladleful at a time, stirring to assist the absorption process.
❡ Cook for 10 minutes then stir in all the vegetables. Continue cooking, adding any remaining stock, and stirring, for about another 10 minutes. Remove from heat, beat in the remaining butter and the Parmesan and serve.

RISOTTO ALLA PARMIGIANA

RICE WITH PARMESAN CHEESE

This is risotto par excellence, *the so-called white risotto that can serve as the basis for many other rice dishes with different flavors. It was originally created to show off the superb quality of Parma's famous cheese, which is very generously used in the dish. Reduce the quantity of cheese used if other ingredients are to be added.*

1 onion, finely chopped
2½ oz (75 g) butter
2½ cups (13 oz/410 g) Carnaroli or Arborio (Italian long-grain) rice

Top: Risotto "Primavera"; bottom left: Risotto con le Rane in Fiore di Zucchino; bottom right: Risotto alla Parmigiana

6 cups (1½ qt/1.5 l) meat stock, heated to a boil
salt
¾ cup (3 oz/90 g) freshly grated Parmesan cheese
SERVES 4

❡ In a high-sided stewpan, which should be made of tinned copper, if possible, gently sauté the onion with half the butter over very low heat. When the onion is translucent, add the rice,

stirring with a wooden spoon until it has absorbed the butter completely. Add the boiling stock, a ladleful at a time, stirring to assist the absorption process. Add a little salt, but not much; the broth is already salted and the Parmesan added at the end will boost the flavor of the dish considerably. When the rice is al dente (after about 14 minutes) turn off the heat. Rapidly mix in the remaining butter and all the Parmesan and serve.

Left: Bomba di Riso alla Parmigiana; right: Riso al Salto (page 68)

BOMBA DI RISO ALLA PARMIGIANA

PARMA RICE MOLD

The people of Parma consider this the pride of the local cuisine, but the dish really originated in Piacenza and is common to other Italian cities as well. Nevertheless the natives of Parma deserve full credit for making it a recipe for great occasions.

5 oz (155 g) butter
1 onion, thinly sliced
2 young pigeons, cleaned and quartered
¼ cup (1 oz/30 g) all-purpose (plain) flour
½ cup (4 fl oz/125 ml) dry white wine
3 ripe tomatoes, peeled, seeded and chopped
2 cups (16 fl oz/500 ml) meat stock, heated
salt
3¼ cups (1¼ lb/625 g) Carnaroli or Arborio (Italian long-grain) rice
1 cup (4 oz/125 g) freshly grated Parmesan cheese
2 eggs, beaten
3–4 tablespoons dried breadcrumbs

SERVES 6

¶ In a casserole, melt 4 tablespoons (2 oz/60 g) of the butter over moderate heat. Add the onion and sauté, without browning, until soft. Dredge the pigeons in the flour and add to the pan. Turn to brown evenly on all sides. Add the wine and cook until evaporated. Add the tomatoes and stock and season with salt. Cook over moderate heat for about 1 hour. When the pigeons are cooked, remove all the bones; strain the cooking liquid, and reserve.

¶ Bring a saucepan of salted water to a boil. Add the rice and cook for 12 minutes; it must be very firm to the bite. Drain. In a large bowl, combine the rice with the remaining butter, the Parmesan, the reserved cooking liquid and the eggs.

¶ Preheat the oven to 350°F (180°C). Butter a 9 in (22 cm) diameter round mold, about 6 in (15 cm) high, with a hole in the center. Sprinkle with the breadcrumbs and line the mold with half the rice, pressing it well against the sides.

¶ Distribute the pigeon meat on top. Cover with the remaining rice. Bake in the oven for about 30 minutes, or until a light crust forms on top. Unmold and serve immediately.

above all, are of the superfine quality essential for a good risotto. The most valuable quality of superfine rices is their capacity to hold their shape during cooking without going mushy.

As with pasta, rice cooking has certain principles that must be observed: first, 4 cups (1 qt/1 l) water for every ½ cup (3 oz/90 g). If the rice is cooked in a small amount of water, the abundant starch released transforms the contents of the saucepan into an unacceptable mush. Remember that as long as the rice is hot, it will continue cooking, even with the heat turned off. Whatever cooking method is used, keep in mind that the heat should be turned off while the rice is still fairly firm to the bite — al dente.

Apart from its presence in a few soups, rice is mostly served in the form of risotto.

RICE

This ancient cereal, cultivated in India as early as 4,000 BC is found in all Italian cooking from north to south, although there is a clear predominance in the northern regions.

After early attempts to grow it in the south, rice production became concentrated wholly in Piedmont and the Veneto, in the provinces of Novara, Pavia, Milan, Mantova and Verona.

In Italy rice is divided into four basic types: common rice, with small round grains that tend to disintegrate during cooking (used mainly in soups); semi-fine, a medium-grain rice (used in molds and croquettes); long-grain or fine rice with larger grains than the previous two (recommended for risottos); and the superfine quality, which has rounder and longer grains again (per-fect for risottos and pilafs).

Each of these groups in turn includes a number of rice types named according to the plants they come from, as displayed on their packaging. Tondo Balilla is a common rice for soups; the names Maratelli and Vialone Nano refer to semi-fine rice; Ribe Ringo and Rizzato are fine quality; Razza 77, Arborio and Carnaroli

1. & 8. *Fine Ribe;*
2. *integrale (brown rice);*
3. & 6. *Vialone Nano;*
4. & 9. *Carnaroli;*
5. *Originario;*
7. & 10. *Arborio*

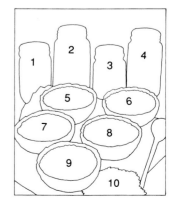

JOTA

BEAN, POTATO AND SAUERKRAUT SOUP

A traditional soup throughout the Friuli–Venezia–Giulia region, Jota has always been a robust and flavorsome dish. In the versions used in modern cuisine there are a few slight changes. The pork fat used with a heavy hand in the past is no longer present, and instead of smoked pancetta we find simple de-fatted prosciutto.

2½ cups (8 oz/250 g) fresh, or 1¼ cups (4 oz/125 g)
   dried borlotti (red) beans
4 or 5 potatoes, peeled
1 celery stalk
1 large onion
2 garlic cloves
2 bay leaves
3 oz (90 g) prosciutto, *with the fat removed*
8 oz (250 g) drained sauerkraut
salt and freshly ground pepper
1 tablespoon all-purpose (plain) flour
3 tablespoons olive oil
pinch of cumin

SERVES 4–6

❡ If using dried *borlotti* beans, soak them for 12 hours in cold water; drain.
❡ Put the beans into a large saucepan of water with the whole potatoes, celery, onion, 1 garlic clove, 1 bay leaf and half the *prosciutto*. Cook slowly for 1½ hours.

Left: Jota; right: Minestrone alla Genovese col Pesto

❡ Meanwhile, brown the flour in a small skillet with a minimum of fat (a few scraps from the *prosciutto*, which are then removed). Set aside.
❡ Squeeze the moisture from the sauerkraut and put it into another saucepan with salt, pepper, 1 bay leaf, 1 garlic clove, the remaining *prosciutto*, the browned flour and water to cover. Cook for 1 hour.
❡ Take 2 or 3 ladlefuls of soup with the celery, some of the beans and 2 potatoes, and blend in a food processor. Return this to the saucepan and add the sauerkraut mixture. Cook for 30 minutes more and adjust the seasoning. Add the olive oil and cumin. Serve warm rather than hot.

MINESTRONE ALLA GENOVESE COL PESTO

GENOESE MINESTRONE WITH PESTO

This is a very simple minestrone, but also rich in garden vegetables, with the all-important addition of a few spoonfuls of pesto just before serving. Adding this strongly flavored Genoese sauce to the soup gives it a character all of its own. It is one of the best-loved dishes in Italian cuisine, and continues to hold a place of honor on the family table and in restaurants.

⅓ cup (2 oz/60 g) dried borlotti (red) beans
⅓ cup (2 oz/60 g) dried cannellini (white) beans
2 zucchini (courgettes), trimmed and diced
2 eggplants (aubergines), trimmed and diced
3 tomatoes, peeled, seeded and diced
1 bunch celery, trimmed and diced
2 potatoes, peeled and diced
2 tablespoons olive oil
1½ tablespoons kosher (coarse) salt
5 oz (155 g) pasta (broken-up spaghetti, shells,
   anolini, *macaroni*, penne *or other*)
2 tablespoons pesto (*see recipe for* trenette al pesto
   page 48)

SERVES 4

❡ Soak the *borlotti* and *cannellini* beans for 12 hours in cold water to cover. Drain. Combine all the vegetables with the oil and salt in a large saucepan. Add cold water to cover. Bring to a boil, cover, reduce the heat to moderately low and cook for about 1 hour, until the beans are tender.
❡ Add the pasta, turn up the heat and cook until the pasta is al dente. Turn off the heat, add the pesto and stir at once with a wooden spoon. Serve immediately.

Left: Acquacotta; right: Garmugia Lucchese

ACQUACOTTA

"COOKED WATER" SOUP

The peasant families of the Maremma region had to contend with chronic poverty. They had bread, the kind of large round loaf that, once the first day's slices had been cut from it, remained permanently stale. They had a little pork fat, to be used sparingly, and a few garden vegetables. Out of this came an economical and simple soup, and it remains so today.

1 oz (30 g) pork fat or prosciutto fat, minced
1 onion, finely chopped
6 cups (1½ qt/1.5 l) water
1 bunch beet (beetroot) greens, cut into thin strips
1 small piece hot chili pepper
1 large sprig mint
salt
¼ cup (2 fl oz/60 ml) oil
8 slices stale bread, toasted

SERVES 4

❡ Combine the pork fat and onion in a saucepan over moderate heat. Lower heat and fry gently until the onion begins to color. Add the water, the beet greens, chili pepper and mint. Add salt to taste. Cook slowly for about 30 minutes. Add the oil and serve in individual soup bowls, each portion poured over 2 slices of toasted bread.

GARMUGIA LUCCHESE

MIXED VEGETABLE SOUP FROM LUCCA

A spring soup of considerable elegance, this one is always made to greet the beginning of the good weather, using the first fresh vegetables from the famous kitchen gardens around Lucca.

3 small white onions, finely sliced
2 tablespoons extra-virgin olive oil
3 oz (90 g) pancetta, diced
5 oz (155 g) ground (minced) lean young beef
   (yearling beef)
3 tablespoons shelled green peas
6 artichokes, cut into wedges
30 asparagus tips
3 tablespoons shelled fava (broad) beans
4 cups (1 qt/1 l) beef stock, heated to a boil
homemade bread, cubed and toasted

SERVES 4

❡ Fry the onions in the oil in a large saucepan until golden. Add the *pancetta* and beef and cook for about 10 minutes.
❡ Add all the vegetables and the boiling beef stock. (The amount of liquid depends on the thickness of soup desired.) Continue cooking for 15 minutes. Serve in soup bowls garnished with the toasted cubes of bread.

Left: Pasta e Ceci all'Olio Crudo; right: Minestrone d'Orzo

PASTA E CECI ALL'OLIO CRUDO

PASTA WITH CHICKPEAS

This is a very old peasant dish from Romagna, and the recipe that follows is the most orthodox one. This version is presented in many elegant restaurants as an example of modern Italian gastronomy. It is, without a doubt, one of the clearest examples of the harmony that exists between country simplicity and the cuisine of the Mediterranean.

1½ cups (10 oz/315 g) dried chickpeas, soaked for 24 hours
3 sage leaves, chopped
a pinch of kosher (coarse) salt
2½ cups (10 oz/315 g) all-purpose (plain) flour
2 eggs
½ cup (4 fl oz/125 ml) lukewarm water
1 cup finely chopped parsley, for serving
1 cup (8 fl oz/250 ml) extra virgin-olive oil

SERVES 6

❡ Drain and rinse the chickpeas. Transfer to a saucepan and add cold water to cover. Add the sage and a pinch of kosher salt. Cover and cook over moderate heat for 2 hours.

❡ Meanwhile, work the flour with the eggs and as much lukewarm water as necessary. Roll out the dough into a thin sheet. Cut the pasta into large, irregular, rectangular shapes.

❡ Drain the chickpeas as soon as they are cooked. Reduce the cooking liquid a little and taste it, adding some meat or vegetable extract, if required, to improve the flavor.

❡ Return the chickpeas to the liquid and bring to a boil. Add the pasta and cook for 5 to 7 minutes. Pour the soup into individual plates, sprinkle with chopped parsley and drizzle some of the olive oil over each serving.

MINESTRONE D'ORZO

MINESTRONE WITH BARLEY

Friuli, the area near the Yugoslavian and Austrian borders, is a gastronomic island with precisely defined features and customs. One requires all the numerous taverns in the area to keep a large pot of minestrone with barley constantly bubbling in a corner of the open fire. Patrons come in at any hour of the day to drink a bottle of wine (and in Friuli the drinking is excellent) accompanied by a plate of minestrone. Traditional recipes always called for a ham bone to be kept in the pot to enhance the flavor. Today there is a tendency to lighten the dish, but without altering the flavors of old.

1 cup (6 oz/185 g) pearl barley
3 oz (90 g) sausage, crumbled
½ oz (15 g) prosciutto, finely chopped
1 celery stalk, diced
1 onion, diced
2 or 3 potatoes, peeled and diced
salt
14 cups (3½ qt/3.5 l) water
½ cup grated Parmesan cheese

SERVES 4

❡ Soak the barley for 12 hours in cold water to cover. Drain, then cook for 45 minutes in boiling, lightly salted water. Blanch the sausage in boiling water and squeeze it to remove all the fat.

❡ In a large saucepan, combine the sausage, prosciutto, celery, onion, potatoes, salt and the water. Simmer for 30 minutes. Add the barley and cook another 45 minutes, until soft and creamy. Add 2 tablespoons Parmesan to each bowl before serving.

LE VIRTÚ

THE VIRTUES

Le virtú is typical of the Teramo area. The ingredients are supposed to be the same in number as the (purely hypothetical) virtues of a perfect mistress of the house:

Left: Le Virtú; front: Pasta e Fagioli (page 80)

love of family, love of her children, fidelity, fear of God, wisdom in the management of the home, and so on.

1 cup (6 oz/185 g) mixed dried legumes (chickpeas, lentils and beans) soaked for 24 hours
1 Belgian endive (witloof), trimmed and thinly sliced
1 bunch beet (beetroot) greens, thinly sliced
1 celery stalk, thinly sliced
2 carrots, thinly sliced
3 oz (90 g) spinach leaves, thinly sliced
6 oz (185 g) pork rind
3 oz (90 g) prosciutto
1 pig's foot
1 pig's ear
1 sprig marjoram
1 sprig mint
1½ oz (45 g) pork fat, chopped
1 tablespoon chopped parsley
1 small onion
2 garlic cloves
1 small piece chili pepper
3 ripe tomatoes, peeled, seeded and chopped
8 oz (250 g) shelled green peas
8 oz (250 g) shelled fava (broad) beans

freshly grated Pecorino cheese, for serving
8 oz (250 g) broken-up spaghetti or bucatini, cooked (optional)

SERVES 6

❡ Cook the drained chickpeas, lentils and beans in boiling salted water for about 1 hour.

❡ Meanwhile, in another saucepan in a small amount of salted water, cook the endive, beet greens, celery, carrots and spinach until just tender.

❡ In a third saucepan, boil the pork rind, prosciutto, pig's trotter and pig's ear in water to cover. When these are all cooked remove the bones, finely chop the meat and return it to the cooking liquid. Add the boiled legumes and a few leaves of marjoram and mint.

❡ In a wide, shallow skillet brown the pork fat, parsley, onion, garlic, chili and tomatoes. Add this mixture to the soup along with the other vegetables and the peas and fava beans. Cook until the peas and beans are tender.

❡ Serve the minestone with freshly grated Pecorino. If you want a richer dish, add the pasta.

PASTA E FAGIOLI

PASTA AND BEAN SOUP

Of all the many Italian soups, this is certainly the most famous, and it is common to a number of regions. There are paste e fagioli in Friuli, Veneto, Lombardy and Tuscany, almost all made by the same method—the beans are cooked first, some of them pushed through a sieve to increase the density of the broth, and the pasta added at the end.

2 lb (1 kb) fresh borlotti (red) beans or ¾ cup (5 oz/
    155 g) dried borlotti beans that have been soaked in
    water overnight
10 cups (2½ qt/2.5 l) water
4 ripe tomatoes, peeled and seeded
1½ cups (12 fl oz/375 ml) olive oil
1 sprig rosemary
1 tablespoon garlic and parsley chopped together
5 oz (155g) short pasta such as penne, small rigatoni
    or tube pasta
salt and freshly ground pepper

SERVES 4–6

❦ Cook the beans in the water, slightly salted, for 1 hour.
❦ Remove a couple of ladlefuls of beans and purée in a blender with the tomatoes. Set the remaining beans aside in their cooking liquid.
❦ Put 1 cup (8 fl oz/250 ml) olive oil in a saucepan, add the rosemary and cook gently to flavor the oil; discard the rosemary. Add the garlic and parsley and the tomato and bean purée. Stir to mix.
❦ Add the rest of the beans and their cooking liquid. Stir in the pasta. Check for salt. Cook until the pasta is just slightly al dente and the soup has a creamy consistency.
❦ Drizzle 1 tablespoon olive oil in a thin stream over each serving, and add pepper if desired. (See photograph page 79.)

ZUPPA DI PORRI E ZUCCA

LEEK AND PUMPKIN SOUP

This is a simple peasant recipe from the Langhe area in Piedmont made with the ingredients that were available to a country household with a limited budget. In earlier versions the pieces of leek and pumpkin were left in the soup after their long cooking.

3 lb (1.5 kg) pumpkin, peeled and cubed
2 teaspoons butter

6 leeks, trimmed
8 cups (2 qt/2 l) milk
salt

SERVES 4

❦ Brown the pumpkin in the butter with the leeks in large stewpan. Add two-thirds of the milk and salt to taste, and cook on very low heat for about 3 hours or until the milk has been absorbed. Place the soup in a blender, add the remaining milk, and whisk. Correct the seasoning, reheat and serve.

Zuppa di Porri e Zucca

POLENTA

POLENTA — BASIC RECIPE

There is no really precise rule for cooking polenta. The same rules apply as for pasta dough: the capacity of the flour to absorb liquid depends on its quality, the climate, the humidity in the air and the composition of the water used. One learns through observation and experience, but here are some basic suggestions to start with.

8 cups (2 qt/2 l) water
1½ tablespoons kosher (coarse) salt

Top: Polenta; bottom: Polenta Pasticciata

5 cups (1¼ lb/625 g) yellow cornmeal (polenta)
butter, for serving
freshly grated Parmesan cheese, for serving
SERVES 5–6

❡ Place the water in a copper cauldron (this is the prescribed vessel for hanging in the fireplace over a wood fire, but if you are in a city house, a steel or heavy metal saucepan will do) over high heat and bring to a boil. Wait until the water begins to boil merrily. Add the kosher salt and start sprinkling in the cornmeal, letting it fall through the fingers of one hand while continually stirring with a wooden spoon in the other. Always stir in the same direction, whether clockwise or counterclockwise, never reversing it. Gradually the mixture will become thicker and thicker, and when you have finished adding the cornmeal, you will need to stir the mixture with both hands. Polenta needs long cooking — at least 40 minutes — and it must never be interrupted. Only constant stirring will make it perfect. It's a dish that is exhausting to make, and was traditionally done by a man.

❡ When it comes out of the pot the polenta is soft and can be served in bowls, coated in butter and Parmesan cheese, and eaten with a spoon. After a while it tends to become more solid and can then be cut into slices, while still warm.

POLENTA PASTICCIATA

BAKED POLENTA

This is a typical Italian winter mountain food, marrying the polenta with butter and the magnificent cheeses produced from summer mountain pasturing. The following recipe is suggested only as an example, for the composition of the dish depends on the taste of the person making it.

12 oz (375 g) cooled, cooked polenta, thinly sliced
6 oz (185 g) thinly sliced assorted cheeses (such as
*   Fontina, Gorgonzola, Taleggio, Asiago)*
5 tablespoons (2½ oz/80 g) butter, cut into thin slivers
2 tablespoons grated Parmesan cheese
SERVES 4

❡ Lightly butter the bottom and sides of a large baking dish or 4 small earthenware or glass dishes and preheat the oven to 400°F(200°C).
❡ Arrange a layer of the polenta slices on the bottom. Arrange half the cheese slices and a few slivers of butter on top. Add another layer of polenta and top with the remaining sliced cheese. Add a final layer of polenta, more butter slivers and sprinkle the Parmesan over the top. Bake in the oven for 30 minutes, until a golden crust forms. Serve immediately.

Top left: bramata oro maize flour; top right: a finer maize flour from the Veneto region; bottom left: cooked polenta; bottom right: mixed maize and buckwheat flour

POLENTA

One of the major foods in the diet right across the arc of the Italian Alps, polenta is made from cornmeal. Corn is the "maize," which in fact came to Italy from Mexico, but at the time of its arrival around the beginning of the sixteenth century, anything from a long way away was "Turkish" by definition: hence the Italian word for corn, *granoturco*.

The origin of the word polenta, on the other hand, is far more ancient. It dates from Roman times and is derived from the Roman *puls*, referring to flour that was cooked in water until all the water was absorbed, and served with various sauces and gravies. But the Roman *puls* was made with flour ground from spelt or other grains, whereas today in Italy the polenta everyone is familiar with is the one made from corn.

Brought to Europe by the Spaniards after the discovery of America, corn met with success immediately because of its ability to adapt to high altitudes and con- sequently to guarantee food even for populations in the poorest areas. Unlike Mexican cooking, where corn is used in a wide range of dishes, in Italian cooking it is used almost exclusively as ground meal and made up as polenta. A few recipes, mostly for desserts and cakes, call for yellow cornmeal.

Various corn hybrids are grown extensively in Italy, both on the Po plains and in the mountains, but the differences between one polenta and another depend largely on the coarseness or fineness of the grind. For a rough kind of polenta with a pronounced "mountain" flavor, the rather coarse *bramata oro* should be used. This is the preferred variety in Bergamo (not far from Milan), which has closer links than any other city with polenta, and indeed its gastronomic emblem is *polenta e osei*, with the polenta served as an accompaniment to a rich and tasty dish of small birds.

The cooking method is the same for all types of cornmeal: A special cauldron called a *paiolo*, which must be made of tinned copper, is filled with water and when the water begins to boil the cornmeal is sprinkled into it and stirred without interruption with a special wooden stick. At this stage the polenta may be softened by adding some milk, or flavored with butter and cheese and eaten on its own. If it is made with water and salt only, it is then poured out onto a board and served, cut in slices with meat dishes that have plenty of sauce (such as *salmis*) or with cheeses. If sliced when cold and put under the broiler (grill), it can again make an excellent accompaniment for dishes like *baccalà mantecato*, Venetian creamed dried salt cod, or broiled (grilled) sardines. It is also marvelous to serve with drinks cut into small stick shapes, fried and served hot with chunks of Parmesan or cubes of mortadella.

POLENTA TARAGNA

BUCKWHEAT POLENTA

This dish is typical of the Valtellina, the valley down which the Adda river flows to form Lake Como. The flour used is buckwheat — coarse-ground, dark in color and strong in flavor — and enriched in this dish with copious amounts of butter and cheese. If we are to be faithful to the dish's origins, it is important to use the characteristic local Bitto cheese, a medium-matured cheese made from cow's milk.

4 cups (1 qt/1 l) water
1¼ cups (10 oz/310 g) butter
1½ tablespoons kosher (coarse) salt
2⅓ cups (9½ oz/300 g) buckwheat flour
13 oz (410 g) Bitto cheese, thinly sliced

SERVES 4–6

❡ Put the water and half the butter over high heat in a cauldron or heavy saucepan. When it boils, add the salt and start sprinkling in the flour with one hand while stirring constantly with a wooden spoon with the other. Cook for about 30 minutes; remove from the heat.

❡ Stir in the remaining butter and all the cheese. Return the pan to the heat and continue cooking and stirring for 15 minutes. Serve in bowls.

INFARINATA

FLOURED SOUP

This is a unique and rather curious one-dish meal, robust and very substantial, which arose out of the experience of the people of Garfagnana, a valley running parallel to the Tyrrhenian coast behind the Apuan Alps, where the famous Carrara marble quarries are located. It is a mixture of soup and polenta, and it is interesting to note that when corn arrived from the New World, the peasants of this area were content to add this yellow meal to their usual soup, without looking for any new recipes.

1 lb (500 g) fresh beans such as borlotti (red) beans,
*   in their shells*
2 sage leaves
2 garlic cloves
2 pieces pork rind, about 2×2 in (5×5 cm)
1 cup (8 fl oz/250 ml) olive oil
2 oz (60 g) pork fat, finely chopped
2 tablespoons basil, chopped
2 tablespoons rosemary leaves, chopped
2 tablespoons parsley, chopped

2 carrots, scraped and finely chopped
½ onion
1 celery stalk, finely chopped
1 red cabbage, cored and shredded
2 or 3 potatoes, peeled and diced
3¼ cups (13 oz/410 g) yellow cornmeal (polenta)

SERVES 6

❡ Shell the beans. In a pot of salted water boil the beans with the sage, garlic and pork rind for about 40 minutes. Heat 1 tablespoon of oil in a large saucepan and melt the pork fat in it. Add the basil, rosemary and parsley; sauté for a moment. Add the carrots, onion, celery, cabbage and potatoes.

❡ Discard the pork rind from the pan of beans. Add the beans and their liquid to the other vegetables. Lower the heat and simmer for 20 minutes or so.

❡ Add the cornmeal, stirring constantly with a wooden spoon. If necessary, add a little boiling water if the soup seems too thick. Cook for 40 minutes, stirring all the time.

❡ The *infarinata* may be eaten immediately, either hot or lukewarm, with 2 tablespoons of olive oil drizzled over each serving. Like polenta, it hardens if left to cool, and in this case it is cut into slices and fried in oil.

Top: Polenta Taragna; bottom: Infarinata

FISH AND SEAFOOD

FISH AND SEAFOOD

THINKING OF A MEDITERRANEAN COUNTRY LIKE ITALY, A PENINSULA WITH ALMOST FIVE THOUSAND MILES (APPROXIMATELY 8,000 kilometers) of coastline, one would imagine its gastronomy to be largely fish-oriented. This is not the case, however, or was not until just a few years ago. Over the centuries the Italians have always had a difficult relationship with the sea, a relationship filled with suspicion and fear. Apart from the unquestionable fondness of the Venetians and the Genoese for navigation and sea trade, Italy's stable populations learned early that the sea was a constant source of danger, not only from storms but because of frequent raids by Saracen pirates.

¶ Nevertheless, Italian fish cookery does have roots in the past. The breeding of edible fish, in particular moray eels and oysters for the tables of the rich, goes back to Roman times, and the populations living near the coast have always fished for food. Thus a gastronomic tradition has grown up, its best-known bases being simple broiled (grilled) versions of the better part of the catch, such as bass and sea bream, and the various fish soups made by cooking whatever was left in the nets and adding herbs and vegetables.

¶ Italian seafood cooking, outside the limited coastal traditions, has only recently assumed major dimensions. This is as a result of technological advances in refrigeration and shipping and consumer awareness of the nutritional benefits of a fish-based diet. The well-known fish markets of old — Chioggia and Ancona on the Adriatic, Mazara del Vallo in Sicily, Fiumicino and Viareggio on the Tyrrhenian — have been far outclassed by the one in Milan, which takes delivery of fresh fish through the night and begins selling it at dawn.

¶ This abundant supply of raw material has inspired creative chefs to experiment with new dishes and to improve on the old classics. The three traditional methods of cooking fish (boiling, frying and broiling/grilling) have been joined by steaming, very light braising, and light forms of marinating. And so a modern seafood cuisine has emerged, building mainly on combinations of fish, vegetables and herbs. The result has been the growth of important cuisine in the cities of the interior such as Milan, Bergamo and Turin and, in turn, the introduction of this great cuisine to the coastal areas where the new dishes have fitted perfectly into place alongside the old. Thus it has become possible to taste and compare the two schools and their capacities to work with different ingredients.

¶ While the modern seafood school of cooking favors the so-called prime-quality fish almost exclusively, the traditional one includes ancient recipes that make skillful use of "second-class" or oily fish as well — anchovies, sardines, mackerel, species that are the true wealth of the Mediterranean.

Previous pages: Italian waters are teeming with anchovies and each region has its traditional way of preparing them. A Ligurian custom is to marinate them in lemon juice and then serve them drizzled with olive oil as an antipasto. APL/OLYMPIA

Opposite: There are many varieties of crustacean in the Mediterranean. The most popular crustaceans in Italian cooking are the aragosto *(spiny/rock lobster), the mantis shrimp and the spider crab.* CARLO CANTINI

STOCCAFISSO ACCOMODATO

DRIED COD STEWED WITH TOMATOES, GOLDEN RAISINS AND PINE NUTS

Genoa, where Italy's first cargoes of dried salt cod arrived from Norway, was one of the first Italian cities to welcome stockfish into its kitchens. This it did with some enthusiasm, combining the fish with the most typical of the local Genoese ingredients. At least five or six recipes still survive that are in regular use along the arc of the Ligurian coast, but stoccafisso accomodato is the most important and best known.

5 tablespoons olive oil
1 garlic clove, bruised
4 pieces dried salt cod, about 1¼–1½ lb/700 g soaked
   weight, bones and skin discarded
salt and freshly ground pepper
3 or 4 ripe tomatoes, peeled, seeded and chopped
2 tablespoons golden raisins (sultanas), softened in
   warm water
2 potatoes, peeled and roughly cubed
2 tablespoons pine nuts

SERVES 6

❡ In a wide, shallow terracotta pan or skillet combine the oil and garlic, and cook until lightly browned. Add the pieces of cod and season with a pinch or two of salt and a grinding of pepper. Stir in the tomatoes. Cover the pan and cook gently

Stoccafisso Accomodato

for about 1½ hours, stirring and adding a little water if the mixture becomes dry. Drain the raisins and squeeze out excess liquid. Stir the potatoes, raisins and pine nuts into the fish mixture. By the time the potatoes are cooked, the sauce should be slightly thick and the dish is then ready to serve.

NASELLO ALLA FONDUTA DI MELANZANE

WHITING WITH EGGPLANT FONDUE

This wonderfully light Ligurian dish is perfectly in line with the latest cooking trends. Whiting (which is sometimes known as merluzzo*) is a so-called second-class fish found in the Ligurian seas and widely appreciated for its extraordinarily delicate flesh. The fish must be absolutely fresh and is cooked simply with a film of oil.*

1 eggplant (aubergine)
salt
½ cup (4 fl oz/125 ml) dry white wine
1 tablespoon extra-virgin olive oil
1½ tablespoons pine nuts
1 whiting, 2½ lb (1.2 kg), cleaned
4 small tomatoes, halved and baked

SERVES 4

❡ Peel the eggplant and cut into ¼ in (5 mm) slices. Sprinkle the slices with salt and set aside on a large plate for 1 hour. Dry the slices and broil (grill) them until al dente. Do not let them get too soft.
❡ In a blender or food processor, combine the eggplant, wine, oil and pine nuts and blend to a delicate, not-too-thick sauce.
❡ Steam or bake the fish, brushed with just a minimum of olive oil until it flakes easily when tested with a fork. Fillet the fish.
❡ Spread the eggplant mixture in a thin layer over the bottom of each heated dinner plate. Place half a fillet on each plate, on top of the eggplant. Garnish with the tomatoes.

PESCATRICE CON MARO' DI FAVE

MONKFISH WITH A PURÉE OF BEANS

The rana pescatrice, *monkfish or anglerfish, is not a particularly attractive looking fish with its very large head. However, despite this, it has a very good flavor.*

Left: Nasello alla Fonduta di Melanzane; right: Pescatrice con Maro' di Fave

Only the tail is eaten. It is almost boneless, and its flesh is white and soft, rather like lobster in taste and texture.

In Ligurian homes use of the mortar is not limited to the making of pesto. It is also used for other sauces and, the sauce in this recipe, based on fava (broad) beans, is an example that marries perfectly with a plain, broiled (grilled) fish. The dish is characteristic of western Liguria, la Liguria di Ponente, between Genoa and the French border. It is made only in late spring when the first fava beans from the kitchen gardens appear in the markets.

7 oz (220 g) fava (broad) beans, shelled
2 oz (60 g) green beans, trimmed
1 green beet (beetroot) leaf, trimmed
1 cup (8 fl oz/250 ml) extra-virgin olive oil
salt

4 small tomatoes, baked and seasoned
    with oregano and oil
4 monkfish or jewfish fillets, skinned and pounded thin
SERVES 4

❡ Skin the fava beans. Blanch the fava beans, green beans and beet leaf in salted water for 2 minutes. Pound the vegetables in a mortar or put through a food mill or blender, adding the oil in a thin stream and beating the sauce as for a mayonnaise. Taste, and season with salt if necessary.
❡ Broil (grill) the fish fillets until just cooked through.
❡ Spread the bean purée in the center of 4 heated serving plates. Place a monkfish fillet in the center of each and garnish with a tomato.

Storione con Sugo d'Arrosto di Vitello

STORIONE CON SUGO D'ARROSTO DI VITELLO

STURGEON WITH THE JUICES FROM A ROAST OF VEAL

Sturgeon are still found today, albeit in reduced numbers, in the Po River, once their favorite habitat. They are now bred in sturgeon farms, and in recent years have reappeared as an item in Lombardian "grand cuisine." They are generally boiled and served with mayonnaise.

9 oz (280 g) shallots, peeled
1½ cups (12 fl oz/375 ml) extra-virgin olive oil
10 tablespoons (5 oz/155 g) butter
1¼ cups (12 fl oz/375 ml) juices from roast veal
1 sturgeon about 3 lb (1.5 kg), cleaned, cut into 4 steaks
10 oz (315 g) zucchini (courgettes), finely sliced

SERVES 4

❡ In a wide, shallow skillet, fry the shallots lightly in the oil and 3 tablespoons (1½ oz/45 g) of the butter until golden. As soon as they begin to color, drain off all the fat. Add the remaining butter, turn up the heat and cook until the butter turns dark brown. Pour in the roasting juices and return to a boil.

❡ Lay the sturgeon steaks in the pan and cover with the zucchini. Cover and cook for 10 minutes or so, turning a couple of times. Turn off the heat and let the fish rest for 5 minutes without removing the lid.

❡ Serve on individual plates, topped with the cooking juices and vegetables.

TORTA DI LUCCIO DI LAGO

PIKE PIE

Pike can be found in many Italian markets, especially those in Milan, Pavia, Mantua and Verona. This pike pie picks up the Renaissance tradition of fish pies made with shortcrust pastry.

2 tablespoons chopped carrot
2 tablespoons chopped celery
2 tablespoons chopped onion
2 tablespoons chopped zucchini (courgette)
2 tablespoons olive oil
7 oz (220 g) boneless pike, cut into pieces
salt and freshly ground pepper
1 egg
⅓ cup (3 fl oz/90 ml) milk
1 tablespoon chopped flat-leafed parsley
6½ oz (200 g) puff pastry

SERVES 4

❡ In a large skillet, gently fry the vegetables in the oil. Add the pike and salt and pepper to taste and cook for 5 minutes. Set aside to cool. Meanwhile, beat the egg and milk together. Beat in the parsley. Add to the fish mixture and mix well.

❡ Preheat the oven to 350°F (180°C). Roll out the puff pastry into a very thin sheet. Line an 8 in (20 cm) round mold with the pastry. Pour in the pike and vegetable filling. Bake in the oven for about 15 minutes, until the pie begins to color a little. Serve immediately.

Torta di Luccio di Lago

PRIME-QUALITY FISH

Gilt-head and other sea bream, sole, turbot, red mullet, monkfish and grouper are among the most prized fish found in Italian cuisine. They are caught in the Italian seas according to cycles governed by a law (for the purpose of safeguarding production) which imposes a ban on fishing in alternate locations throughout the year.

Orata, gilt-head sea bream, is caught year-round, but the most sought-after are the small variety caught between October and January. The best season for *pagello*, sea bream, is spring and summer.

Branzino, sea bass, is a particularly delicate fish that spends a period of its life in freshwater. It reaches peak quality in January/February, June/July and in December. It is suitable for farming and for some time now there has been a sizeable production from fish farms.

Caught more or less all around the Italian peninsula the best *sogliola*, sole, are from the Adriatic which, particularly early in the season when they are still quite small, are known as *sfoge* (a dialect word meaning a thin layer). *Sfoge* are fried and then preserved in a marinade of wine and vinegar to which onions and herbs are added.

Rombo, turbot or brill, is a large fish with speckled skin and characteristic bony protuberances. Its fine white flesh lends itself to steaming and baking. If the fish is particularly big it is advisable to let it ripen in the refrigerator for a day or two before cooking, to soften its texture.

There are two varieties of *triglia* — the deep-sea mullet and the striped surmullet that lives among the rocks. The latter is the more sought-after because its flesh has a more refined flavor. The major difference between the two is the color of the skin, which in the rock mullet is a more definite red, while the deep-sea variety is paler with a slight gray tinge. During August, fishermen along the Apulian coast in the southern Adriatic bring in vast quantities of newborn deep-sea mullet. These are no more than ¾ inch (2 centimeters) long, and are simply dipped in flour and fried.

Rana pescatrice, monkfish or anglerfish, is not a pretty fish, with its very large head, but it is very tasty. Only the tail is eaten. It is almost boneless, white, and soft and full of flavor — rather similar to lobster.

1., 5. & 6. orata (gilt-head sea bream); 2. & 3. pagello (sea bream); 4. branzino (sea bass); 7. sogliola (sole); 8. rombo (turbot and brill)

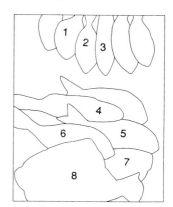

FILETTI DI TRIGLIE ALLA CREMA DI ZUCCA

RED MULLET FILLETS WITH CREAMED PUMPKIN

Red mullet has always been highly thought of in Italy. It has good flavor but it contains many bones. There are two varieties of red mullet — triglia di fango (mud mullet) and triglia di scoglio (rock mullet).

This recipe is from the Marches, and represents a reversal of the usual method of treating such a delicate fish. Traditionally in this region red mullet is first marinated in oil and lemon, then it is baked with butter, sage and slices of prosciutto, which results in a very tasty but rather heavy dish. In this version the red mullet is briefly fried and then served with a puréed pumpkin sauce, in homage to the wonderful pumpkins of the Marches region.

For the pumpkin sauce:
1¼ lb (625 g) pumpkin, unpeeled
  and cut in large pieces
½ cup (4 fl oz/125 ml) extra-virgin olive oil
1 garlic clove
1 onion, minced
For the fish:
12 medium red mullet, filleted
salt and freshly ground pepper
1 egg, beaten
¾ cup (3 oz/90 g) dry breadcrumbs
1 ripe tomato, peeled, seeded and diced
1 tablespoon dried fennel seeds
3 tablespoons (1½ oz/45 g) butter

SERVES 4

❡ Cook the pumpkin until tender in lightly salted boiling water. Drain, remove the skin and finely chop.
❡ In a wide, shallow pan, combine half the oil and the garlic and cook until garlic browns. Discard the garlic. Add the onion and cook until wilted. Add the pumpkin and cook for a few minutes. Purée the contents of the pan in a blender or food processor; set aside and keep hot.
❡ Rub the fish fillets with salt and pepper, dip them in the beaten egg and then in the breadcrumbs mixed with the fennel seeds. Melt the butter with the remaining oil in a large skillet. Brown the fillets on both sides. Drain on paper towels.
❡ Place some of the pumpkin sauce in the center of each heated serving plate; place 6 hot mullet fillets on top of the sauce on each plate. Scatter the tomato over the fish, and serve.

RAZZA AI FILETTI DI POMODORO E BASILICO

SKATE WITH SAUTÉED TOMATO AND BASIL

The best versions of this dish are made in the restaurants of Fiumicino, an important fishing center near Rome airport. It was a typical fisherman's meal in the days when skate that had been caught in the nets remained unsold because there was no market for them. Skate is a good quality fish and is often served with a tomato sauce (as in this recipe) or with anchovy sauce or black butter (butter cooked over low heat until it turns dark brown). Usually only the wings are eaten.

2 lb (1 kg) skate, cleaned
8 cups (2 qt/2 l) water
3 tablespoons vinegar
approximately 3 cups (24 fl oz/750 ml) dry white wine
1 bay leaf
1 tablespoon chopped flat-leafed parsley
1 teaspoon thyme
pinch of salt
pinch of peppercorns
2 tablespoons extra-virgin olive oil
1 shallot, chopped
1 lb (500 g) ripe tomatoes, peeled, seeded and
  cut into strips
2 tablespoons chopped basil
freshly ground pepper

SERVES 4

❡ Give the fish a preliminary cooking by covering it with the water and vinegar, putting it on the heat and removing it as soon as the water begins to boil.
❡ Fill another saucepan with two-thirds water and one-third white wine. Add the bay leaf, parsley, thyme, salt and peppercorns, bring to a boil and boil for 10 minutes. Set aside to cool. When cooled, immerse the skate in it and put it back on the heat. Remove the fish as soon as the stock returns to a boil.
❡ Fillet the fish and arrange the fillets on warmed dinner plates.
❡ Meanwhile, put a small pan on the heat with the oil and shallot. When this is very hot, add the tomato and barely sauté before quickly removing them from the heat. Adjust the salt. Spoon the mixture over the skate. Sprinkle with chopped basil and a grinding of pepper.

Top: Filetti di Triglie alla Crema di Zucca; bottom: Razza ai Filetti di Pomodoro e Basilico

FILETTO DI ROMBO CON CREMA DI PEPERONI

TURBOT FILLETS WITH BELL PEPPER PURÉE

½ cup (4 fl oz/125 ml) extra-virgin olive oil
1 onion, sliced
1 garlic clove, minced
3 yellow or red bell peppers (capsicums), seeded, deribbed
   and chopped
1 tomato peeled, seeded and chopped
salt and freshly ground pepper
2 cups (16 fl oz/500 ml) water
4 turbot (flounder) fillets, about 6 oz (185 g) each
¼ cup (2 fl oz/60 ml) dry white wine

SERVES 4

❡ Heat half the olive oil in a stewpan or casserole,
add the onion and garlic and cook over low heat
for a couple of minutes until softened but not
browned. Add the bell peppers and tomato;
season with salt and pepper. Stir in the water,
cover and cook for 30 minutes over moderate
heat. Set aside to cool.
❡ When cool, blend the sauce in a blender or
food processor. Put through a sieve to remove
any solids.
❡ Preheat the oven to 350°F (180°C). Arrange
the fish fillets in a baking dish. Season with
salt and pepper and sprinkle with the remaining
oil and the white wine. Bake in the oven for
6 minutes. Serve the fish on the bell pepper sauce.

DENTICE AI CARCIOFI

PORGY WITH ARTICHOKES

*Italy is the world's major producer of artichokes, which
are used in many recipes. This dish arose out of the
experience of the people and also that of restaurant own-
ers in the countryside around Rome, where the famous
romaneschi, round artichokes with purple-tinged green
leaves and no spikes, are picked throughout most of the
year.*

8 young artichokes
½ cup (4 fl oz/125 ml) extra-virgin olive oil
1 cup (8 fl oz/250 ml) fish stock
4 porgy (red bream) fillets, about 9 oz (280 g) each
all-purpose (plain) flour, for dredging
salt and freshly ground pepper
1 cup (8 fl oz/250 ml) dry white wine, such as Frascati
1 tablespoon chopped flat-leafed parsley

SERVES 4

❡ Trim the artichokes, removing the tough outer
leaves. Cut each into 4 wedges. In a wide, shallow
pan combine half the olive oil, ½ cup (4 fl oz/
125 ml) of the fish stock and the artichokes. Cook

Top: Filetto di Rombo con Crema di Peperoni; bottom: Dentice ai Carciofi

for 10 minutes; remove from heat and keep warm.
¶ Dredge the fish fillets in flour and season with salt and pepper. Brown them in the remaining olive oil and moisten with the white wine. Cook

until the wine has almost completely evaporated. Add the artichokes and the remaining fish stock. Cook for 10 minutes on low heat, until tender. Serve, sprinkled with chopped parsley.

OILY FISH

All of the "second class" or oily fish are the ones most frequently consumed in coastal areas, because they are so easy to catch. Anchovies, sardines and mackerel are caught in teeming hundreds of thousands all along the coasts of Italy, with seasonal peaks in spring and autumn. Fishing for swordfish is a picturesque ritual in the Straits of Messina, between Calabria and Sicily, while the tuna finish up in nets laid mainly off Liguria, southwestern Sardinia and western Sicily. Ordinary nets are used to catch more limited quantities of bonito or *palamita*, a smaller fish of the tuna family (weighing on average from 2 to 12 pounds/ 1 to 5 kilograms).

All of these fish belong to the large family known as *pesce azzurro*, "blue fish," whose flesh is notably oilier than that of other fish. Every Italian region has its own traditions for preparing them, especially in the case of anchovies and sardines. On the Adriatic coast, for instance, people get together to eat sardines grilled over charcoal, either as they are (in Emilia and the Marches) or with polenta grilled in the same manner (in the lagoon areas between Venice and Trieste).

In Liguria, small anchovies are cleaned, gutted and preserved in jars with salt. When the anchovies are fresh and plentiful in the markets, a typical Ligurian custom that now has spread all over Italy is to gut the fish, bone them and remove the heads, and then lay them on a plate for a few hours covered in lemon juice. Anchovies treated in this way are served drained and dressed with a drizzle of olive oil, as a light antipasto.

It is also common to put sardines in salt, but they are used only for immediate cooking. There is a popular old Italian saying that claims sardines have 24 virtues, and they lose one every hour — in other words, this is a fish that should be cooked within a day of being caught.

The consumption of tuna in its fresh state has always been limited to using what is left over from processing in the areas where canning in oil takes place. Only in Sicily is one likely to find freshly caught sliced tuna being sold. The same is true of swordfish. The large slices are usually cooked on the broiler (grill) and dressed with *salmoriglio*, a simple sauce of oil, salted water, lemon and oregano.

1. pesce spada (swordfish);
2. & 8. scorfano (scorpion fish); 3. anguilla (eel);
4. & 9. sgombro (mackerell);
5. triglie (red rock mullet);
6. aguglie (garfish);
7. sardine; 10. acciughe (anchovy)

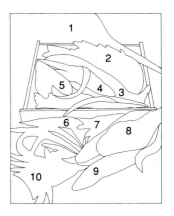

ORATA ROSA ALL'ACQUA PAZZA

GILTHEAD BREAM

This is one of Capri's most famous dishes. The term acqua pazza (crazy water) refers to the simplest method of all for cooking fish, poaching, which respects the flavor of the fish completely.

1 cup (8 fl oz/250 ml) olive oil
1 onion, halved
1 gilthead bream or porgy (red bream),
*   about 5½ lb (2.2 kg), cleaned*
13 oz (410 g) canned, peeled tomatoes
salt

SERVES 4

§ In a fish poacher, combine the oil and onion. Add the fish and water to cover and bring to a boil. Cook over moderate heat for 15 minutes. Add the tomatoes and taste for salt. Continue cooking until the fish is white and flakes easily when tested with a fork.

§ Transfer the fish to a serving platter. Garnish with toast squares and sprinkle the strained cooking liquid over both.

SARDE A BECCAFICO

STUFFED SARDINES

This Sicilian dish is the best known Italian recipe for sardines. The sea surrounding Italy is teeming with sardines which are widely used in home cooking because they are always fresh and are inexpensive.

1½ lb (750 g) sardines
1 cup (8 fl oz/250 ml) olive oil
1 cup (4 oz/125 g) dry breadcrumbs
⅓ cup (2 oz/60 g) golden raisins (sultanas), soaked
½ cup (2 oz/60 g) pine nuts
¼ cup chopped flat-leafed parsley
6 anchovy fillets, minced
salt and freshly ground pepper
3 bay leaves

SERVES 4

§ Gut the sardines and wash well under running water. Half-open each one by slitting the belly side and leaving the back intact. Remove the central bone, head and tail, wash them again and drain on paper towels.

§ Heat three-quarters of the oil in a skillet over moderate heat until hot. Add two-thirds of the breadcrumbs and brown well, stirring constantly. Transfer the crumbs to a plate. Add the drained and squeezed raisins, pine nuts, parsley, anchovies and salt and pepper to taste. Stir to mix well. Place a small amount of the mixture on top of each opened sardine, then close it up and press down gently. Arrange the stuffed sardines in an oiled baking dish and scatter the bay leaves on top.

§ Preheat the oven to 350°F (180°C). Sprinkle the remaining breadcrumbs over the fish and drizzle with the remaining olive oil. Bake in the oven for 30 minutes. Serve immediately.

Left: Orata Rosa all'Acqua Pazza; right: Sarde a Beccafico

Top: Sogliola al Basilico; bottom: Seppie con Piselli

SOGLIOLA AL BASILICO

SOLE AND BASIL

This decidedly modern dish comes from Liguria, and its major feature is the sauce that uses the basil and pine nuts from the classic Genoese pesto. Here, however, the sauce is finished with a reduction of the cooking juices from the fish, added to the marinade in which the fish soaked prior to cooking.

4 sole, about 8 oz (250 g) each
4 tablespoons olive oil
juice of ½ a lemon
1¼ cups (10 fl oz/315 ml) dry white wine
salt and freshly ground pepper
1 celery stalk, chopped
1 carrot, chopped
1 leek, washed, trimmed and chopped
½ cup (4 fl oz/125 ml) water
2 bunches basil leaves
¼ cup (1 oz/30 g) pine nuts
green beans and tomatoes for garnish

SERVES 4

❡ Fillet the sole, making 4 fillets from each fish. Reserve the bones and trimmings. In a wide shallow bowl, marinate the fish fillets in 2 tablespoons olive oil, a few drops of lemon juice, ½ cup (4 fl oz/125 ml) white wine, and salt and pepper for 15 minutes.
❡ Meanwhile, in a small skillet, brown the celery, carrot and leek with the fish bones and trimmings in 1 tablespoon olive oil. When browned, add

½ cup (4 fl oz/125 ml) white wine and the water. Continue cooking until the mixture reduces to a small amount of thick sauce. Put this through a fine strainer.
❡ Drain the fish fillets, reserving the marinade. Brown them for 4 minutes in a skillet with 1 tablespoon olive oil, then pour in ¼ cup (2 fl oz/60 ml) of white wine. Cook for a further 4 minutes then place the fish on a serving dish and keep warm. Add the marinade to the cooking juices in the skillet and simmer for a few minutes, stirring with a wooden spoon.
❡ Put the basil leaves and pine nuts in the bowl of a food processor. Add the marinade and cooking juice mixture. Blend until the sauce is smooth and a pale green color. Pour the sauce into a small terracotta or earthenware saucepan and return it to the heat. Stir in the strained fish and vegetable mixture and a few drops of lemon juice and cook for 3 minutes. Spoon the mixture over the sole fillets and serve with a garnish of boiled green beans alternating with thin strips of raw tomato.

SEPPIE CON PISELLI

CUTTLEFISH AND PEAS

Cuttlefish stewed with peas is a permanent component of Italian gastronomy along the shores of the Tyrrhenian Sea. In season, when the tender baby cuttlefish that have been caught during the night, using special night-fishing lamps, and the first fresh peas from the kitchen gardens come into the markets, you will find this dish appearing in homes and restaurants.

1 lb (500 g) small cuttlefish
1 cup (8 fl oz/250 ml) extra-virgin olive oil
1 medium onion, minced
1 lb (500 g) shelled green peas
½ cup chopped flat-leafed parsley
salt

SERVES 4

❡ Skin the cuttlefish and discard the eyes, intestines and beaks. Reserve the sacs with their black liquid. In a wide, shallow nonstick skillet, heat the oil and fry the onion until golden. Add the washed cuttlefish, still dripping with water, and cook for a few minutes. Add the liquid from the cuttlefish sacs, the chopped parsley and the peas. Adjust the salt and bring to a boil over high heat. Reduce the heat, cover the pan and cook slowly for about 30 minutes, until the cuttlefish is tender when tested with a fork. Serve at once.

FRESHWATER FISH

The most common freshwater fish in Italian cooking are trout, sturgeon, tench, *lavarello*, *agone*, carp, pike, catfish, river perch and eel. Today's breeding techniques mean that trout and sturgeon are found more or less continuously on the market and on restaurant menus. The others are still caught in lakes and rivers, and consequently their availability is much more limited and is linked for the most part to the traditions of the Italian lakeside fishing communities.

Agone and *lavarello* are mainly caught in Italy's three major lakes: Lake Maggiore, Lake Como and Lake Garda. At Lake Maggiore there is a tradition of preparing *lavarello in carpione*. The fish is cleaned and gutted, dipped in flour and fried, and then preserved in a marinade of vinegar (with or without white wine), herbs and spices. On Lake Como, cleaned and gutted *agoni* are threaded onto fine skewers and put out to dry in the breeze coming down from the Alps. *Agoni*

treated this way keep for long periods, and are eaten simply broiled (grilled) and accompanied by toasted polenta.

Another tradition still surviving in the Brianza area, near Milan, is that of a risotto with perch, really two separate dishes presented on the same plate. The risotto is the classic one, *alla parmigiana* — rich with cheese — and on it are laid fillets of river perch coated in breadcrumbs and fried in butter.

But as far as freshwater fish are concerned,

the richest of the Italian lakes is certainly Lake Trasimeno, where the famous *carpa regina*, queen carp, is found, each fish weighing 35 to 45 pounds (15 to 20 kilograms). They are baked in the oven stuffed with herbs and vegetable flavorings, exactly as for *porchetta*. This is also the home of a traditional soup known as *tegamaccio*, which includes more or less all the species of edible fish found in the area. To make it, tench, trout, river perch, eel and pike are placed on a rich bed of oil and fresh tomatoes cooked for almost an hour with garlic and parsley, and served on oven-toasted bread.

Frogs' legs, although from amphibians, should be mentioned here too. Frogs' legs are also a delicacy in Italy.

In northern Italy, where they are mainly found in cooking, frogs' legs are cooked either *in guazzetto* (with butter and wine) or fried after marinating (*rane fritte*).

1. storione (sturgeon);
2. carpe (carp); 3. rane (frogs' legs); 4. tinca (tench);
5. lupo di mare (catfish);
6. anguilla (freshwater eels);
7. pesce persico (river perch)

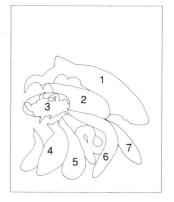

with salt and pepper and dredge in flour. Add to the pan and brown on each side. Pour in the wine and let it evaporate completely. Add the stock, sage, mushrooms, peas, and tomatoes. Lower the heat and cook, covered, for 30 or 40 minutes, until the fish flakes easily when tested with a fork.

Top: Tinca con Piselli alla Lariana; bottom: Filetto di Trota ai Finocchi

TINCA CON PISELLI ALLA LARIANA

LAKE COMO TENCH WITH PEAS

The fishermen of Lake Como cook tench in this manner, and to eliminate its muddy taste they make the fish swallow a spoonful of vinegar, taking advantage of the ability of the tench to survive for a few hours out of water. If the fish is already dead, the same result may be obtained by immersing it in boiling salted water for a few minutes before starting to cook it according to this recipe.

3 tablespoons (1½ oz/45 g) butter
3 tablespoons olive oil
1 tench or trout, about 2 lb (1 kg), cleaned and cut into
    2 in (5 cm) pieces
salt and freshly ground pepper
all-purpose (plain) flour, for dredging
2 cups (16 fl oz/500 ml) dry white wine
2 cups (16 fl oz/500 ml) veal and chicken stock
1 sprig sage
8 oz (250 g) champignons (button mushrooms)
8 oz (250 g) shelled green peas
8 oz (250 g) ripe tomatoes, peeled, seeded and diced
SERVES 4

❡ In a wide, shallow pan combine the butter and olive oil over moderate heat. Sprinkle the fish

FILETTO DI TROTA AI FINOCCHI

TROUT AND FENNEL

One of the most interesting dishes in modern Italian cuisine, this recipe was created on the shores of Lake Garda and brings to this inland region two cooking methods that are typically Mediterranean. Although vastly different, they are both tied to the use of wild fennel. The Sicilian method uses this herb with sardines, and the method from Provence combines it with sea bass. The following recipe uses the fragrant fennel fronds and the whole bulb as well.

2 salmon trout, about 1 lb (500 g) each, filleted
salt and freshly ground pepper
2 fennel bulbs, thinly sliced
juice of 2 lemons
1 bunch wild fennel (fennel leaves)
½ cup (4 fl oz/125 ml) oil
SERVES 4

❡ Preheat the oven to 400°F (200°C). Arrange the trout in a baking dish well coated with the olive oil. Season the fillets with salt and pepper and top with the fennel bulb slices. Season, then sprinkle with lemon juice and add a few wild fennel fronds.
❡ Cover the dish with foil. Bake in the oven for 7 to 8 minutes. Remove the foil and serve from the baking dish.

FILETTI DI SGOMBRO AL MIRTO DI SARDEGNA

MACKEREL FILLETS WITH SARDINIAN MYRTLE

Although relegated to the rank of a second-class fish because of its rather fatty flesh, mackerel is an excellent food. It is usually broiled (grilled), or boiled, and served with oil and lemon juice or a mayonnaise, but in this recipe from the island of Maddalena in northern Sardinia, it is baked in the oven and enhanced with myrtle, a typically Sardinian herb which is used to produce a local aromatic liqueur with good digestive properties.

Left: Filetti di Sgombro al Mirto di Sardegna; right: Scaloppa di Branzino alle Zucchine

2 tablespoons extra-virgin olive oil
1½ lb (750 g) medium-size mackerel, filleted
salt and freshly ground black pepper
1 garlic clove, cut into slivers   ,
¼ cup (2 fl oz/60 ml) myrtle liqueur

SERVES 4

❡ Preheat the oven to 400°F (200°C). Brush the bottom of a baking dish with the oil and lay the fish fillets in it, skin-side down. Season with salt and pepper to taste; scatter with the garlic. Bake in the oven for about 5 minutes. Take the dish from the oven, sprinkle the myrtle liqueur over the fillets, return them to the oven for another couple of minutes, then serve.

SCALOPPA DI BRANZINO ALLE ZUCCHINE

SEA BASS STEAKS WITH ZUCCHINI SAUCE

Zucchini (courgettes) take on a new dimension in this typically Ligurian dish, becoming a simple, elegant sauce to make the most of the mellow flavor of the sea bass.

1 garlic clove, minced
⅔ cup (5 fl oz/155 ml) extra-virgin olive oil
3 oz (90 g) fresh tomatoes, peeled, seeded and diced
1 cup (8 fl oz/250 ml) fish stock
8 sea bass steaks, about 2½ oz (75 g) each
salt and freshly ground pepper
9 oz (280 g) zucchini (courgettes), trimmed and cubed
1 bunch basil

SERVES 4

❡ In a wide, shallow skillet, fry the garlic in 2 tablespoons olive oil on low heat until golden. Add the tomatoes, fish stock and fish steaks; season with salt and pepper to taste. Cover and cook gently for a few minutes.
❡ In a saucepan, barely cover the zucchini with water. Add 10 basil leaves and 3 tablespoons olive oil and cook slowly for 12 minutes, covered. When everything is ready, purée the zucchini in a food processor. Taste the purée for salt, and mix in 2 tablespoons olive oil in a thin stream. Cover the bottom of each plate with this sauce, add 2 fish steaks per serving and spoon over a little of the fish cooking juices. Serve, garnished with basil leaves.

CRUSTACEANS

Although a rich family of crustaceans exists in the Mediterranean, including shrimp (prawns) and crayfish among others, only a few are identified with Italian eating traditions.

Let us start with the *aragosta*. The use of the English term "lobster" on restaurant menus to describe *aragosta* is sometimes a cause of confusion, since the Mediterranean *aragosta* bears no relation to the American lobster, which is known as *homard* (from the French), and in Italian as *astice*, and is very rare in Italian

waters. The *aragosta*, found mainly in the waters of Alghero in Sardinia and along the southwestern coast of Sicily between Trapani and Agrigento, is usually rather small, rarely more than 2 pounds (1 kilogram) in weight, and although it lacks claws it has instead two huge antennae. Of all the crustaceans of this family it is the one with the tenderest and most flavorful flesh.

The mantis shrimp is a typical Mediterranean crustacean caught mainly in the Adriatic, whose muddy depths provide an

ideal habitat. It is about 8 inches (20 centimeters) long, with a pale yellow shell and two distinct purplish patches on the tail. The mantis shrimp is mainly caught in winter, when the flesh is at its meatiest, and generally arrives on the market still alive. It is only eaten boiled. They are very popular as an antipasto.

The spider crab, typical of Venice, is a large crab with a roundish body about 8 inches (20 centimeters) in diameter. Its peak season is between December and February. The females of the species have more

meat and are more popular for this reason, but gourmets prefer the males, because their flavor is far more delicate. Like all crustaceans, they are found at the markets live. To preserve the tenderness of the meat, the crab is plunged directly into boiling salted water. For serving, the shell of the crab is emptied and the meat is cut up and returned to the shell dressed with oil and lemon.

Shrimp known as *gamberetto* and *scampi* are also features of Italian cooking. When very fresh *gamberetto* are boiled in salt water with a slice of lemon juice shelled at the table.

Jumbo shrimp (king prawns), *gamberoni*, are traditionally found near the coast of Latium where they are served fried.

Abundant in the northern Adriatic sea, fresh *scampi* have a very delicate flavor and a solid meaty flesh. A popular cooking method is coating shelled *scampi* in egg and flour and then frying them in oil.

1. live aragosta; 2. cooked aragosta; 3. mantis shrimp; 4. scampi; 5. gamberoni (jumbo shrimp/king prawns)

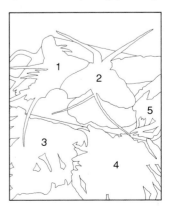

Cacciucco alla Livornese

CACCIUCCO ALLA LIVORNESE

FISH SOUP IN THE STYLE OF LIVORNO

The name of this dish is derived from the Arab word shakshoukli *meaning a mixture of ingredients cooked in a tegame (a wide, shallow terracotta pan). It is common to the entire Mediterranean coast.*

3 lb (1.5 kg) assorted fish and seafood, such as red
   mullet, octopus, scorpion fish, whiting, moray eel,
   cuttlefish, mussels, lobster and squid
3 ripe tomatoes, coarsely chopped
2 onions
2 celery stalks
2 carrots
salt
2 cups (16 fl oz/500 ml) olive oil
1 sprig parsley, chopped
1 small piece of chili pepper, chopped
2 garlic cloves, minced
1 cup (8 fl oz/250 ml) dry white wine
2 tablespoons tomato paste dissolved in
   ½ cup (4 fl oz/125 ml) hot water
8 slices coarse whole wheat (wholemeal) home-style
   bread, toasted

SERVES 4

❡ Clean and wash the seafood. Remove the heads of the larger fish and put them on the heat in a saucepan with a few discarded small fish, the tomatoes, 1 onion, 1 celery stalk, 1 carrot, a pinch of salt and some cold water. Cook for at least 30 minutes, or until fairly thick. Put the stock through a fine strainer held over another pan and keep warm.

❡ Meanwhile, thinly slice the remaining onion, celery and carrot. Brown them in the oil in a large, wide, shallow pan (terracotta if possible). Stir in the parsley, chili pepper and garlic and let the flavors blend. Add the squid and cuttlefish cut in strips and cook until their liquid evaporates. Add the white wine and cook until evaporated. Add the tomato paste, followed by the rest of the ingredients in the following order: first the fish, then the mussels and lobster. Cook, covered, over moderate heat for about 15 minutes.

❡ Meanwhile, place 1 slice of bread on the bottom of each plate, or put all of them in the bottom of a soup tureen. Ladle the hot fish stock over the bread. Lift the pieces of fish and seafood one by one from the cooking pan and arrange on top of the bread, with a coating of the cooking juices to finish.

FAGOTTINO DI ZUCCHINE E GAMBERI

BAKED JUMBO SHRIMP AND ZUCCHINI

A modern dish from Calabria, this is a first-class example of contemporary Italian cuisine using ingredients typical of the region.

3 zucchini (courgettes)
½ cup (2 oz/60 g) crumbled stale bread, crusts removed
½ cup flat-leafed parsley, thyme, oregano and mint, chopped together
2½ tablespoons (20 g) freshly grated Parmesan cheese
1 teaspoon chili powder
⅓ cup (3 fl oz/90 ml) olive oil
12 jumbo shrimp (king prawns), thoroughly cleaned
salt

SERVES 4

❡ Thinly slice the zucchini lengthwise, using a slicer if you have one. Mix the crumbled bread with the chopped herbs, Parmesan and chili powder.
❡ Preheat the oven to 400°F (200°C).
❡ Brush 4 ramekins or other individual ovenproof dishes with some of the olive oil. Place a layer of the zucchini slices on the bottom and sprinkle with half the bread and herb mixture. Arrange 3 shrimp on top of each, scatter a little more of the bread and herbs over them, add salt to taste and moisten with a thin stream of oil. Cover with more zucchini slices, then the remaining bread mixture, drizzle on more oil and salt lightly. Cover the ramekins tightly with foil and poke a few holes in the foil with a toothpick. Bake in the oven for 5 minutes. Serve at once.

CALAMARO IMBOTTITO

STUFFED SQUID

This is a Neapolitan recipe for squid. There are many recipes for squid from all over Italy. Squid can be stuffed, as in this recipe, or can be stewed. They are also delicious when fried. The most basic version does not include cheese, eggs or bread, let alone peas. The usual filling consists merely of the chopped-up tentacles mixed with breadcrumbs, black olives, capers and herbs. It is also frequently served with tomato sauce.

2 cups (16 fl oz/500 ml) oil
1 cleaned squid, about 1½ lb (800 g), tentacles chopped and mantle intact

1 cup shelled peas, fresh or frozen
2 eggs
¼ cup (1 oz/30 g) freshly grated Parmesan cheese
¼ cup (1 oz/30 g) crumbled bread, crusts removed
salt and freshly ground pepper
1 sprig flat-leafed parsley, chopped
½ cup (2 oz/60 g) pine nuts
9 oz (280 g) green olives, for garnish

SERVES 6

❡ In a wide, shallow pan heat half the oil and the chopped tentacles. Cook until lightly browned. Add the peas and cook for 2 minutes; remove from the heat.
❡ In a bowl, beat the eggs with the Parmesan, bread and salt and pepper to taste. Stir in the parsley and pine nuts. Add the chopped squid and mix well.
❡ Preheat the oven to 350°F (180°C).
❡ Fill the squid mantle with this mixture, sew up the opening with kitchen thread and lay it in a baking dish. Pour on the remaining oil and the olives. Bake for about 30 minutes. Remove and set aside to cool for 10 to 15 minutes.
❡ Cut into slices and serve just warm, surrounded by the olives.

POLIPI IN PURGATORIO

OCTOPUS IN PURGATORY

The part of the Adriatic that is best known (the stretch between Ancona and Venice) is not particularly rich in octopus, but they are found in abundance further south along the Abruzzi and Apulia coasts. This very old recipe comes from Termoli and is part of the gastronomic heritage of the local fishing communities.

2 lb (1 kg) small octopus, cleaned
2 lb (1 kg) onions, sliced
½ cup (4 fl oz/125 ml) extra-virgin olive oil
1 garlic clove, minced
salt
½ cup (4 fl oz/125 ml) white wine vinegar (optional)

SERVES 6

❡ In a wide, shallow pan, combine the octopus, onions, oil, garlic and a little salt. Cook over moderate heat for about 2½ hours, stirring from time to time. Do not add water during the cooking.
❡ If a sharper flavor is desired, the vinegar may be added.

Top: Fagottino di Zucchine e Gamberi; bottom: Calamaro Imbottito; right: Polipi in Purgatorio

cooked in the simplest ways, for example, mussels or clams are sautéed briefly with oil, garlic and parsley and served piping hot, still in their shells, with the strained cooking juices poured over them.

The small clam, *tartufi di mare* is a mollusk of the family Veneridae, which includes *vongola. Tartufi di mare* is said to possess aphrodisiac properties which makes it very popular. When fresh it is best eaten raw with a squeeze of lemon juice, although some people make sauces for spaghetti with it.

Oysters, *ostrica* are best broiled (grilled) and dressed with oil, pepper and lemon juice. However, coated with flour and fried in oil they are also delectable.

Squid or calamari is a favorite food in Italy which is prepared in a variety of ways. They are best cooked by frying or by inclusion in a *fritto misto di pesce*, to which they add a delicious sweet taste.

SHELLFISH AND MOLLUSKS

Mollusks in the broad sense of the term, meaning all those sea animals with soft bodies, with or without shells, are very common in all Italian regional cuisines. Squid, large and small octopus, cuttlefish, limpets, razor shells, sea dates, clams, mussels and venus shells offer the consumer a truly extraordinary range of tastes. Italians also love oysters, but the local production is limited to just a few farms of no significant size.

Also belonging to the copious mollusk phylum is the famous *coquille St Jacques*, so named because in medieval times pilgrims visiting the sanctuary of St James of Compostella in northern Spain wore this shell around their necks and used it as a spoon for drinking water from the springs, or for eating the soups they were offered at monasteries along the route. In Italy the mollusk is known as *capa santa* — holy shell.

All the mollusks without shells are generally either boiled and served with oil, or fried or, particularly in the case of squid and cuttlefish, stewed or stuffed. The shellfish, on the other hand, are eaten both raw and cooked. For serving raw, they must be absolutely fresh, still alive if possible. In this form they constitute the favorite antipasto in coastal areas. They are

1. *mussels*; 2. *octopus*;
3. *tartufi di mare*; 4. *vongola (clams)*; 5 & 6. *capa santa (coquilles St Jacques)*;
7. *oysters*; 8. *calamari*

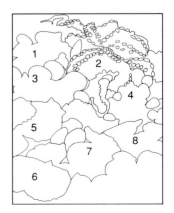

Involtini di Pesce Spada

INVOLTINI DI PESCE SPADA

STUFFED SWORDFISH ROLLS

This is a typical Sicilian dish. It is mainly found in Messina and the surrounding area, but you will also find it served in many other parts of the island, especially in family-run trattorie.

3 tablespoons olive oil
1 onion, minced
5 oz (155 g) lean swordfish, minced
1 basil sprig
1 tablespoon chopped flat-leafed parsley
³/₄ cup (3 oz/90 g) dry breadcrumbs
3 oz (90 g) sharp provolone cheese, finely diced
2 eggs
salt
pinch of minced hot chili pepper
8 oz (250 g) thinly sliced swordfish

SERVES 4

❦ Put a skillet on moderate heat with a little oil. Add the onion and gently fry. As soon as the onion begins to color add the minced swordfish, basil, parsley and breadcrumbs. Fry gently for 5 minutes so the flavors will blend.

❦ Put the mixture through a food mill. Add the provolone, eggs, a pinch of salt and minced chili, and mix well.

❦ Lightly flatten the sliced swordfish with a meat mallet. Spread a little of the prepared filling on each and roll up and fasten with toothpicks.

❦ Either barbecue the *involtini* or broil (grill) them and serve with *salmoriglio*.

SALMORIGLIO
This is Sicily's simplest and most widely used sauce for broiled (grilled) fish.
1 cup (8 fl oz/250 ml) extra-virgin olive oil
½ cup (4 fl oz/125 ml) hot water
juice of 2 lemons
pinch of salt
1 garlic clove, crushed
1 teaspoon oregano
Pour the olive oil into a small saucepan. Working quickly with a fork or a small whisk, gradually add the hot water (purists insist that it must be sea water, but most people use ordinary water), and the lemon juice. Add the salt, garlic and oregano. Put the saucepan over another containing hot water, and cook the sauce in this bain marie for 5 minutes. Pour it into a heated sauceboat and serve.

Top left: baccalà; bottom left: baccalà cut into pieces ready for cooking; right: stoccafisso

STOCKFISH AND SALT COD

There is some confusion in Italy between *stoccafisso* (stockfish) and *baccalà* (salt cod). In most places the appropriate term is used, but in the Veneto, where the local cuisine is rich in dried cod dishes, what should be called *stoccafisso* is also known as *baccalà*. In any event the two names apply to the same fish, cod, treated by different methods.

Stockfish is preserved the way the ancient Vikings used to do it: dehydration through exposure to air. *Baccalà* is salted and packed in barrels according to the custom of Portuguese fishermen, which is where the name (*bacalao*) came from. In both cases the fish cannot be cooked until after it has soaked under running water for a long period (up to six or seven days in the case of *stoccafisso*, two or three days for *baccalà*). In Italy this operation is carried out by the shopkeepers who have special marble vats for the purpose, but it can be done in the home using a basin placed under a thin stream of water from the tap. Italy is the world's largest consumer of *stoccafisso*, a product that first reached the Italian market via the sea, and found instant favor last century for its taste, its nutrient value and its cost, which at the time was relatively low. Today, however, it is in great demand and so, inevitably, its price has risen.

To recognize good stockfish you must check that there are no yellowish parts. The flesh must be unmistakably white. The best type is called *ragno* after the most famous Norwegian exporter, Ragnar. The recipes given in this chapter are the most common and significant ones, chosen from the 60 or more usually given in the best recipe books.

ARAGOSTA ARROSTO IN SALSA VERDE

BAKED LOBSTER WITH GREEN SAUCE

In Italy the best lobsters are caught along the coastal areas of the western Mediterranean, especially in Sardinia and Sicily. One of the most important lobster fishing centers is Alghero on the northwest coast of Sardinia, where lobsters are boiled and served with an uncooked sauce of finely sliced tomatoes and onions in an oil and lemon juice dressing.

This recipe comes from the area around Cagliari in the south of Sardinia and makes use of the typically Sardinian fragrances of thyme, marjoram, basil and parsley.

1 cup (8 fl oz/250 ml) fish stock
salt and freshly ground pepper
1 sprig flat-leafed parsley, chopped
1 bunch basil, chopped
1 sprig mountain thyme, chopped
3 marjoram leaves
1 cup (8 fl oz/250 ml) extra-virgin olive oil
1 lobster, about 2 lb (1 kg)
SERVES 4

⚓ In a saucepan, combine the fish stock, salt and pepper, parsley, basil, thyme, marjoram and olive oil. Beat with an immersion mixer or in an electric blender to give a rather thick green sauce.
⚓ Cook the lobster, whole, directly on a grill, or under the broiler (grill) with the heat not turned up too high, allowing 15 minutes per side.
⚓ When cooked, break the lobster in half lengthwise, remove the flesh from the shell and discard the stomach sac and intestines from the head section. Cut the flesh into cubes and dress with the green sauce. Return the lobster meat to the shell and serve.

GAMBERI DI FIUME CON CRESPELLE DI PATATE

FRESHWATER CRAYFISH WITH POTATO PANCAKES

In this recipe the crayfish are only lightly and simply cooked, the amount of butter used is reduced to a minimum, and the ever-present garlic is missing.

Top: Aragosta Arrosto in Salsa Verde; bottom: Gamberi di Fiume con Crespelle di Patate

1½ lb (750 g) live freshwater crayfish
2 bay leaves
2 carrots
2 onions
2 celery stalks
2 cups (16 fl oz/500 ml) water
1 teaspoon butter
1 shallot
9 oz (280 g) shelled peas, fresh or frozen, parboiled
2 or 3 ripe tomatoes, peeled, seeded and mashed with
    a fork
salt and freshly ground pepper
1 sprig flat-leafed parsley, chopped
For the pancakes:
1½ cups (6 oz/185 g) puréed potatoes
⅓ cup (3 fl oz/90 ml) milk
1 egg plus 1 egg yolk
salt, freshly ground pepper and nutmeg
olive oil, for frying

SERVES 4

❡ Blanch the live crayfish in salted water flavored with 1 bay leaf, 1 carrot, 1 onion and 1 celery stalk. Remove the shells and reserve the heads.

Place the heads in a saucepan with the water and remaining bay leaf, carrot, onion and celery stalk and bring to a boil. Boil for a few minutes until a reduced stock is formed.

❡ In a skillet, melt the butter. Add the shallot and remove it as soon as it begins to color. Add the crayfish and sauté rapidly. Add the peas. Stir in the tomatoes. Adjust the salt and pepper. Pour in the crayfish stock and cook for a few minutes more. Remove the crayfish and peas and set aside. Reduce the cooking juices. Flavor the sauce with the fresh parsley.

❡ Make the pancakes: Beat the puréed potatoes with the milk, egg and egg yolk. Stir in a sprinkling of salt, pepper and nutmeg. The potato mixture should form a thick cream, which is then pushed through a strainer. In a skillet over high heat, fry the potato mixture spoonful by spoonful in just enough oil to cover the base of the skillet. Each spoonful will form a pancake about 2 in (5 cm) across.

❡ Place a pancake in the center of each plate and arrange the crayfish and peas on top. Coat with the sauce made from the cooking juices and serve.

MEAT, POULTRY AND GAME

Meat, Poultry and Game

ALL THE MEAT CONSUMED AT THE ITALIAN TABLE IS PREPARED ALONG THESE BASIC lines: roasting, frying, boiling, braising and stewing. Then there are the ground (minced) or thinly sliced raw meats dressed in various ways that belong to the Piedmontese tradition, and there is the Venetian *carpaccio*, a recent creation that has spread throughout the world.

❡ Roasting and frying are the cooking methods reserved for finer cuts of meat to be consumed as soon as they are cooked and the roast or broiled (grilled) meat leftovers do not form the basis of another dish — at most the leftovers might end up ground in a rissole. Similarly, fried dishes are meals in themselves and, because fried meat is not reusable, do not combine with other ingredients to form new dishes.

❡ Boiling, braising and stewing present a different story. Here the requirements of good taste and those of the family budget come together in a marriage suggested by centuries of experience in the kitchen. In Italian homes both the meat and the stock of a *bollito* (boiled meats) can be used. The stock can be used to make soups or risottos, or to contribute to other types of cooking, and the meat provides a rich and substantial meal. This is also true for the various types of braises and stews, which all come under the category of *in umido*, meaning they have an abundance of rich cooking juices that can be used as a sauce with pasta, or to finish a pasta *timballo* baked in the oven, or to flavor the filling of *tortellini* or *agnolotti*.

❡ Although braising and stewing use similar methods of combining ingredients, they differ in both structure and cooking. Braises and the type of stew known as *stracotto* use a single piece of meat that is first browned in fat (oil, butter or lard) with onion and other ingredients, and then cooked with added liquid (stock, wine, water or the marinade previously used for the meat). The other type of stew, *stufato*, may be made with smaller pieces of meat and thus allows the use of cheaper cuts to produce delicious dishes known as *spezzatini*, which are very popular and usually served in the more modest *trattorie*. The most famous of these is without doubt *goulasch*, which in Trieste and surrounding regions is a legacy of the long period spent under the Hapsburgs and of their geographical proximity to the Hapsburg Empire. Unlike the Hungarian version, flavored with sweet paprika, which is more a soup than a main dish, the Trieste *goulasch* is a true *spezzatino*, rendered spicy with the addition of chili pepper and hot paprika.

❡ Moving south, red meats such as beef give way to white, with a predominance of animals belonging to the peasant and pastoral traditions — sheep, goats, rabbits, turkeys, chicken and geese.

Previous pages: Prosciutto *is the leg of the pig that has been treated with a mixture of salt and spices and left to age in well-aired surroundings. It can be eaten raw* (prosciutto crudo) *or cooked* (prosciutto cotto). JOHN CALLANAN

Opposite: Prosciutto *is traditionally served in paper-thin slices, often with melon or figs.* CATHERINE KARNOW

FILETTO ALLA CARBONADE

CARBONNADE OF BEEF FILLET

In the old days in the Val d'Aosta, the harshness of mountain life was such that the peasants could only now and then include red meat in their diet. Oxen were precious working companions and were slaughtered only when they were too old to pull the plough, and then their meat would be preserved in salt in barrels and consumed very sparingly. That is how the Valdostan carbonade was born — out of the needs of poor people. Today the dish is cooked in the traditional manner with a red wine sauce, but a beef fillet is more often used.

2 cups (16 fl oz/500 ml) dry red wine
2 carrots, coarsely chopped
1 onion, coarsely chopped
1 celery stalk, coarsely chopped
1 lb (500 g) beef fillet, cut into 4 slices
5 tablespoons (2½ oz/75 g) butter
1 sprig rosemary, minced
1 garlic clove, minced
salt and freshly ground pepper

SERVES 4

❡ In a saucepan, boil the wine, carrots, onion and celery until the wine is reduced to a delicate thin sauce. Strain the sauce and discard the vegetables. In a skillet, sauté the beef slices in half the butter, with the rosemary, garlic, salt and pepper. Pour the wine sauce over the meat and let the flavors blend for a few moments. Remove the meat. Thicken the sauce with the remaining butter, pour it over the meat again and serve.

Filetto alla Carbonade

COSTATA DI MANZO ALLE ERBE AROMATICHE

SIRLOIN STEAK WITH HERBS

This Tuscan dish is enriched with aromatic wild herbs and served with an uncooked tomato sauce.

3 tomatoes, peeled and seeded
1 sprig marjoram
⅓ cup (3 fl oz/90 ml) olive oil
salt and freshly ground white pepper
1 T-bone steak, about 3 lb (1.5 kg)
1 sprig savory, minced

SERVES 4

❡ In a blender, combine the tomatoes with half the marjoram and 2 tablespoons of olive oil. Add salt and pepper to taste and blend until smooth.
❡ Heat the remaining olive oil in a large skillet. When it is hot, add the steak and cook for 10 minutes on each side. When turning the meat, sprinkle it with the savory and the remaining marjoram and season with salt and pepper. The steak should be rare. Thinly slice it. Spread some of the sauce over the bottom of each heated plate, top with slices of steak and serve. Slivers of fresh boletus (*porcini*) mushrooms make a good accompaniment.

GOULASCH FRIULANO

FRIULAN GOULASH

All the cuisine of the Friuli and Venezia Giulia regions bears the mark of centuries of Hapsburg rule. This goulash is just one example. Whereas in Hungary it is looked upon as a meat soup in Friuli it becomes an important main course. Its encounter with Italian tradition has, however, led to a few changes. The classic recipe uses butter and pork fat which are here replaced by olive oil, and the original vinegar becomes white wine. Moreover, the rather sweet Hungarian paprika gives way to the very Italian touch of hot chili pepper.

2 large onions, thinly sliced
½ cup (4 fl oz/125 ml) olive oil
a pinch of ground cumin
1 garlic clove, minced
2 tablespoons dry white wine
2 lb (1 kg) yearling beef, cut up for stewing and trimmed well
1 red chili pepper, minced

Top: Costata di Manzo alle Erbe Aromatiche; bottom: Goulasch Friulano

2 cups (16 fl oz/500 ml) hot water
salt
1 tablespoon all-purpose (plain) flour

SERVES 4–6

¶ In a large skillet, fry the onions gently in the oil. Add the cumin, garlic, white wine, and beef.

Brown the meat, stirring, and continue cooking, adding the chili pepper and pouring in the hot water a little at a time. Simmer for 1½ hours. Adjust the salt. Just before the end of cooking dissolve the flour in a ladleful of the cooking liquid, and stir into the goulash to give it a dense, creamy sauce. Serve with boiled potatoes.

BOLLITO MISTO

MIXED BOILED MEATS

Because of climate and environmental features, the great food belts in Europe tend to develop horizontally. The clearest example of this phenomenon is the boiled meat tradition. The French pot au feu *comes into Italy through Piedmont, where it becomes* bollito misto *and extends over the entire Po River plain where it takes on princely dimensions both quantitatively and qualitatively. It is a dish for large numbers, very difficult to make at home, and restaurants that offer it daily on their menu base their fame and reputation on it. It is usually accompanied by at least two sauces.*

1 cotechino *sausage, about 1¾ lb (800 g)*
2 onions, chopped
3 carrots, chopped
1 celery stalk
1 bunch flat-leafed parsley
4 cloves
1 chicken, cleaned and halved
3 lb (1.5 kg) beef brisket, in 1 piece
8 oz (250 g) veal breast
8 oz (250 g) calf's head
8 oz (250 g) veal tongue
2 tablespoons kosher (coarse) salt

SERVES 8–10

¶ Cook the *cotechino* separately in boiling water for 2½ hours, pricking the casing so it will not pop. Meanwhile, place the vegetables and 1 tablespoon kosher salt into a large saucepan and fill it with water. Bring to a boil and then add the beef and cook, covered, for about 1 hour. Add the veal meats, cover and cook for a further 30 minutes and then add the chicken. Cover and cook for 30 minutes, then add the *cotechino* and cook for another 15 minutes. Continue cooking until all meats are quite soft. Place the meats on a large heated tray, sprinkle with kosher salt and

moisten with a ladleful of boiling stock. The meat is carved at the table. Serve with green or red sauce, or with *mostarda di Cremona.*

SALSA VERDE
Green sauce
This is the best known sauce for serving with boiled meats. In a deep dish, very finely chop 2 oz (60 g) of parsley and add 2 anchovy fillets. Cut the crusts off a bread roll and soak it in vinegar. Squeeze out and add to the parsley. Beat with a wooden spoon to mix well. Add plenty of olive oil in a thin stream, beating to make a sauce that is quite liquid. Season with salt to taste. Serve.

SALSA ROSSA
Red sauce
Peel and seed 7 or 8 ripe tomatoes. Chop them finely together with 2 onions, 1 carrot and 2 or 3 garlic cloves. Put all these into a deep pan and add a pinch of hot chili powder, 1 tablespoon of sugar, 1 teaspoon vinegar, some salt and a little olive oil. Cook slowly over very low heat for at least 3 hours. Push the sauce through a sieve, add a little more oil and some salt if required and mix well. Serve as an alternative to green sauce.

Left: Bollito Misto; right: Bistecca alla Fiorentina

BISTECCA ALLA FIORENTINA

FLORENTINE T-BONE STEAK

The primary aspect of this celebrated dish is the quality of the meat. It must be beef from one of the Chianina *cattle farms in the Val di Chiana near Arezzo. Equally important is the type of heat used: it must be cooked over charcoal, or embers of olive-tree or grapevine wood. Finally, the steak must be large, weighing at least 2 pounds (1 kilogram), and cut with the bone in, to include both fillet and sirloin sections.*

2 T-bone steaks each about 2 lb (1 kg), cut at least
   1 in (2.5 cm) thick
salt and freshly ground pepper

SERVES 4

❡ Prepare a charcoal grill.
❡ When the coals are ash-covered and glowing, lay the steaks on the grill. Let the heat seal the meat for 30 seconds or so, to prevent the juices from running out; then turn the steaks to seal the other side. Sprinkle salt and pepper over the steaks and cook for 4–5 minutes. Turn, sprinkle with salt and pepper and continue cooking for a further 4–5 minutes, until the surface of the meat is well browned. Serve immediately. (While the meat is cooking it will shed drops of fat, and as these come into contact with the embers they cause the fire to flame up and scorch the meat. Tuscan cooks scatter handfuls of kosher/coarse salt on the embers, to prevent this from occurring.)

Left: braising or stewing cut of beef; center back: Florentine T-bone steak; center front: lean beef cut for bollito; right: beef fillet

RED MEAT

The term "red meat" is used in Italy to mean the meat from fully grown cattle, whether ox, cow or bull, as well as horsemeat and mutton (from older sheep, both ordinary rams and the *castrati* that are castrated early and raised solely for their meat). Sometimes added to these are animals that should rightly be called game, but are nowadays usually raised for eating purposes, such as boar and venison. The main feature of red meat is that, in comparison with the white meats, it may be used for prolonged cooking, such as roasting and braising, or for shorter cooking *al sangue*, as in broiled (grilled) fillet or *entrecôte*.

The variety of red meat cuts ranges in quality and in price. The parts of the animals where the muscles are least used, such as buttocks and back, are more tender and therefore more highly regarded. The parts subjected to greater use — the legs, shoulders and neck — are tougher and require much longer cooking times. Another

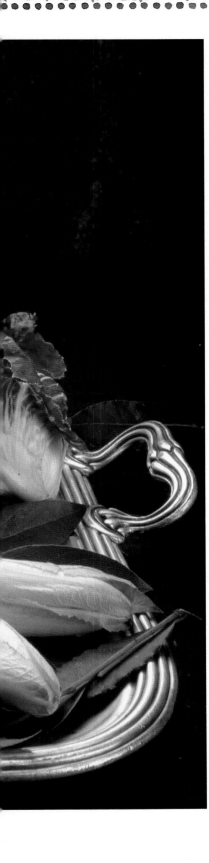

important factor is the animal's age: cattle slaughtered when they are old will give meat that is more difficult to cook. This is why, especially in mountain areas like the Valle d'Aosta, Valtellina and Trentino where oxen were used as working beasts for as long as possible and only put down when they could no longer pull the plough, there evolved a tradition of storing red meats over a long period before consumption. In Valle d'Aosta and Trentino the meat used to be divided into pieces and preserved in salt in wooden barrels, to be cooked a little at a time. In the Valle d'Aosta they would make a *carbonade* with strips of meat cooked for a long time in wine and flavorings, while in Trentino the custom is to sauté very thin slices of the salted meat in a skillet with a little fat, and serve it accompanied by boiled beans dressed with oil and salt. In Valtellina the best parts of the animal are salted and preserved using a method similar to the one used for ham.

The breeds of beef cattle most prized for their meat in Italy are the Chianina, Marchigiana, Piemontese and Romagnola, all of which take their names from their major breeding region. Then there are the Bruno Alpina, the Pezzata Nera, and the Frisona Italiana, which are also used for milk. Absolute supremacy among Italian meats belongs to the meat from the Chianina cattle, originally from the Chiana Valley in the southern part of Tuscany, between Arezzo and the border with Umbria and Lazio. These imposing beasts are distinguished by their small, forward-pointing horns and their black skin hidden beneath a white coat. They are unlike any other breed of cattle existing in Europe, all of which are descended from the *Bos primigenius*. The Chianina bears a closer resemblance to the *Bos indicus*, ancestor of the Asian breeds, but despite a great deal of research, no one has yet been able to find out how it came to Italy. Given that Italy is situated in the heart of ancient Etruria, a possible explanation is that these animals arrived in the wake of the Etruscans. The flesh of the Chianina is soft and compact, lightly marbled with threads of pure white fat which quickly melt during cooking.

In recent times attempts have been made to standardize cuts of beef throughout Italy, but even so the same piece of meat will still be found under different names in different cities. For example, the Milanese *biancostato*, one of the cuts generally used in the *bollito misto*, becomes *spezzato* in Turin, *costata* in Bologna and *spuntatura* in Rome. The *Enciclopedia Illustrata della Gastronomia (Illustrated Encyclopedia of Gastronomy)* which has recently been published in Italy gives a comprehensive overview of these differences. In fact there is one division of beef and veal cuts common to Milan, Como and Bergamo, and others for Venice, Trento, Torino, Genoa, Macerata and Ascoli Piceno, Florence, Rome, and so on. In this absolute Babel of nomenclatures a cook wanting to buy meat in various parts of Italy would need to know the terms used in at least fourteen areas from Lombardy to Sicily, and these in turn are subdivided (for example, the names used in Genoa are different from those used in nearby Imperia).

With the number of cookbooks in existence, it is frequently difficult to be sure which piece of meat is being specified for a given recipe. The national classification system proposed by the Italian National Breeders' Association suggests twenty-two "official" cuts. Ten of these are from the "posterior quarter" of the animal, and these are preferred for their quality and ease of cooking. Among them are the loin (*lombata*), which includes the fillet, leg (*fesa*) and best end (*noce*) making up the *sottofesa* or under part of the leg, and the rump (*scamone*) and topside (*girello*) from the upper leg. These cuts of meat are mainly used for broiling (grilling), roasting and braising.

The forequarter, which embraces another twelve cuts, is used for more everyday dishes. The part known as the "anterior muscle," for example, the front leg, is sliced horizontally to obtain the *ossobuco* so beloved of the Milanese. The larger the bone and the more marrow it contains, the more prestigious the dish. Other parts from this portion of the animal — partly because of their fattier texture — end up in a *bollito misto* (mixed boiled meat) or cut up for a homemade stew.

FALSOMAGRO

STUFFED BEEF ROLL

Falsomagro *in Italian means "mock lean," and the name derives from the fact that the roll of meat looks lean, whereas in fact it conceals a very rich filling.*

6 oz (185 g) prosciutto, chopped
6 oz (185 g) fresh pork and veal sausage, chopped
1 slice pancetta, chopped
2 oz (60 g) soft cow's milk cheese, such as Bel Paese, Stracchino or mozzarella, chopped
2 oz (60 g) Sicilian black pepper Pecorino cheese, chopped
1 egg plus 1 egg yolk
1 sprig flat-leafed parsley, minced
1 garlic clove, minced
salt and freshly ground pepper
1¼ lb (600 g) round steak in a single large slice, pounded ⅛ in (3 mm) thick
2 hard-cooked eggs, thinly sliced
1 cup (8 fl oz/250 ml) oil
1 onion, thinly sliced
½ cup (4 fl oz/125 ml) dry red wine

SERVES 6

❦ In a bowl, combine the *prosciutto*, sausage, *pancetta*, soft cheese, Pecorino, egg and egg yolk, parsley, garlic, and a pinch each of salt and pepper. Mix well.
❦ Spread the stuffing mixture carefully over the meat, taking care to cover the slice completely. Distribute the egg slices on top. Roll up the meat and tie with kitchen string.
❦ In a wide, shallow pan, heat the oil with the onion and fry until onion is golden. Add the roll of beef and brown on all sides. Pour the wine over it and cook over slow heat for about 1 hour.
❦ As soon as it is cooked, remove the string, transfer the meat to a serving dish and slice it at the table. Serve with the cooking juices. This is also very good cold.

MANZO IN VESCICA

BEEF IN A BAG

A speciality of northern Italy, probably Lombardic in origin, this dish was first transcribed in recipe collections of the eighteenth century, but is similar to an even older one from Padua that features capon instead of beef. The original version calls for a pig's bladder, but a plastic oven bag may be substituted.

1¼ lb (625 g) beef shank (cut from the inner leg), trimmed and cubed
1 lb (500 g) cipolline (small onions), trimmed
1 celery stalk, strings removed and thinly sliced
5 or 6 carrots, thinly sliced
4 garlic cloves, peeled
5 bay leaves
salt and freshly ground pepper
½ cup (4 fl oz/125 ml) water

SERVES 4

❦ In a plastic oven bag, combine the meat, onions, celery, carrots, garlic, bay leaves, salt and pepper to taste and the water. Tie the bag securely and immerse in a pot of cold water. Bring to a boil and cook for 3½ hours over low heat. If the bag swells too much, untie it, let out the air and re-tie.
❦ At the end of the cooking time, open the bag and serve the meat and vegetables.

NOCETTE DI MAIALE AI SEMI DI SENAPE

PORK NOISETTES IN MUSTARD-SEED SAUCE

This is a traditional recipe from the area straddling the border between Veneto and Friuli in the Adriatic hinterland northeast of Venice. It is a rich and complex one-dish meal; however, for an important dinner it could be preceded, for example, by a light antipasto such as San Daniele prosciutto (thus keeping to the same area) and followed by dessert.

For the pork:
1¼ lb (625 g) whole fillet of pork
3 tablespoons (1½ oz/45 g) butter
1 sprig rosemary
2 sage leaves
salt and freshly ground pepper
For the sauce:
¼ cup (2 fl oz/60 ml) juices from a roast of veal, or strong meat stock
3 tablespoons (1½ oz/45 g) butter
2 tablespoons crushed fresh mustard seeds
salt and freshly ground pepper
For the onion *gnocchi*:
1 lb (500 g) potatoes
2 onions, thinly sliced
3 tablespoons (1½ oz/45 g) butter
1 bay leaf
¾ cup (3 oz/90 g) all-purpose (plain) flour
3 eggs
¾ cup (3 oz/90 g) freshly grated Parmesan cheese

Left: Falsomagro; top right: Manzo in Vescica; bottom right: Nocette di Maiale ai Semi di Senape

salt and freshly ground pepper
2 tablespoons melted butter, for serving
2 tablespoons chopped chives, for serving

SERVES 4

❡ Prepare the meat: In a skillet, cook the pork for about 20 minutes in the butter, rosemary and sage, turning frequently to brown it on all sides. It should remain a little pink.

❡ Make the sauce: In a skillet combine the veal juices with the butter, and whisk in the mustard seeds and salt and pepper to taste.

❡ Make the *gnocchi:* Boil the potatoes in their skins. Peel and mash them through a potato ricer.

Meanwhile, stew the onion gently in the butter with a bay leaf without letting it color. Discard the bay leaf; season with salt and pepper. Add the potatoes and work into a dough along with the flour, eggs and Parmesan. Form the dough into ¾ in (2 cm) *gnocchi*. Cook the *gnocchi* in plenty of boiling, salted water. They are cooked when they rise to the surface of the water. Drain.

❡ Slice the pork about ½ in (1.5 cm) thick. Arrange the slices over half of each heated dinner plate; coat carefully with the sauce. On the other half of the plate, arrange the onion *gnocchi*, boiled and dressed with melted butter and the chopped chives.

LONZA DI MAIALE AL LATTE

PORK COOKED IN MILK

Widely used throughout Italy, this dish originated in the Marches region. It is one of the few Italian dishes in which milk and cream appear as major ingredients, and it apparently arose out of the peasant custom of slaughtering huge pigs that were bred for salami and sausagemaking and whose rather compact flesh required the addition of something to soften both the texture and the flavor of the meat during cooking.

3 tablespoons (1½ oz/45 g) butter
2 onions, finely chopped
2 lb (1 kg) pork loin, in 1 piece
salt and freshly ground pepper
2 cups (16 fl oz/500 ml) milk
1 cup (8 fl oz/250 ml) heavy (double) cream

SERVES 4

¶ In a high-sided terracotta pan over low heat, combine the butter and onions. Cook until the onion colors. Add the pork, sprinkle with salt and

Top: Lonza di Maiale al Latte; bottom left: Stinco di Maiale alla Tirolese; bottom right: Carne 'Ncantarata

pepper and brown, turning several times.

❡ Preheat the oven to 400°F (200°C). When the meat is well browned pour in the milk and cream and mix. Cover the pan and transfer it to the oven and bake for about 1 hour. Check the cooking from time to time and turn the pork.

❡ To serve, slice the pork, arrange the slices on a serving dish and coat with the pan juices. Serve accompanied by puréed potatoes.

STINCO DI MAIALE ALLA TIROLESE

TYROLEAN PORK SHANK

The people of the Trentino–Alto Adige region are of Germanic background and language, and quite a number of Middle European traditions are preserved in their cuisine, particularly the use of pork in dishes of every description. Pork shank, small enough to be served as a single portion, has come into common use in many restaurants and trattorie and has won a place of importance in Italian gastronomy.

4 bone-in pork shanks, about 13 oz (410 g) each
2 tablespoons (1 oz/30 g) butter
2 celery stalks, finely chopped
1 onion, finely chopped
1 carrot, scraped and finely chopped
2 garlic cloves, finely chopped
1 sprig sage
1 sprig rosemary
2 juniper berries
1 cup (8 fl oz/250 ml) dry white wine
⅓ cup (3 fl oz/90 ml) grappa
salt and freshly ground pepper
¾ cup (6 fl oz/185 ml) meat stock
1 teaspoon all-purpose (plain) flour

SERVES 4

❡ Preheat the oven to 400°F (200°C). Clean, trim, wash and dry the shanks. Arrange them in a high-sided casserole with half the butter and surround with the celery, onion, carrot and garlic. Add the sage, rosemary and juniper berries and cook over high heat, stirring until the meat browns evenly.

❡ Add the wine and grappa, taste for seasoning and cook until the alcohol evaporates.

❡ Add the stock and the remaining butter worked with the flour. Mix well once more.

❡ Bake in the oven, uncovered, for 2 hours.

❡ Remove the shanks and set aside. Put the pan

juices through a food mill. Cook over high heat until reduced. Serve the shanks with the sauce poured over them, accompanied by boiled or roast potatoes.

CARNE 'NCANTARATA

PRESERVED MEAT

Derived from the Greek khantaros, the word 'ncantarata means "preserved in a jar." Carne 'ncantarata is an old Calabrian recipe that uses preserved meat. Its origins go back to the time of the Greek civilization of southern Italy, and it has hardly changed since that time. Used up to the beginning of the last century, it has only reappeared in modern times.

1 whole pork loin fillet, about 1½ lb (750 g) or
If preserving the meat (optional):
salt
½ teaspoon chopped dried chili pepper
1 teaspoon wild fennel seeds
For preparing the meat:
2 cups (16 fl oz/500 ml) dry white wine
1 cup (8 fl oz/250 ml) olive oil
1 teaspoon wild fennel seeds
zest (rind) of 1 orange, grated
¼ cup (3 oz/90 g) honey
1 teaspoon chili powder

SERVES 4

❡ For preserving the meat (optional): Slice the pork into 8 pieces. Sprinkle each slice with salt, chili pepper and fennel seeds. Pile the slices in a terracotta container and cover the meat with a circle of wood that just fits inside the container. Press down by placing weights on the wooden lid. Store for at least 15 days (the meat will last for many months). Remove the slices, wash them in several changes of cold water.

❡ Preheat the oven to 400°F (200°C).

❡ Either take the 8 slices of preserved pork, or slice the fresh pork into 8 pieces and put them into a wide, shallow, terracotta pan. Add the wine and olive oil to cover. Add the fennel seeds and orange zest and bake for 20 minutes. Serve with green salad.

❡ Drain off the cooking juices and stir into them the honey and chili powder. Pour this mixture over the meat, return to the oven to bake for a further 20 minutes. Serve with green salad.

CASTRATO ALLA GRIGLIA E CROSTINI ALLO SCALOGNO

BROILED MUTTON WITH SHALLOT-FLAVORED CROÛTONS

The castrato is a male sheep castrated to be raised for meat. This practice, applied when the animal is very young, fosters the development of tender flesh that is full of flavor. However in Romagna, where this type of meat is most commonly eaten, the meat from ordinary adult sheep is also sold as castrato. This is another reason for letting the meat ripen for five or six days before cooking.

For the mutton:
4 castrato *(mutton) cutlets*
¼ cup (2 fl oz/60 ml) extra-virgin olive oil
1 sprig rosemary
3 basil leaves
salt and freshly ground pepper
For the sauce:
4 ripe tomatoes, peeled, seeded and diced
1 shallot, chopped
For the croûtons:
8 slices coarse-textured bread
1 shallot
¼ cup (2 fl oz/60 ml) olive oil

SERVES 4

❡ Prepare the mutton: Beat the cutlets lightly with a mallet. In a wide, deep dish combine the cutlets with the oil, rosemary, basil and salt and pepper. Set aside to infuse for 10 minutes. Remove and reserve the cutlets; strain the oil marinade and reserve.
❡ Make the sauce: Combine the tomatoes, shallot and the strained oil from the marinade. Set aside to infuse briefly.
❡ Prepare the croûtons and finish the dish: Broil (grill) the cutlets for 2 to 3 minutes each side. Toast the bread slices. Rub the toast with the shallot and sprinkle with olive oil. Cut the toast slices into small squares. Serve the cutlets surrounded by these croûtons, with a little tomato sauce alongside.

AGNELLO CON SALSA ALL'AGLIO

LAMB WITH GARLIC SAUCE

One of the few cases in Italian cooking where the use of heavy (double) cream is acceptable is this decidedly modern recipe which clearly illustrates the lightening process currently under way in the new Italian gastronomy. Traditionally a baked lamb is flavored directly with things like garlic, rosemary and other herbs finely chopped and mixed with salt and pepper. Here these flavors are limited and tempered by the cooking in cream, which then becomes a delicate sauce.

2 cups (16 fl oz/500 ml) heavy (double) cream
6 garlic cloves, sliced
2 bay leaves
1 sprig rosemary

Left: Castrato alla Griglia e Crostini allo Scalogno; right: Agnello con Salsa all'Aglio

1 tablespoon potato flour
2 saddles (racks) of lamb with 6 cutlets each
salt and freshly ground pepper
½ cup (4 fl oz/125 ml) extra-virgin olive oil

SERVES 4

❡ In a saucepan, heat the cream, garlic, bay leaves and rosemary. Cook for 3 to 4 minutes; remove the bay leaves and rosemary. Process the cream and garlic in a blender. Add the potato flour and mix until moderately thick.

❡ Preheat the oven to 400°F (200°C). Season the lamb with salt and pepper. Put it in a baking dish with oil and bake in the oven for about 15 minutes, until when pricked with a fork the meat is tender and the juice is not pink. Divide the saddles into cutlets, arrange these in a fan shape (3 to a plate) and coat with the garlic sauce.

AGNELLO IN SCOTTIGLIA

LAMB COOKED WITH WINE AND HERBS

In Tuscany, in the countryside around Arezzo, a scotti-glia is a robust peasant dish of mixed meats (veal, pork, chicken, pigeon) stewed in a strong red wine sauce. In the hills of Romagna, near the border with the Arezzo countryside, the same cooking procedure is applied to the lighter meat from the lamb.

1 lb (500 g) boneless lamb, trimmed and cubed
3 tablespoons (1½ oz/45g) butter
⅓ cup (3 fl oz/90 ml) olive oil
1 garlic clove, minced
1 sprig rosemary, chopped

Left: Scaloppine alla Perugina; top: Agnello in Scottiglia; bottom: Abbacchio alla Romana

4 sage leaves
1 cup (8 fl oz/250 ml) dry red wine
13 oz (410 g) potatoes
curly endive (chicory), for serving

SERVES 4

❡ In a skillet, brown the lamb cubes in the butter and olive oil with the garlic, rosemary and sage for 2 to 3 minutes. As soon as the lamb colors, pour in the wine. Cook until evaporated. Continue cooking over moderate heat for 15 to 20 minutes, until when pricked with a fork the meat is tender and the juice is no longer pink. Keep the meat and the cooking liquid warm.
❡ Meanwhile, peel the potatoes and cut them into little balls using a melon baller. Cook in boiling salted water; drain.
❡ Push the meat cooking juices through a fine strainer. Arrange a few leaves of curly endive on each dinner plate. Arrange some of the meat on these, sprinkle with a little of the cooking liquid, and garnish with the potato balls.

SCALOPPINE ALLA PERUGINA

PERUGIA VEAL ESCALOPES

An easy dish from the family cuisine of Umbria, this one has one unusual feature: whereas meats are usually browned first and then enriched with various sauces or pan juices, here the meat is added to a rich layer of base ingredients before cooking begins. This enables each of the components to mingle its flavors and fragrances with the other ingredients, resulting in a most interesting blend.

3 tablespoons olive oil
juice and grated zest (rind) of ½ lemon
2 or 3 sage leaves
3 anchovy fillets, minced
2 oz (60 g) prosciutto, chopped
1 chicken liver, trimmed and chopped
2 tablespoons capers, drained and chopped
1 garlic clove, chopped
8 slices veal scaloppine, about 1½ lb (750 g) total weight
salt and freshly ground pepper

SERVES 4

❡ In a wide, shallow pan, combine the olive oil, lemon juice, sage leaves and grated lemon zest. Add the anchovies, ham, chicken liver, capers and garlic. Lay the veal on top and sprinkle with salt and pepper. Put the pan on moderate heat and

cook for about 15 minutes, turning the meat several times. (If the pan is not large enough to accommodate the 8 scaloppine, divide the ingredients that make up the sauce into 2 batches, and cook half at a time.) Serve the meat hot, in the sauce.

ABBACCHIO ALLA ROMANA

ROMAN ROAST LAMB

Of all the dishes in classical Roman cuisine, abbacchio (the dialect term for lamb that has been fed exclusively on its mother's milk) is probably the oldest and most traditional. These same ingredients — olive oil, herbs such as garlic and rosemary — were in common use at the time of the Roman Empire. The anchovies are a modern addition, probably replacing garum, the universal ancient Roman sauce the composition of which is unknown, although according to some scholars it was made with fish (anchovies and mackerel) macerated in salt and wine.

2 lb (1 kg) milk-fed lamb
3 tablespoons olive oil
2½ garlic cloves, peeled and bruised
salt and freshly ground pepper
1 sprig rosemary
2 anchovy fillets
2 to 3 tablespoons white wine vinegar

SERVES 4

❡ Cut the lamb into small pieces. In a skillet over low heat, combine the oil and 2 of the garlic cloves. Fry gently until the garlic begins to color. Add the meat and brown evenly on all sides over moderate heat. Add a pinch of salt and a grinding of pepper (although many people prefer to use chili pepper, which is healthier) and cook over moderate heat.
❡ Meanwhile, pound the rosemary leaves with the anchovies and half a garlic clove in a mortar or food processor. Add the white wine vinegar and mix well.
❡ As soon as the lamb is cooked (all the pieces must be done to an even degree of tenderness), drain off the excess pan juices, if any, leaving only a small amount. Pour the anchovy sauce over the meat, stir to mix, and cook until the vinegar completely evaporates. Arrange the pieces of lamb on a serving platter and sprinkle with the cooking juices. Serve hot, with roast or fried potatoes.

VITELLO FARCITO

STUFFED VEAL

Veal is a very popular meat in Italy, especially in the north. The best veal comes from calves killed when only three months old, when they are still milk fed. The meat should be very pale pink in color.

In Piedmont, there are many recipes for veal. This is a very rich Piedmontese dish belonging to the tradition of Turin, which means that it was created (as were similar dishes found in French cooking) in the kitchens of the Royal Palace or of some aristocratic family in the eighteenth century, when the splendors of the Court of Versailles dictated fashions for all of Europe.

3 tablespoons (1½ oz/45 g) butter
4 oz (125 g) lean veal
2 slices pickled tongue
2 oz (60 g) salt pork
1 truffle
1 garlic clove, peeled
1½ cups of sprigs flat-leafed parsley
½ oz (15 g) dried mushrooms, soaked and squeezed dry
1 bread roll softened in 1 cup (8 fl oz/250 ml) milk and squeezed dry
1 egg, beaten
2 tablespoons freshly grated Parmesan cheese
salt and freshly ground pepper
1¼ lb (625 g) veal breast with a pocket cut in it
3 oz (90 g) prosciutto, thinly sliced
3 tablespoons olive oil
1 cup (8 fl oz/250 ml) Barolo wine
2 cups (16 fl oz/500 ml) beef or veal stock

SERVES 6

❡ In a wide, shallow pan over moderate heat, melt 1 tablespoon butter and brown the lean veal.
❡ Put the veal through a meat grinder twice, together with the tongue, salt pork, truffle, garlic, parsley and mushrooms. Add the bread, the egg, Parmesan and salt and pepper to taste. Mix well and fill the pocket of the breast, alternating layers of the stuffing with a few slices of prosciutto. Sew the opening up with kitchen thread and tie the meat into a cylinder shape.
❡ Heat the remaining butter with the oil in a wide, shallow pan. Lay the rolled veal on top and brown on all sides. Season with salt and pepper, cover and continue to cook over moderate heat for at least 40 minutes, basting from time to time first with the Barolo, and then with the stock. Move the meat around often and sprinkle with the cooking juices.
❡ Serve hot, sliced and coated in its sauce.

UCCELLETTI SCAPPATI

"ESCAPED BIRDS"

A very well-known dish from Milan, these little veal rolls are served with polenta in place of the traditional small birds. The curious name of the dish derives from this substitution, which arose, according to popular legend, because the real birds had flown.

1¼ lb (625 g) leg of veal, thinly sliced
3 oz (90 g) pancetta, thinly sliced
20 sage leaves
3 oz (90 g) pancetta, cubed
5 tablespoons (2½ oz/75 g) butter
salt and freshly ground pepper

SERVES 4

❡ Flatten the veal with a meat mallet. Lay 1 slice of pancetta and 1 sage leaf on each. Roll up the meat and thread the rolls onto long wooden skewers, placing a sage leaf and a cube of pancetta at each end. Continue in this way, so you have a series of skewers with 4 or 5 rolls on each.
❡ Place the butter in a skillet over moderate heat. When the butter is foaming, add the skewers and sprinkle with salt and pepper. Cook on high heat for 15 minutes, turning several times. Serve with broiled (grilled) polenta slices.

VITELLO TONNATO

COLD VEAL WITH TUNA SAUCE

A speciality of Milan and Piedmont, vitello tonnato is a typical summer dish. It has a cool, fresh taste and is equally good as an antipasto or as the main course of a light lunch, enjoying wide popularity not only in restaurants but also on the family table. There are any number of recipes with personal variations introduced by every cook. The version given here may be taken as the universally accepted formula in professional kitchens.

2 lb (1 kg) lean veal, such as topside
1 carrot, sliced
1 onion, sliced
3 or 4 cloves
2 bay leaves
salt and freshly ground pepper
3 cups (24 fl oz/750 ml) dry white wine
For the sauce:
2 egg yolks
6 oz (185 g) tuna packed in olive oil, drained, with oil reserved

Top left: Vitello Farcito; top right: Uccelletti Scappati; bottom: Vitello Tonnato

juice of 1 lemon
2 tablespoons dry white wine
1 to 2 tablespoons white wine vinegar
1 tablespoon capers, drained and minced

SERVES 4–6

§ Put the veal in a bowl along with the carrot, onion, cloves, bay leaves and salt and pepper. Pour on wine to cover. Cover and set aside to infuse overnight.

§ Next morning, wrap the meat in a white napkin, lay it in a casserole or saucepan and pour on the marinade. Place over moderate heat and cook for about 40 minutes, or until the meat is soft and tender. Remove the napkin (which serves to keep it in shape) and set the meat aside to cool.

§ Meanwhile, prepare a good quantity of mayonnaise by beating the egg yolks with the olive oil and the lemon juice. Push the tuna through a strainer or process it in a food processor until very fine, and fold it gently into the mayonnaise. Dilute the sauce with the white wine and vinegar; stir in the capers.

§ Slice the veal, arrange it on a serving dish and coat it with the sauce. Refrigerate until serving time.

Ossobuco alla Milanese

MILANESE STEWED SHIN OF VEAL

An immensely popular dish in Milan, this is served as a main course with an accompaniment of risotto alla milanese or as a meal on its own. The term ossobuco *refers to the rear hock of the animal sawed by the butcher into chunks at least 1½ in (4 cm) thick. The most delicious part of this dish is the marrow which is extracted with a special tool, a kind of long thin spoon popularly labeled the "tax agent" because it can take everything from the bone right down to its innermost recesses.*

Back: Ossobuco alla Milanese; front: Stinco di Vitello in Umido

3 tablespoons (1½ oz/45 g) butter
1 garlic clove, halved
4 chunks veal shank, each about 12 oz (375 g)
all-purpose (plain) flour, for dredging
1 cup (8 fl oz/250 ml) dry white wine or meat stock
salt and freshly ground pepper
1 sprig flat-leafed parsley
grated zest (rind) and juice of ½ a lemon
SERVES 4

❡ In a wide, shallow pan, combine the butter and half the clove of garlic. Meanwhile, dredge the veal in flour. When the garlic begins to brown, discard it, and add the veal. Brown the meat on all sides. Reduce the heat, cover the pan and cook slowly, adding a few spoonfuls of white wine from time to time. Cook for about 1½ hours, turning the pieces to ensure that they cook evenly and become golden brown all over. Season with salt and pepper.

❡ Meanwhile, chop the remaining half clove of garlic with the parsley and lemon zest.

❡ When the meat is cooked, sprinkle the parsley mixture and the lemon juice over it and cook for 10 minutes. Serve sprinkled with the cooking juices.

STINCO DI VITELLO IN UMIDO

SHIN OF VEAL WITH CELERY AND POTATOES

Shin of veal is one of the secondary cuts of meat that has been lifted to the ranks of a true specialty thanks to the imagination of ordinary people. This dish is characteristic of Emilia Romagna, but it differs very little from others belonging to the cuisine of the Trentino and Veneto regions. The modern version given here eliminates the butter of old, and replaces the meat stock once used in generous amounts with a little of the juice from a roast.

1 veal shank
rosemary leaves
sage leaves
garlic slivers
salt and freshly ground pepper
1 lb (500 g) potatoes, peeled and cut into large cubes
½ cup (4 fl oz/125 ml) olive oil
1 bunch celery, trimmed and chopped
2 tablespoons (1 oz/30 g) butter
2 cups (16 fl oz/500 ml) dry white wine
¼ cup (2 fl oz/60 ml) of the juices from a roast
SERVES 4

❡ Preheat the oven to 350°F (180°C). Make cuts in the meat with the point of a knife and insert rosemary, sage, garlic and season with salt and pepper. Lay the shank in an oiled baking dish and brown over high heat.

❡ In a skillet, sear the potatoes briefly in olive oil over high heat. Set aside. Briefly sear the celery in the butter. Set aside.

❡ Pour the wine over the meat and bake until evaporated. Cover and cook for 1 hour. Add the potatoes, celery and roasting juices and cook for a further 30 minutes or so, until the meat is tender. Slice the veal lengthwise and serve the slices hot, surrounded by the potatoes and celery.

FRITTO CROCCANTE DI POLLO E CONIGLIO

CRUNCHY CHICKEN AND RABBIT FRITTERS

The great tradition of frying chicken and rabbit in the Tuscan manner continues to hold the limelight in all Italian cuisine. Dishes like this one are found everywhere, but there is general agreement that no one can match the craftsmanship of the Tuscan cook in the simple perfection of this delicate creation.

½ cup (2 oz/60 g) all-purpose (plain) flour
½ cup (2 oz/60 g) durum wheat flour
½ cup (2 oz/60 g) cornstarch (cornflour)
salt
1 cup (8 fl oz/250 ml) water
10 oz (315 g) boneless chicken, cut into 10 pieces
10 oz (315 g) boneless rabbit, cut into 10 pieces
all-purpose (plain) flour, for dredging
olive oil
SERVES 4

❡ Make the batter: Dissolve the all-purpose flour, the durum wheat flour, the cornstarch and a pinch of salt in the water, and stir until you have a creamy batter that is not too thick, adding more water if necessary.

❡ Sprinkle the chicken and rabbit pieces with a little salt, dredge in flour and dip into the batter, which must be quite cold. In a large skillet, shallow-fry the meat pieces in the olive oil at 320°F (160°C) and drain on paper towels when they are evenly browned. (Fritters prepared this way are crisp on the outside and at the same time soft and succulent within.) Serve with a green salad. (See photograph page 133.)

Left: Misto Padovano alla Griglia; right: Pollo Ripieno alle Noci

drain well and cook on the grill. The chicken and rabbit will need to be cooked 3 to 5 minutes each side; the pheasant and the duck only require about 1½ minutes each side.

§ Slice the meat and serve the slices alternating in a fan shape in the center of the plate, garnished with grilled vegetables in season, such as zucchini (courgettes), eggplants (aubergines), tomatoes and radicchio.

MISTO PADOVANO ALLA GRIGLIA

PADUA-STYLE MIXED GRILL

The idea for this grill, consisting exclusively of farmyard animals and birds, arose out of the culinary tradition of Padua with its strong peasant links. It is a simple dish with fats reduced to a minimum and a skillful interplay of flavors resulting from the different marinades.

6 oz (185 g) each of skinless, boneless breast of chicken, duck and pheasant, and fillet of rabbit, sliced thinly
1 cup (8 fl oz/250 ml) olive oil
½ teaspoon grated ginger root
2 garlic cloves, bruised
1 teaspoon grated orange zest (rind)
2 bay leaves
8 black peppercorns
2 tablespoons red or white wine vinegar
1 sprig rosemary

SERVES 4

§ The four meats should be marinated separately as follows:
• the chicken in ¼ cup (2 fl oz/60 ml) olive oil, with the ginger and a garlic clove;
• the duck in ¼ cup (2 fl oz/60 ml) olive oil, with the grated orange zest, a bay leaf and 4 peppercorns;
• the pheasant in ¼ cup (2 fl oz/60 ml) olive oil, with a bay leaf and 4 peppercorns;
• the rabbit in ¼ cup (2 fl oz/60 ml) olive oil, with the vinegar, a garlic clove and the rosemary sprig.
§ Leave the meat to marinate for 24 hours, then

POLLO RIPIENO ALLE NOCI

WALNUT-STUFFED CHICKEN

This is a very rich dish typical of the cuisine of Trento. In a region whose gastronomy is basic and mainly of mountain origin, this stuffed chicken takes on particular importance. Its origins are patrician, and the use of exotic ingredients such as nutmeg leads us to suppose that the bishop-princes that ruled the city for many hundreds of years had something to do with it.

2 bread rolls, crusts removed
¼ cup (2 fl oz/60 ml) beef stock
½ cup (1½ oz/45 g) shelled walnuts
⅓ cup (1½ oz/45 g) pine nuts
1 chicken, about 3 lb (1.5 kg), cleaned with gizzard reserved
5 oz (155 g) beef marrow
3 oz (90 g) chicken livers
salt and freshly ground pepper
1 tablespoon freshly grated Parmesan cheese
1 egg, beaten
grated nutmeg
1 bouquet garni

SERVES 6

§ Soften the rolls with beef stock. Squeeze dry. Immerse the walnuts in boiling water for a few moments to loosen their fine skins; remove the skins. Crush the walnuts with the pine nuts.
§ Wash the chicken under running water. Cook the gizzard for a few minutes in lightly salted boiling water. Put the gizzard, beef marrow, chicken livers and well-squeezed bread through a meat grinder. Add the nut mixture, a pinch each of salt and pepper, the Parmesan, egg and very little nutmeg.
§ Stuff the bird with the mixture; sew up with kitchen string. Place the chicken in boiling salted water with a bouquet garni and cook for about 1 hour over moderate heat. Serve the chicken cut into 4 pieces, with legs and wings separated, with the stuffing in the center of the serving dish.

Top: Gallina alla Borragine; bottom: Fritto Croccante di Pollo e Coniglio (page 131)

GALLINA ALLA BORRAGINE

CHICKEN AND BORAGE

It is important in this recipe to immerse the bird in water that is already boiling, so that the shock of the heat closes all the pores in the skin and allows it to cook without leaking anything into the water. Putting the chicken into cold water yields an excellent stock and boiled meat of inferior quality.

1 bunch borage
1 dressed boiling fowl, about 2½ lb (1.2 kg)

6 small round onions
3 carrots, sliced
5 oz (155 g) small new potatoes
¼ cup (2 fl oz/60 ml) olive oil

SERVES 4

❡ Place the borage inside the bird. Place the chicken in a saucepan of boiling salted water and cook slowly for about 1 hour. Then add the vegetables. Continue cooking for a further 15 minutes or until the vegetables are cooked. Divide the chicken into quarters and serve surrounded by the vegetables, with olive oil drizzled over it.

WHITE MEAT AND POULTRY

Along with pasta, white meat forms the true backbone of Italian cuisine. The origins of Italian gastronomy are to be found in the traditions of its ordinary folk, and the country's eating habits are the result of what the land has to offer.

Veal, lamb, kid, rabbit, chicken, turkey and goose are considered white meat. The meat of the young donkey is also white, but its consumption is limited to small areas of Piedmont, in the country around Novara and Asti.

Veal must be young, from calves fed only on their mother's milk, and the meat will be pinkish in color. If the color is stronger and there is a significant amount of fat, it means the animal has also been fed meal, grain or grass, and it will not be of such high quality.

Veal has a delicate flavor, less pronounced than red meats, and adapts well to a great variety of combinations. It is this feature that has led to the many variations of veal *scaloppine*, where it is cooked with mushrooms, tomatoes, artichokes, broccoli or other vegetables, or simply enriched by the addition of white wine to the pan.

Veal is eaten mainly in the north, in Piedmont, Lombardy, the Veneto, Emilia and Romagna. In Piedmont, in particular, the animals are raised for twelve months on cow's milk without weaning, and sometimes their diet is enriched with egg yolks added to the mother's milk. Although an animal fed this way (known locally as *sanato*) grows to a considerable size, its flesh retains a delicate flavor that is much sought after by gourmets. Veal is the basis of one of the most famous dishes in Lombardian cuisine, the *costoletta alla milanese*, crumbed and fried in butter.

Lamb and kid are also popular. The animal is best when fed only on milk and slaughtered at about four weeks of age when it weighs around 22 to 25 pounds (10 to 12 kilograms). Larger lambs and kids, ones that are allowed to graze in the pastures up to the age of ten weeks or so, weigh about 30 pounds (14 kilograms). Their meat is a little less tender and slightly more flavorful than that of the smaller animals.

Kid tends to be more

associated with peasant dishes and is eaten mainly in central and southern regions, as in Calabria where a common method of preparation is to stuff a whole kid with vermicelli and roast it in the oven. The best eating is to be had from the leg and shoulder, which are usually cooked whole on the spit, or in the oven surrounded by new potatoes. The loin can be cooked whole or divided into cutlets that are generally broiled (grilled) quickly and served piping hot. These are the famous *scottadito* (burn the fingers), so-named because they are eaten as soon as they come off the broiler (grill), held in the fingers using the slender bone as a handle. In the south of Italy lamb is served in many ways. Cut up into pieces it may be baked in the oven with potatoes and tomatoes after a much-loved recipe from Apulia, or served in the manner known as *cacio e uova*, a simple version of the fricassée with a mixture of beaten eggs and grated cheese added to the lamb after it has been stewed with oil, garlic, herbs and wine.

The meat of the rabbit, a constant presence on every farm, is especially popular in Liguria, Piedmont, Lombardy and Tuscany. Rabbits are easy to breed, although they are delicate animals and were once subject to raging epidemics. Wild rabbit is more flavorsome, however, because of the wild herbs and berries it feeds on.

From the nutritional point of view rabbit is held in high regard because it contains more protein than beef or veal (approximately 21 per cent as against 18 per cent), and a far lower fat and cholesterol content. It used to be traditional in Italian families to feed rabbit stock to convalescents. Rabbit lends itself to stewing in wine and stock, after a preliminary browning in oil with flavorings. In Liguria it marries wonderfully with olives; in Tuscany it is cut up and presented with or without artichokes as a famous "fry." In the Marches it is cooked the same way as *porchetta*, completely boned and stuffed with a rich filling of eggs, cheese, herbs and other ingredients, and then sliced thinly for serving either hot or cold.

Like rabbit, chicken and turkey belong to the farmhouse tradition. They are creatures of the barnyard, allowed to scratch about freely in the spaces around the house and closed in at night, mainly to keep them from such nocturnal predators as foxes and martens.

Turkey is more popular in the north and in Milan it features as traditional Christmas fare. Turkey with pomegranate, however, is a specialty of Venice.

The best chickens are corn-fed and their flesh, consequently, has a slightly yellow hue. Tuscany has long been renowned for the quality of its free-range chickens and for the variety of its chicken recipes. One such that uses the whole chicken is *pollo alla diavola*, for which the chicken is sliced down the breast, opened out and flattened and then cooked preferably over an open wood or charcoal fire. Most recipes in Italian cooking, however, use chicken pieces, for preference.

In the past, only the wealthy could afford to eat chicken, and the birds were mainly kept for laying eggs. As a result, most people would only kill the birds when they had stopped laying and were quite old; so, the bird would usually be boiled up to make stock.

Fegatini (chicken livers) feature in a number of recipes, particularly in Tuscany, and are used in risottos and for making sauces to accompany pasta.

Intensive breeding has led to an unlimited distribution of these two birds, but they are almost always prepared according to recipes that belong to the popular tradition.

More unusual and interesting is the return to eating goose, particularly evident in Milan and Lombardy in recent years. Although goose was popular during the Middle Ages and the Renaissance, its popularity subsequently underwent a decline because the meal was considered too fatty.

The major goose farms are in the area of Mortara, in the countryside around Pavia, where a Jewish colony settled during the height of the Renaissance and began producing kosher foods. Today Mortara is a production center for salamis made with *foie gras* and goose meat. In autumn each year there is a lively festival dedicated to the goose and the products derived from it.

In northern country regions local people have a tradition of preserving geese in autumn so that they last during the winter months.

1. chicken; 2. rabbit; 3. rib of veal; 4. lamb cutlets

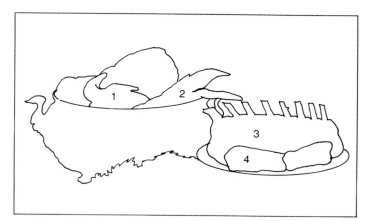

FEGATO GRASSO D'ANITRA CALDO ALLA CREMA DI BORLOTTI

HOT FOIE GRAS OF DUCK WITH BEAN PURÉE

Do not be misled by the term foie gras. *Although this dish belongs to the more modern school of Italian cooking,* its roots are deep in the past.

Around the Mortara area to the west of Milan, the tradition of breeding geese and ducks was first introduced in the sixteenth century by a Jewish community settled there, and it still continues. And a few miles further west is Vigevano, which has always been famous for its high-quality borlotti (red) beans.

Other interesting ingredients included in this recipe are

Top: Fegato Grasso d'Anitra Caldo alla Crema di Borlotti; bottom: Anatra Ripiena

the wonderfully sweet Tropea onions from Calabria, and balsamic vinegar which adds to the character of the dish. The very limited use of fats is also worthy of note here.

½ red Tropea onion, or a white onion, chopped
2 oz (60 g) pancetta, chopped
1 garlic clove, peeled
2 tablespoons olive oil
1¼ lb (600 g) fresh borlotti (red) beans, shelled
3 cups (24 fl oz/750 ml) water
salt and freshly ground pepper
4 slices duck foie gras, each about 2½ oz (75 g)
balsamic vinegar

SERVES 4

❦ In a small saucepan, fry the onion, pancetta and garlic gently in the oil, but do not let them color. When the onion is translucent and the pancetta rendered, add the beans and stir to coat with the fats. Add the water, bring to a boil and cook over low heat for about 30 minutes, or until very tender. Taste for salt toward the end of cooking only.
❦ Process the beans in a blender or with an immersion beater to make a soft, thick cream. Adjust the salt and pepper if necessary.
❦ Wrap the liver slices in heatproof plastic and steam for 5 minutes.
❦ Spread some bean purée over the bottom of each heated serving plate. Place a slice of foie gras in the center, brush with a little balsamic vinegar, add salt and pepper and serve.

ANATRA RIPIENA

STUFFED DUCK

This dish is one of the great classics of regional gastronomy — so much so that it can be found written on menus in the local dialect, anara col pien. There are two versions of it, the strictly traditional one in which the duck is boiled, and another where it is roasted with various ingredients; both are accompanied by equally typical Venetian sauces. Featured among the ingredients is the Venetian soppressa, an item of local charcuterie that can be replaced by another type of salami without too much garlic.

1 onion, coarsely chopped
1 carrot
1 celery
¼ cup kosher (coarse) salt

½ cup flat-leafed chopped parsley
1 garlic clove, chopped
3 oz (90 g) duck or chicken livers, chopped
2 oz (60 g) soppressa, Milano salami, or fresh pork and veal sausage, chopped
table salt
pinch of ground nutmeg
2 eggs, beaten together
½ cup (2 oz/60 g) freshly grated Parmesan cheese
½ cup (2 oz/60 g) dry breadcrumbs
1 duck, about 4 lb (2 kg)

SERVES 6

❦ Fill a large saucepan with water, add the onion, carrot, celery and kosher salt and set over moderate heat.
❦ Meanwhile, in a deep dish, combine the parsley, garlic, liver, soppressa, a pinch of table salt and nutmeg. Add the eggs and Parmesan and mix. Stir in the breadcrumbs until the stuffing is quite firm.
❦ Fill the duck with the stuffing and sew up the opening with kitchen thread. When the water in the saucepan is boiling, put in the duck and cook for about 2 hours until perfectly tender.
❦ Open the duck down the middle, and remove the stuffing. Slice the stuffing. Divide the duck into serving pieces, arrange them on a serving dish together with the stuffing, and serve with pearà sauce.

PEARÀ SAUCE
This is a sauce from the Veneto region suitable for boiled meats. It also goes very well with duck. Its name comes from one of its essential ingredients — pepper.
2 oz (60 g) bone marrow, from beef, veal or pork bones
2¾ cups (11 oz/345 g) dry breadcrumbs
4 tablespoons (2 oz/60 g) butter
2 cups (16 fl oz/500 ml) meat stock, heated to a boil
salt and freshly ground pepper
Put the marrow on low heat in a small shallow pan and let it melt, then add the breadcrumbs, remove from the heat and beat rapidly with a wooden spoon, incorporating the butter at the same time.
When everything is thoroughly amalgamated, return the pan to the heat and, stirring constantly, add boiling stock, a ladleful at a time. Cook on very low heat for 1½ hours.
About 10 minutes from the end of the cooking time add salt and a generous grinding of pepper. Serve in a hot sauce boat.

GAME

Pheasant, hare, partridge, boar, and, to a lesser degree, thrush, woodcock and snipe make up the typical range of Italian game. In the mountainous areas of the north along the Alps, limited numbers of chamois and roebuck are also caught.

The best season for eating game is from September to the late northern winter, coinciding with the hunting season. Farm-bred pheasants that taste similar to chicken can be found on the market, but to appreciate pheasant you need to taste the wild variety, preferably one caught during November or December when it has fed on wild berries and its muscles have developed. Such pheasants are gutted and left to ripen in a cool place for at least three or four days. Nearly all the recipes in Italian cooking suggest that the bird, whether male or female (the latter has a better flavor), be wrapped in thin slices of pork fat or *pancetta* to enhance the flavor and soften the texture, which is otherwise a bit tough.

The hare is the other major player in the Italian hunting season. It needs at least five or six days to ripen, and is nearly always cooked *in salmis*, that is, it is left to marinate in wine, spices and herbs for a day and then cooked on a bed of fats and flavorings with the marinade and other ingredients added.

Wild ducks are a less frequent catch for Italy's hunters, but they can be found on the market either imported from the Baltic countries or frozen. The difference between a wild duck and one that has been commercially bred lies in the flavor and the consistency of the flesh, which in the wild variety is much firmer and more compact. It is important to select a young bird, and experienced Italian cooks will always test the beak, which should be flexible. The beak of a duck that is too old will have ossified, and its legs will be wrinkled. Old ducks are only used for pâtés and terrines, where the meat is ground (minced). Duck is cooked *in salmis*, braises, and in various stews using sauces that vary from region to region. Wild duck needs to be cooked a little longer than domestically bred duck. The other game birds — thrush, woodcock, snipe and partridge — are rarer than duck because there are no breeding stocks to complement supplies in the wild. They are difficult to catch and are found only in a hunter's kitchen or in specialty restaurants.

The large animals such as boar and chamois are rarely eaten in the home; you will find them almost exclusively in major restaurants.

1. boar; 2. hare; 3. male pheasant; 4. duck; 5. female pheasant; 6. partridge; 7. quails

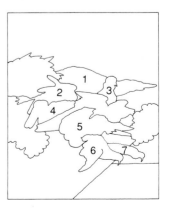

Petti di Quaglia con Ciliegie

PETTI DI QUAGLIA CON CILIEGIE

QUAIL BREAST WITH CHERRIES

Although today quail are commercially bred, they are still looked upon as game. The following dish comes from the country area to the north of Novara, close to Lake Maggiore, where cherries are grown in quantity. In this unusual combination, the slightly tart flavor of the cherries brings out the very delicate flavor of the quail.

4 quail, dressed
4 slices pancetta
4 sage leaves
1 carrot, chopped
1 celery stalk, chopped
1 onion, chopped
2 tablespoons oil
½ cup (4 fl oz/125 ml) dry white wine
½ cup (4 fl oz/125 ml) meat stock
6½ oz (200 g) sweet red cherries, pitted
1 or 2 teaspoons butter
For the puréed potatoes:
2 potatoes, unpeeled
1 bunch flat-leafed parsley, chopped
¾ cup (6 fl oz/185 ml) milk, heated
2 tablespoons freshly grated Parmesan
salt and freshly ground pepper

SERVES 4

❡ Preheat the oven to 350°F (180°C). Wrap each quail in a *pancetta* slice with a leaf of sage. Brown the birds and the carrot, celery and onion in a wide, shallow pan in the oil. Pour on the wine and the stock, little by little, alternately, and cook for 2 minutes more. Add three-quarters of the cherries and transfer to the oven for 5 minutes. The cherries will disintegrate completely during cooking.

❡ Remove the quail from the pan and set aside to keep warm. Place the pan on the stove top over high heat to reduce the cooking juices a little. Put the resulting sauce through a strainer, firmly mashing any remaining cherry pulp. Reduce the sauce further, and bind with 1 teaspoon butter, if necessary.

❡ Meanwhile, prepare the puréed potatoes: Cook potatoes in boiling, salted water until tender. Peel and mash while still warm. Whisk the parsley in with the milk. In a saucepan over moderate heat, combine the potatoes and milk, stirring vigorously. Add the Parmesan, continuing to stir until the mixture is smooth. Season with salt and pepper. Sauté the remaining cherries in a small skillet with 1 teaspoon butter, and use for garnish.

❡ Serve the quail halved and partially boned with the sauce poured over, garnished with cherries and accompanied by parsleyed potato purée.

Tacchinella Ripiena alle Castagne

TACCHINELLA RIPIENA ALLE CASTAGNE

TURKEY WITH CHESTNUT STUFFING

This is the traditional star of the Christmas dinner table and is very rich. In the classical Italian family recipe collection it calls for sausage and pancetta *to be included in the stuffing, but the version given here is the one generally used today.*

For the stuffing:
8 oz (250 g) lean pork, ground (minced)
8 oz (250 g) turkey, ground (minced)
4 oz (125 g) salt pork, cut into small cubes
½ cup (4 fl oz/125 ml) heavy (double) cream
1 egg white
salt and freshly ground pepper
⅓ cup (1½ oz/45 g) shelled walnut pieces, chopped
3 tablespoons (1½ oz/45 g) golden raisins (sultanas),
    plumped in water
1 oz (30 g) black truffles, minced
4 oz (125 g) glacéed chestnuts, minced
For the turkey:
1 small young turkey, about 5 lb (2.5 kg)
salt and freshly ground pepper
1⅓ cups (11 oz/345 g) butter
4 sage leaves

1 sprig rosemary
1 celery stalk, coarsely chopped
1 carrot, coarsely chopped
1 onion, coarsely chopped
1½ cups (12 fl oz/375 ml) dry white wine
SERVES 8

❡ Prepare the stuffing: In a bowl, combine the pork, turkey, salt pork, cream, egg white and salt and pepper; mix well. Stir in the walnuts, raisins, truffles and chestnuts. Mix well and set aside.

❡ Meanwhile, prepare the turkey: Slit the turkey down the back and bone it, taking care not to break the skin. Season the inside with salt and pepper, put in the stuffing and sew up the bird with kitchen thread.

❡ Preheat the oven to 350°F (170°C). In a roasting pan, melt one-third of the butter with the sage and rosemary. Add the celery, carrot and onion and sprinkle the white wine over all. Bake in the oven for 2½ hours. Add a little water if needed.

❡ Remove the turkey from the oven and let it rest in a warm place. Meanwhile, push the contents of the roasting pan through a strainer into a bowl and bind with the remaining butter to make a sauce.

❡ Serve the turkey cut into slices, with 2 slices per portion coated in the sauce and garnished with fresh baby onions and *marrons glacées* and accompanied by *mostarda di Cremona*.

MOSTARDA DI CREMONA

The word mostarda *derives from the French* moutarde, *which in turn comes from* mout ardent, *meaning "burning must," a term used to describe ground mustard seeds dissolved in grape must. Mostarda di Cremona is an ancient condiment, its origins lying in the Middle Ages and the Renaissance tradition of sweet and sour dishes. When the ships of the Venetian Republic brought candied fruit from the Near East, cooks working in the Italian Courts developed dishes that used them to great effect. Mostarda di Cremona is served, in the place of sauce, with bollito misto, or any other form of boiled meat dish and is a traditional accompaniment to roast turkey. It is made by mixing mustard powder in wine and honey, and combining the mixture with cooked fruit, such as apples, peaches, pears, apricots, oranges and lemons. Best prepared in large quantities, it is not suited to being made at home, but it can be found in specialist food shops. The mostarda should be bought in small quantities as it loses its strong, spicy taste as it ages.*

Top: Pernici in Salmì' (page 142); bottom: Piccione in Agrodolce

PICCIONE IN AGRODOLCE

SWEET AND SOUR PIGEON

This is a most interesting dish from Piedmont which enjoyed great popularity last century but then went out of fashion. It was recently re-introduced with resounding success and is offered in restaurants around the Asti area.

4 pigeons
1½ tablespoons honey
1 tablespoon vinegar
1 garlic clove, chopped
3 tablespoons (1½ oz/45 g) butter
salt and freshly ground pepper

SERVES 4

☙ Bone the pigeons but leave the bones in the legs.
☙ Combine the honey, vinegar and garlic and brush the birds with the mixture. Set aside for 24 hours, brushing several times with the mixture.
☙ Melt the butter in a wide, shallow pan. Season the pigeons with salt and pepper. Cook until browned on all sides. Add the honey and vinegar marinade and cook over low heat for 20 minutes, or until the pigeons are tender when tested with a fork.
☙ Serve the meat cut in slices, accompanied by cabbage sautéed in butter.

PERNICI IN SALMI'

SALMIS OF PARTRIDGE

An important dish with great style prepared in the Langhe during late autumn when the hunters bring down partridges and the truffle pickers come to the markets with their most fragrant white truffles. A salmis is a mixture of wine and vegetables in which meat is marinated and cooked, or just cooked, and the ingredients then sieved or puréed to make a sauce for the meat.

1 onion, finely chopped
3 carrots, scraped and finely chopped
1 celery stalk, finely chopped
1×4 in (10 cm) sprig rosemary
7 tablespoons (3½ oz/105 g) butter
4 tablespoons olive oil
4 partridges, dressed, with livers reserved
2 bay leaves
3–4 tablespoons dry Marsala or dry sherry
1 white truffle

SERVES 4

❡ In a bowl, combine the onion, carrot, celery and rosemary leaves and mix well. Fill the partridges with half the mixture. In a large pan melt 5 tablespoons (2½ oz/75 g) of the butter with 3 tablespoons of the olive oil. When hot, add the birds and brown on all sides.
❡ Meanwhile, add the bay leaves to the remaining stuffing mixture. In a skillet, combine the remaining butter and oil over moderate heat. Add the stuffing mixture and cook until browned. Add the partridge livers and brown. Sprinkle with the dry Marsala and cook, covered, for a few minutes. Purée the livers and vegetable mixture in a food mill and add to the pan containing the partridges.
❡ Continue cooking the birds for 30 minutes or so until they are tender when tested with a fork. Serve, coated in their sauce, topped with paper-thin slivers of white truffle. They may be served alone, or as a fabulous main dish with a small serving of risotto. (See photograph page 141.)

SELLA DI CONIGLIO ALL'ARANCIO IN CREMA DI FINOCCHIO

SADDLE OF RABBIT WITH ORANGE SAUCE AND CREAMED FENNEL

Rabbit is a common meat in regions where cattle are bred as working animals, and thus animals such as rabbits are bred for food. The flesh of the rabbit is also favored as it is light and easily digestible. All this explains why Italian cooks have tended to look for new ways of preparing rabbit. The following recipe, from the countryside around Arezzo, succeeds with considerable elegance in combining a variety of typically Italian flavors.

1 saddle of rabbit
½ cup (4 fl oz/125 ml) extra-virgin olive oil
1 cup (8 fl oz/250 ml) any meat stock
salt and freshly ground pepper
1 lb (500 g) fennel, cut into wedges
juice of 1 orange

SERVES 4

❡ Preheat the oven to 350°F (180°C).
❡ Very carefully remove the 2 fillets from the saddle of rabbit and trim them, removing every trace of fat and any surplus ends of meat. Lay them in a baking dish with 2 tablespoons of the olive oil and half the stock. Season with salt and pepper, cover with foil and bake in the oven for about 15 minutes. The meat must remain very soft as it cooks.
❡ Cook the fennel in boiling salted water. Purée until creamy in a food processor; put the purée through a food mill. Taste for salt and pepper.
❡ Combine the orange juice with the remaining olive oil and beat until thoroughly blended.
❡ Slice the rabbit fillets into rounds, and arrange 3 on each individual plate resting on a bed of the creamed fennel. Drizzle a thin stream of the olive oil and orange mixture over the meat and decorate with fronds of fresh fennel.

COSCE DI CONIGLIO AI FUNGHI

LEG OF RABBIT WITH MUSHROOMS

A dish originating from the area around Pisa, this teams rabbit, which features in many Tuscan recipes, with boletus (porcini) mushrooms so plentiful in the wooded hills north of the city. Linking the two flavors is the fragrance of calamint, a herb that grows all over Tuscany. Note the absence of garlic, an almost inseparable companion of rabbit.

4 boned rabbit legs
all-purpose (plain) flour, for dredging
1 cup (8 fl oz/250 ml) olive oil
salt and freshly ground pepper
1 cup (8 fl oz/250 ml) dry white wine
1 cup (8 fl oz/250 ml) meat stock

Left: Sella di Coniglio all'Arancio in Crema di Finocchio; right: Cosce di Coniglio ai Funghi

3 calamint or mint leaves, minced
5 oz (155 g) fresh boletus (porcini) *mushrooms, sliced*

SERVES 4

℘ Dredge the rabbit legs in flour. Brown the rabbit in the hot oil, in a large deep skillet. Season with salt and pepper. Pour in the wine, cover the skillet and let the rabbit cook slowly for 30 minutes, moistening it now and then with a little stock. Add the calamint and mushrooms and continue cooking for 15 minutes. Serve.

CAPRETTO AL VINO BIANCO

KID IN WHITE WINE

In the Langhe area around the town of Alba, the home of this dish, a particular local white wine called Arneis is used. It has a light, delicate taste and kid prepared this way becomes soft and yet crisp and is totally devoid of fat.

1 leg of kid or lamb, all traces of fat removed, cut into
    serving pieces and patted dry
12 garlic cloves
4 sprigs rosemary
6 bay leaves
½ cup (4 fl oz/125 ml) olive oil
½ cup flat-leafed parsley
1 carrot, scraped and minced
½ onion, minced
1 bottle Arneis or other light dry white wine

SERVES 4–6

❡ Put the meat into a wide, shallow pan with 6 cloves of the garlic, 2 rosemary sprigs and 3 bay leaves and cook over gentle heat until the meat has given off all its juices. Remove the kid from the pan and discard the flavorings. Wash the pan.

❡ In the clean pan, combine the oil, parsley, carrot, onion, celery and the remaining garlic, rosemary and bay leaves. Cook until well browned. Add the kid and cook for 40 minutes, until tender, turning the meat from time to time and adding the white wine little by little. Serve hot with a green salad or baked potatoes.

BRACIOLINE DI CAPRETTO IN CROSTA DI PATATE

KID CUTLETS IN POTATO CRUST

An interesting dish from Alto Adige; the potato crust enveloping these kid cutlets combines the tradition of cooking meat in a crumb coating and the classic German–Austrian röstli, *the famous grated potatoes browned in butter. No fats are used other than light oil for the cooking.*

1 medium-size loin of kid or lamb, about 4 lb (2 kg),
    divided into chops or cutlets
salt and freshly ground pepper
2 cups (16 fl oz/500 ml) fruity white wine, such as
    Gewürztraminer
1 sprig thyme
1 garlic clove, crushed

2 potatoes, peeled and chopped
4 tablespoons fresh white breadcrumbs
2 tablespoons whole wheat (wholemeal) flour
2 eggs beaten
palm oil, sunflower or other seed oil, for frying

SERVES 4

❡ Season the chops with salt and pepper. Place in a dish, add the wine, thyme and garlic and marinate for about 6 hours.

❡ When ready to cook the chops, mix the potatoes with the breadcrumbs, season with salt and a little thyme. Remove the chops from the wine marinade and pat dry. Dip them first in the flour, then in the beaten eggs and then in the breadcrumb and potato mixture, pressing down well so it will adhere to the meat.

❡ Fry the chops in 350°F (180°C) oil until golden. Serve hot.

FAGIANO CON TARTUFO IN CREMA DI BROCCOLI

PHEASANT AND TRUFFLES WITH BROCCOLI PURÉE

For this recipe the black truffles typical of Norcia in Umbria, similar to the French ones from Perigord, are used. The dish has been part of Tuscan cooking, and in particular that of Arezzo, since the fourteenth century. It appears to have been imported from France thanks to the contacts of the wealthy Ariati family of Arezzo with some high-ranking prelates who had followed the Pope to Avignon.

1 well-ripened pheasant, cleaned and gutted
5 oz (155 g) black truffle, thinly sliced
10 sage leaves
salt and freshly ground pepper
6 oz (185 g) pancetta, very thinly sliced
2 cups (16 fl oz/500 ml) meat stock
1 lb (500 g) broccoli, cut into florets

SERVES 4

❡ Using a small sharp knife, carefully detach the skin of the pheasant from its flesh. Insert the truffle slices beneath the skin. Put the sage leaves and a pinch each of salt and pepper inside the bird. Wrap the bird in the *pancetta* and secure with kitchen string.

❡ Place the pheasant in a baking dish and bake at 350°F (180°C) for about 50 minutes, basting from time to time with a ladleful of stock.

Top left: Capretto al Vino Bianco; top right: Fagiano con Tartufo in Crema di Broccoli; bottom: Bracioline di Capretto in Crosta di Patate

❡ Cook the broccoli in boiling, salted water until tender but still green, drain. Purée in a food processor and then push through a sieve. Season with salt and pepper. If the purée is too thick, dilute it with a little stock.

❡ When the pheasant is cooked, remove the *pancetta* and cut into small squares. Bone the bird and cut the meat into thin slices. Pour a little of the broccoli purée onto each plate. Arrange 4 or 5 slices of pheasant on top. Scatter with a few squares of the *pancetta*, and serve, accompanied by steamed potatoes.

VARIETY MEATS

Italian "poor" cuisine has developed a substantial number of dishes created by the imaginative cook to use up parts of animals which are often considered unusable. Such is the case with variety meats or offal.

The term "variety meats" extends well beyond just liver and kidney. It is interesting to note that at the time of the splendor of ancient Rome, variety meats were not regarded as second-class or cheaper meat. Apicius, the highest authority on gastronomic matters in Imperial Rome and author of the exhaustive work *De Re Coquinaria* — possibly the oldest known work on culinary matters — considered many variety meat dishes good enough to be included in the chapter he dedicated to "sumptuous meals."

Today some of the most interesting Italian recipes use animal intestines (the innards of lamb and kid in Apulia and Sardinia, and of milk-fed calves in Rome), rolled into a ball and cooked over charcoal, or by other means, together with the heart and lungs, and tripe.

The term tripe refers to the three stomachs of ruminants, known respectively as the rumen, the reticulum and the omasum. Of the three, the last is the most sought-after, having the most delicate taste.

Tripe goes under various names in Italian, including dialect terms such as *busecca* and *foiolo*, and more imaginative descriptions like *centopelli* ("a hundred skins") and *millefoglie* ("a thousand leaves"). It is sold by butchers already half-cooked. When choosing tripe avoid any that is particularly white — an indication that it has been precooked for too long with additives to whiten it. The grayish type that has just been washed and scalded in boiling water is to be preferred.

In the Calabrian region pig or calf giblets are cooked with tomatoes and hot red chilies to prepare *morseddu*, and thinly sliced veal or lamb kidneys are sautéed to obtain *rognoni trifolati*.

In Apulia an interesting recipe is *quagghiariddi*, sheep's tripe stuffed with eggs, liver, salami, cheese and parsley.

But it is Roman cuisine that offers the greatest number of preparations using a range of variety meats. The popular *trippa alla romana* has been offered as Thursday's "dish of the day" by most of the Roman *trattorie* since the time of Apicius. Prepared with tomato sauce, onions, celery and carrots, it is flavored with grated Pecorino cheese and fresh mint leaves, or alternatively with a less sharp blend of Pecorino and Parmesan.

Frittura di cervella (fried brains of calf or lamb) is another favorite with the gourmets of the eternal city, who are traditionally enamored of all fried foods.

Lamb and veal sweetbreads are prepared in many different ways, all recipes sharing the same name — *alla romana* — "in the Roman style."

Although seemingly unappealing to many people, the *testine in forno* (the head of lamb or kid halved and baked in the oven with parsley, garlic, stale country-style bread, lard, olive oil, salt and pepper) is a delicacy.

Probably easier to accept and also very popular is another Roman specialty, *coda alla vaccinara* (braised ox tail). The simplest of the two variants of this dish requires for its preparation: olive oil, garlic, peeled tomatoes, celery and wine. Other characteristic preparations are : liver *alla macellara* ("butcher's style"), broiled (grilled) ox heart, *and pajata* (roasted veal heart). All these dishes form part of an experience an adventurous gourmet would find well worth sampling.

1. tripe; 2. cooked tripe; 3. veal kidney; 4. sausages; 5. spiedino, a dish of skewered kidney and sausages

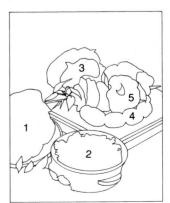

Left: Fegato allo Stefani; right: Lingua di Vitello in Salsa

citron, pine nuts, raisins, chopped herbs, a pinch of cinnamon, 1 teaspoon of sugar and salt and pepper in a large bowl. Bind with the egg yolks and mix thoroughly. Sprinkle the liver slices with salt, pepper, 1 teaspoon of sugar and a pinch of cinnamon. Spread 1 tablespoon of the filling on each, roll it up and wrap individually in pig's caul.

❡ Melt 3 tablespoons (1½ oz/45 g) of butter in a large skillet. Brown the rolls, moistening with the wine, and cook over low heat for 15 to 20 minutes, until just cooked through. Transfer to a lightly buttered baking pan and bake in a preheated 475°F (250°C) oven for 5 to 6 minutes, just long enough to color.

❡ Serve, sprinkled with the de-fatted cooking juices thickened with 2 tablespoons (1 oz/30 g) butter.

FEGATO ALLO STEFANI

CALF'S LIVER STEFANI

Bartolomeo Stefani, cook to the Gonzaga Court in the Duchy of Mantua, has left a lasting impression on the cuisine of Italy. This is one of his recipes, and except for a slight reduction in the quantity of pork fat and the use of calf's rather than pig's liver, it gives us a precise replica of one of the courses always served at banquets in the Renaissance.

pig's caul fat
6 oz (185 g) calf's liver, ground (minced)
2 oz (60 g) pork fat, ground (minced)
2 oz (60 g) boiled bone marrow, diced
⅓ cup (2 oz/60 g) candied citron or lemon peel, grated
3 tablespoons pine nuts
1½ tablespoons golden raisins (sultanas) softened in water and squeezed dry
1 cup finely chopped sage leaves, rosemary, tarragon, shallot and lemon zest (rind)
2 pinches of cinnamon
2 teaspoons sugar
salt and freshly ground pepper
2 egg yolks
4 large slices calf's liver, about 6 oz (185 g) each
5 tablespoons (2½ oz/75 g) butter
1 cup (8 fl oz/250 ml) dry white wine

SERVES 4

❡ Roll up the pig's caul fat and immerse it in warm water for a few minutes. Open and pat dry. Cut into squares large enough to wrap around the liver slices when they are rolled.

❡ Combine the ground liver, pork fat, marrow,

LINGUA DI VITELLO IN SALSA

VEAL TONGUE IN BUTTER SAUCE

A Piedmontese classic, this dish is served hot as a main course or cold as an antipasto. In other areas, and particularly in Lombardy, it is more commonly eaten cold as a first course at lunch. Most specialist salumerie (delicatessens) make it and sell it by the slice.

1 veal tongue, about 2 lb (1 kg)
1 lb (500 g) onions, thinly sliced
1 carrot, chopped
1 celery stalk, chopped
2 cups (16 fl oz/500 ml) dry white wine
1 cup (8 fl oz/250 ml) water
juice of 1 lemon
salt and freshly ground pepper
5 tablespoons (2½ oz/75 g) butter mixed with 1 teaspoon all-purpose (plain) flour

SERVES 4

❡ Cook the tongue in boiling, salted water for 1 hour. Drain, remove all the skin. In a casserole, combine the tongue, onions, carrot, celery, white wine, water, lemon juice, salt and pepper. Cover and cook over moderate heat for about 1 hour, until the tongue is tender when pricked with a fork.

❡ Remove the tongue and keep warm. Strain the cooking liquid and discard the solids. Return the liquid to the heat. Stir in the butter and flour mixture and stir to dissolve. Cook until the sauce is reduced to a creamy consistency.

❡ Slice the tongue and serve immediately, coated with the sauce.

ROGNONE AI PORCINI

VEAL KIDNEYS WITH MUSHROOMS

In this interesting recipe from the Euganei hills, not far from Padua and the famous Abano Terme, the kidneys are cooked in an unusual and elegant combination with boletus (porcini) mushrooms.

2 garlic cloves, finely chopped
2 tablespoons finely chopped flat-leafed parsley
⅔ cup (5 fl oz/155 ml) olive oil
6 oz (185 g) fresh boletus (porcini) mushrooms,
    thinly sliced
2 veal kidneys, well cleaned, trimmed and thinly sliced
1 tablespoon prepared mustard
pinch of salt
2 teaspoons lemon juice
1 tablespoon sweet liqueur such as Alpestre, Strega or
    Galliano
1 sprig basil, minced
2 tablespoons (1 oz/30 g) butter

SERVES 4

❡ Gently fry half the garlic and half the parsley in half the olive oil in a skillet. Add the mushrooms and cook for 10 to 15 minutes.

❡ Coat the sliced kidneys with the mustard. In another skillet, heat the remaining olive oil and add the kidneys. Brown rapidly, and then lower the heat. Add the salt, remaining garlic, the lemon juice and liqueur and cook until the liqueur evaporates. Add the mushroom mixture and stir to heat through. Turn off the heat and finish the dish by adding the remaining parsley and basil and beating in the butter until it melts. Serve with slices of toasted polenta.

FEGATELLI DI MAIALE ALLA TOSCANA

TUSCAN SKEWERED PIG'S LIVER

The original home of this recipe is Garfagnana, a valley of great gastronomic importance which runs from the city of Lucca up towards Liguria, along the inland side of the Apuan Alps. But it has been adopted by the whole of the region and is normally to be found in all the typical Tuscan trattorie. These days for practical reasons the livers are threaded onto ordinary skewers. To be faithful to the original recipe one should use little sticks of wood from the bay tree, carefully stripped of their bark.

6 oz (185 g) pig's caul fat
¼ cup (1 oz/30 g) fennel seeds, pounded
2 bay leaves, chopped
½ cup (2 oz/60 g) dry breadcrumbs
½ cup (2 oz/60 g) freshly grated Parmesan cheese
salt and freshly ground pepper
1¼ lb (600 g) pork liver, cut into 2 in (5 cm) cubes
small slices fried home-style bread (optional)
8 whole bay leaves
3 tablespoons olive oil, for frying (optional)

SERVES 4

❡ Roll up the pig's caul fat and immerse it in warm water for a few minutes. Open and pat dry. Cut into squares large enough to wrap around the cubes of liver.

❡ On a plate, combine the fennel seeds, bay leaves, breadcrumbs, Parmesan and salt and pepper. Mix together well. Roll the cubes of liver in the mixture and lay each one on a square of pig's caul. Close up the caul and secure with a toothpick.

❡ When all the *fegatelli* are ready, select the method for cooking them: if you have a spacious oven or a good-size fireplace, thread them on a long skewer alternately with slices of fried home-style bread and bay leaves, and cook them in the traditional manner. Otherwise, thread them onto shorter skewers, with bay leaves between, and brown them over high heat in good quality olive oil in a skillet, or bake them in the oven. The oven should be preheated to 400°F (200°C) and the meat will need to cook for 5 to 8 minutes.

TRIPPA ALLA FIORENTINA

FLORENTINE STEWED TRIPE

Tripe enjoys great popularity in Florence. All the restaurants serve it, and especially the numerous traditional osterie where everyone sits at one long table and the staff bring flasks of Chianti one after another, replacing them immediately they are emptied. Among the breakfasts served in particular in fruit and vegetable markets there is plain boiled tripe on a slice of bread, dressed with olive oil for flavor. The recipe given here is for classic stewed tripe as it is found in most Italian cities, sometimes with one or two variations in the ingredients.

2 lb (1 kg) partially cooked tripe, washed well and cut
    into thin strips
3 tablespoons (1½ oz/45 g) butter
⅓ cup (3 fl oz/90 ml) olive oil
1 garlic clove, peeled
1 onion, finely chopped
1 carrot, finely chopped

Bottom left: Trippa alla Fiorentina; top: Rognone ai Porcini; bottom right: Fegatelli di Maiale alla Toscana

1 celery stalk, finely chopped
1 sprig basil, finely chopped
1 cup (8 fl oz/250 ml) dry white wine
1 cup (4 oz/125 g) freshly grated Parmesan cheese
13 oz (410 g) ripe tomatoes, peeled, seeded and chopped
salt and freshly ground pepper
2 cups (16 fl oz/500 ml) meat stock, heated

SERVES 4

❡ Put the tripe into a large saucepan of boiling salted water and cook for about 20 minutes. Drain and put into cold water.
❡ In a terracotta casserole, heat 1 teaspoon of butter, the olive oil and garlic. Add the onion, carrot, celery and basil and brown gently. Add the wine and cook until absorbed. Add the drained tripe, 2 tablespoons Parmesan, tomatoes, and salt and pepper to taste. Cook over moderate heat, moistening every now and again with the hot meat stock for 30 to 40 minutes or until the tripe is tender.
❡ Preheat the oven to 300°F (150°C). When the tripe is ready, divide among 4 small ovenproof containers, top with the remaining butter and remaining Parmesan. Bake in the oven for 10 minutes before serving.

VEGETABLES, SALADS, HERBS, OILS AND VINEGARS

VEGETABLES, SALADS, HERBS, OILS AND VINEGARS

GARDEN PRODUCE IS OF GREAT IMPORTANCE IN THE EATING HABITS OF ITALIAN FAMILIES. THE VERY FOUNDATIONS OF THE MAJOR cuisines are built around vegetables.

❡ However, vegetables are rarely served as an accompaniment to other dishes in Italy. Generally they are served as a separate dish.

❡ Vegetable soups, made with some surprisingly successful combinations of ingredients (vegetables with fish, for example, or other seafood), are a basic feature of the cuisine in regions like the Marches, Latium and Tuscany. It is interesting to note that in spite of the emergence of large-scale agricultural companies, the major consumption of vegetables today still revolves around the produce from family kitchen gardens.

❡ This is due in particular to the natural suitability of the Italian soil for growing top-quality vegetables. Perhaps no other country in the world produces artichokes as good as the Italian ones, and the same can be said for radicchio, asparagus, watercress and lettuce. Certain products — such as artichokes and asparagus from Albenga, asparagus from Bassano and Fucecchio, onions from Tropea and beans

Previous pages: Zucchini (courgette) flowers are often served stuffed with ricotta or more exotic ingredients such as lobster mousse. They may also be fried in batter or simply steamed. IMAGE BANK/ANTINOZZI/ACTION PRESS

Opposite: The foundations of Italy's major cuisines are built on vegetables. Despite the immense popularity of vegetables, the major consumption still revolves around the produce of family kitchen gardens. IMAGE BANK/
PEDONE/ACTION PRESS

from Lamon, are considered true gems whose quality cannot be equaled.

❡ In general however, the first vegetable image that comes to mind is of a salad, and this brings us to a curious aspect of Italian eating habits.

❡ A salad is generally understood as a number of ingredients brought together according to the season and the imagination of the person in the kitchen: the Ligurian *condiglione alla Ligure* in this chapter, for example, is a classic salad containing tomatoes, anchovies, hard-cooked eggs, and so on. On the other hand the French *salade niçoise*, renowned along the Cote d'Azur, is the same dish with boiled potatoes and one or two other ingredients added.

❡ Food customs along the coast from Genoa to Marseilles are fundamentally similar. Thus the term salad indicates a union of various ingredients, vegetable and non-vegetable, raw and cooked. But in everyday use the word "salad" is used to mean simply a collection of green leaves. Any waiter in an Italian restaurant when asked simply for *un'insalata* will bring an exclusively vegetable mixture of one or more greens chosen from among the six classic types of chicory grown in Italy: *catalogna* (asparagus chicory), Belgian endive (witloof), *spadona* (sword-leaved chicory), curly endive (chicory), escarole (Batavian endive) and *cicorietto*, to which should be added the three more common radicchios (Treviso, Castlefranco and Verona) plus watercress, two types of lettuce (*lattuga* and *lattughino*) and *soncino* or hare's lettuce.

❡ Concerning dressing, there is no doubt: only olive oil and salt, with a little vinegar or lemon juice, plus freshly ground pepper as an optional extra. No other kind of dressing has a rightful place on the Italian table.

Left: Involtini di Peperoni; right: Peperonata

INVOLTINI DI PEPERONI

STUFFED BELL PEPPERS

This recipe is an old speciality from Daunia, a historic area of Apulia inland from Cape Gargano with a wealth of premium-quality agricultural products. Involtini di peperoni is still made regularly today in both homes and restaurants, served either as a vegetarian course on its own, or sometimes even in smaller quantities as an appetizing antipasto.

4 yellow bell peppers (capsicums)

1 tablespoon pine nuts

1 tablespoon golden raisins (sultanas), soaked in hot water for 15 minutes and squeezed dry

1 tablespoon capers, drained

4 anchovy fillets, finely chopped

2 or 3 tablespoons olive oil

1 slice fresh bread without crust

1 bunch flat-leafed parsley, chopped

SERVES 4

¶ Roast the bell peppers directly over a flame, or under a hot broiler (grill) until charred. Remove the skins and cut the bell peppers lengthwise in half, removing the inner ribs and seeds.

¶ In a deep plate, mix the pine nuts, golden raisins, capers, and anchovies. Add the olive oil, and mix well. Work in the bread and the parsley. The mixture should be fairly firm.

¶ Preheat the oven to 350°F (180°C).

¶ Fill the peppers with the mixture. Arrange in an oiled baking dish. Bake in the oven for about 20 minutes.

¶ Serve hot or cold.

PEPERONATA

STEWED BELL PEPPERS

A typical summer vegetable dish that lends itself to a variety of interpretations, this one is from Sicily but it is found throughout Italy.

The version given here emphasizes the original of the peperonata by using the typically Sicilian green olives in brine. Elsewhere, and particularly in the north, in Lombardy and Piedmont, olives are not included. To make the dish attractive as well as tasty, the bell peppers (capsicums) used should be the rather large yellow and red ones of the kind found in abundance on the Po River plains at Voghera, near Pavia, and in Carmagnola near Turin. A peperonata like this one can be blended in a food processor to become a splendid sauce for roast meats, or added to a risotto alla parmigiana (see page 72) with a little oregano to produce a wonderfully tasty risotto.

1 cup (8 fl oz/250 ml) olive oil
3 large onions, thinly sliced
15 oz (410 g) tomatoes, seeded and chopped
4 large yellow and red bell peppers (capsicums), seeded and coarsely chopped
salt
2 oz (60 g) pitted green olives in brine, coarsely chopped

SERVES 4

¶ Put the oil into a wide, shallow pan, preferably of terracotta, heat it and add the onions. Fry gently over low heat without burning until nicely golden. Add the tomatoes and bell peppers, mix, and season with salt. Cover the pan and cook over low heat for 15 minutes. Stir in the olives and cook for 20 minutes until the peppers are soft but not mushy. Serve hot or cold.

FAGIOLI CON LE COTICHE

BEANS AND PORK RIND

This recipe comes from the country areas of Lombardy, where families have always raised one or two pigs for domestic consumption all the year round. The cotiche are strips cut from the tough pork rind, which had been specially treated, in line with an old saying, del maiale non si butta via niente — no part of the pig is wasted.

This dish also uses the borlotti (red) beans that have always been grown in abundance in the vegetable gardens on the plains around Milan. Many different varieties of beans have been developed. However, borlotti is the most popular. Having a creamy texture they are most suited for cooking in stews or soups.

Traditionally a single-dish meal, today fagioli con le cotiche is served in moderate quantities with roast meats. It still appears on the menus of trattorie, however, as a main course.

1 cup (6 oz/185 g) dried borlotti (red) beans
1 lb (500 g) fresh pork rind
2 onions, coarsely chopped
2 celery stalks
2 carrots
2 garlic cloves, peeled
salt
2 tablespoons ground (minced) pork fat
1 tablespoon (½ oz/15 g) butter
2 tablespoons olive oil
2 tablespoons homemade tomato sauce
freshly ground pepper

SERVES 4

¶ Cook the beans in boiling water until soft.

¶ Meanwhile, wash the pork rind well. Cut into thin strips.

¶ In a saucepan, combine the pork rind, 1 onion, coarsely chopped, 1 celery stalk, 1 carrot, chopped, and 1 garlic clove. Add cold water to cover and a pinch of salt. Cover and cook over moderate heat until the pork rind is soft. Drain, reserving the cooking liquid.

¶ Finely chop the remaining onion, celery and carrot. Heat the ground pork fat, butter and olive oil in a large stewpan. Add the vegetables and the remaining garlic clove. Cook until the vegetables are nicely browned, remove the garlic clove. Add the drained beans and rind.

¶ Heat a couple of ladlefuls of the reserved cooking liquid. Stir in the tomato sauce and the stock/tomato sauce mixture. Reduce the heat to very low and simmer for about 30 minutes. Taste for pepper, and serve. (See photograph page 156.)

FAGIOLI ALL'UCCELLETTO

TUSCAN BEANS AND TOMATOES

This typically Tuscan peasant dish is also widely used as a vegetable accompaniment to meat dishes in family homes. It is a classic example of a rich and tasty sauce into which the Tuscans dip their famous unsalted bread.

2 lb (1 kg) small fresh white beans (such as toscanelli
   or cannellini), shelled, or 2¼ cups (11 oz/345 g)
   dried white beans
⅓ cup (3 fl oz/90 ml) olive oil
5 or 6 fresh sage leaves
2 garlic cloves, peeled and gently bruised

1 lb (500 g) ripe tomatoes, peeled, seeded and chopped
Salt and freshly ground pepper

SERVES 4

¶ If using dried beans, soak them in cold water for 12 hours; drain. Place the beans in cold water to cover and bring to a boil. Drain when they are soft. Pour the oil into a wide, shallow terracotta pan or skillet. Add the sage leaves and garlic and fry till the garlic browns. Add the beans, mix and cook for 4 or 5 minutes to blend the flavors. Add the tomatoes, salt and a grind of pepper; cover the pan and cook over moderate heat for about 20 minutes. Serve as an accompaniment to broiled (grilled) meat or sausages.

Left: Fagioli con le Cotiche (page 155); right: Fagioli all'Uccelletto

TOMATOES

The tomato practically holds pride of place in Italian cuisine. The chief merit of the tomato and the prime reason for its success is its infinite adaptability. It can change not only the taste of many foods but also their appearance, simply by enlivening it with color, while the characteristics of the ingredients it accompanies, be they fish, meat, eggs or even such strong flavors as onion and garlic, are maintained. The Neapolitan pizza was merely a focaccia sprinkled with cheese before the tomato appeared on the scene.

Another valuable characteristic of the tomato is its ability to be preserved. Simply pushed through a sieve and collected in tins or bottles tomatoes retain their taste and color almost unchanged for lengthy periods, and can thus be used out of season.

As an antipasto fresh tomatoes are served with alternating slices of fresh mozzarella cheese, or stuffed with beans or rice. Another popular way of serving tomatoes is to halve them and stuff them with parsley, garlic, and oregano, sprinkle them with breadcrumbs and bake them in the oven. Perhaps pride of place, though, should be given to the juicy Italian tomato *au naturel*, lightly dressed with olive oil and decorated with fresh basil.

The most common table tomatoes are the *cuore di bue* (ox heart), so called because of their characteristic heart shape, and the *costoluto genovese* which is round, with ridges marking it into segments.

The round tomato, ridged or unridged, is the one usually used for stuffing. Tomato paste is used extensively in Italian cuisine. Before commercial production started, tomato concentrate was made at home, as it still is today in southern Italy and Sicily. It can only be made in summer when tomatoes and sun are at their best. The tomatoes are cut in half, sprinkled with rock salt and spread in large baskets to soften in the sun. After a few days they are puréed and placed in the sun again for the liquid to evaporate. Oil is added to the purée, which is then stored in sealed jars.

The most popular variety suitable for preserving is the popular San Marzano plum or egg tomato, also known as *perino* because it is shaped like a small pear. This is the type used by most major processors of *pelati* (peeled tomatoes), as it ripens evenly all over, peels easily, and the removed stem leaves no hole. Other less important varieties are Ventura, Roma, Lampadina and Vesuvio.

A special type of tomato also found in Italian markets is the one preserved in clusters; these are hung in kitchens and barns in their natural state. Botanists have bred different varieties, such as the Sicilian "Principe Borghese," commonly known as cluster tomatoes, ideal for making quick, simple pasta sauces or enriching a minestrone or a stewing sauce for fish. Often sold still on the stem, *pomodori da grappolo* are found in Southern Italy — Puglia and Sicily — and are very good for making sauces.

Left: pomodori di grappolo; top center: cuore di bue; top right: costoluto genovese; bottom right: San Marzano

POMODORI RIPIENI

STUFFED TOMATOES

This method of serving tomatoes is common to all of central and southern Italy and especially popular in Rome, around Naples, and in Sicily. This dish began life as a main course and subsequently became both an accompaniment to more important dishes, and an antipasto.

4 large, ripe tomatoes
salt and freshly ground pepper
1 cup (8 fl oz/250 ml) olive oil
1/3 cup (2 oz/60 g) raw rice
1 sprig flat-leafed parsley, minced
basil leaves, minced
1 garlic clove, peeled and bruised
1 teaspoon oregano
2 or 3 potatoes, sliced

SERVES 4

¶ Wash the tomatoes and slice horizontally across the top to make a cap that will serve as a lid. Scoop out the centers and reserve the pulp. Sprinkle a pinch each of salt and pepper and 1 teaspoon of the oil on the bottom of each tomato case.

¶ In a bowl, combine the rice, tomato pulp, parsley, basil, garlic, oregano and 4 tablespoons of the oil. Mix well and divide the mixture among the 4 tomato cases. Cover with the tomato caps and arrange in an oiled baking dish on a bed of potato slices. Sprinkle with the remaining oil. Bake in a preheated 350°F (180°C) oven for 45 minutes, until tender. Serve hot or cold.

CAPONATA ALLA SICILIANA

SICILIAN VEGETABLE STEW

In all Sicilian restaurants patrons are welcomed with large, brightly colored ceramic dishes piled high with caponata.

2 lb (1 kg) medium-size eggplants (aubergines)
salt
1 lb (500 g) onions, thinly sliced
1/3 cup (3 fl oz/90 ml) olive oil
1 lb (500 g) ripe tomatoes, seeded and cut into strips
2 tablespoons capers, drained
2 or 3 celery stalks, chopped
6 oz (185 g) olives in brine, pitted

1/3 cup (3 fl oz/90 ml) vinegar of any kind
1 teaspoon sugar

SERVES 4

¶ Wash the eggplants, cut them into small pieces, put them into a large strainer and sprinkle with salt. Set aside to drain for at least 1 hour.

❡ Meanwhile, combine the onions with one-third of the olive oil in a wide, shallow pan. Cook until golden. Add the tomatoes, capers, celery and olives. Mix well and cook for 15 minutes, set aside.

❡ Rinse the eggplant and dry completely. Heat the remaining oil in a skillet over high heat. When the oil reaches its maximum temperature, add the eggplant pieces and fry until well browned. Drain.

❡ Stir the eggplant into the tomato mixture. Sprinkle on the vinegar and sugar and return to low heat. Cook until the vinegar completely evaporates. Serve cold.

Front: Pomodori Ripieni; back: Caponata alla Siciliana

RADICCHIO

Of all the products in the Italian kitchen garden, radicchio is undoubtedly the most characteristic. Unlike the vegetables that begin appearing in late spring, radicchio is a winter vegetable, eaten from the end of November through to March. Sowing takes place in late June and early July. The seedlings are picked at the beginning of November with roots intact, put into special containers of sand in rooms kept at 65°F (18°C) and watered regularly. During this period, which lasts only a few days, they acquire (depending on the variety) their typical reddish variegated appearance. They are then prepared for market; damaged leaves are trimmed off and the longish, bitter-tasting roots are trimmed to form a conical stump. The radicchio is then ready for the road.

From a botanical viewpoint radicchio is merely a form of chicory distinguished by the techniques used to cultivate it. There are several varieties but the most typical is the one grown in Venice's hinterland, in the country areas around Treviso, Castelfranco Veneto and Chioggia, with little differentiation occurring between these areas. The Trevisan variety known as "the red chicory of Treviso," with elongated red leaves and white ribs, is the best known of all. It is used in risottos and soups, but most often is served simply broiled (grilled) as an accompaniment to baked fish or meat dishes. The Castelfranco Veneto radicchio, on the other hand, which has densely packed leaves and is shaped like a rose, is used in salads as well. No matter how the radicchio is prepared, only the leaves should be served. The roots are very bitter and should be discarded.

In the cuisine of the Veneto radicchio holds a place of honor and features in numerous recipes. For serving raw as a salad its usual dressing is one part wine vinegar to three parts olive oil (6 tablespoons of oil to 2 of vinegar), seasoned with salt and pepper. In its many cooked versions, radicchio is first blanched in water and then prepared according to the recipe. It may be baked in butter for five minutes and coated with cheese sauce, or cooked in a Bolognese risotto.

Back: Trevisan radicchio; front: Castelfranco Veneto radicchio

INSALATA DI RADICCHIO ALLA MELAGRANA

RADICCHIO SALAD WITH POMEGRANATES

In Italy the use of pomegranates in cooking goes back to the time of the Renaissance when various dishes gracing the tables of patrician families — particularly at the Gonzaga court in Mantua and the Este court in Ferrara — featured pomegranate seeds added for reasons of taste or esthetics. Neglected then for a couple of hundred years, the pomegranate has recently resurfaced in recipes by the most modern and innovative cooks.

4 radicchio heads, leaves separated
2 pomegranates
⅓ cup (3 fl oz/90 ml) extra-virgin olive oil
salt
1 teaspoon green peppercorns in brine, rinsed

SERVES 4

❦ Trim the radicchio, discard the outer leaves, pull off the inner leaves and wash and dry thoroughly. Combine in a large salad bowl with the seeds and juice of the pomegranates. Sprinkle with the oil, a little salt, and the green peppercorns. Toss and serve.

Top: Insalata di Radicchio alla Melagrana; bottom: Insalata di Cavolfiore (page 162)

INSALATA DI CAVOLFIORE

CAULIFLOWER SALAD

This cauliflower salad, typically served in Naples during the Christmas period, is also known as "reinforcing salad" because it is seen as one more rich addition to the Christmas dinner. Its origins go back to the seventeenth century.

1 cauliflower, trimmed
8 or 10 anchovy fillets in olive oil
2 oz (60 g) black Gaeta olives, pitted
2 oz (60 g) green olives, pitted
1 tablespoon chopped flat-leafed parsley
1 garlic clove, minced
3 tablespoons capers, drained
salt
1 cup (8 fl oz/250 ml) olive oil
2 tablespoons red or white wine vinegar

SERVES 4

¶ Cut the cauliflower into florets and cook until al dente in boiling salted water. Drain and set aside to cool.

¶ In a small bowl, combine the anchovy fillets, black and green olives, parsley, garlic, capers and a pinch of salt. Mix well. Add the olive oil and vinegar and whisk until combined. Place the cauliflower in a salad bowl and dress with the sauce. (See photograph page 161.)

INSALATA DI PORCINI CON BASILICO E PARMIGIANO

MUSHROOM SALAD WITH BASIL AND PARMESAN

This dish is common to many areas along the hilly Apennine strip running from Liguria to central Italy. Some people marinate the mushrooms in oil and vinegar, while others prefer to use oil alone, and still others merely sprinkle the sliced mushrooms with oil. Serve this dish either as an antipasto or as an elegant accompaniment for white meat.

5 tablespoons olive oil
1 tablespoon wine vinegar
salt and freshly ground pepper
10 basil leaves
10 oz (315 g) porcini (boletus) mushrooms, thinly sliced
2 oz (60 g) fresh Parmesan cheese (aged under 18 months), sliced wafer thin

SERVES 4

watercress leaves, for garnish

¶ Whisk together the oil, vinegar, salt and pepper and 6 basil leaves. Add the mushroom slices and marinate for 30 minutes.

¶ To serve, arrange the mushroom slices in the center of each dinner plate in a fan or bouquet shape. Tuck small slices of Parmesan between the mushroom slices. Lay a basil leaf on top and garnish with a few leaves of watercress. Sprinkle lightly with the marinade.

Left: Insalata di Porcini con Basilico e Parmigiano; right: Radicchio alla Trevigiana

RADICCHIO ALLA TREVIGIANA

GRILLED RADICCHIO, TREVISO STYLE

As the name indicates, this recipe comes from Treviso, where the extraordinary and flavorful radicchio with the purplish-red leaves is grown.

8 radicchio heads
⅓ cup (3 fl oz/90 ml) olive oil
freshly ground salt and pepper
SERVES 4

❡ Trim the radicchio, discarding damaged or wilted leaves. Halve or quarter them lengthwise, and wash them carefully under the tap. Drain them thoroughly — for perfect cooking they must be dry, and you may find a salad spinner useful for this. Sprinkle the radicchio with olive oil, salt and pepper.
❡ Grill the radicchio over charcoal for 4 to 5 minutes or cook them in a cast-iron pan over moderate heat for 4 to 5 minutes. If a cast-iron pan is used, cook uncovered for a crisp result, or covered if you prefer them soft.

Sformato di Porri in Salsa di Zucchini

SFORMATO DI PORRI IN SALSA DI ZUCCHINI

LEEK MOLD WITH ZUCCHINI SAUCE

An example of modern Florentine cuisine which brings together two thick soups from the ancient Tuscan peasant tradition, and presents them in a much lighter form. By using leeks and ricotta, a dish of considerable refinement is achieved. The ricotta provides an agreeable substitute for the usual butter, and the purest oil acts as a thickener for the dressing.

3 lb (1.5 kg) leeks
10 oz (315 g) ricotta
2 eggs
⅔ cup (3 oz/90 g) freshly grated Parmesan cheese
pinch of nutmeg
1 cup (8 fl oz/250 ml) extra-virgin olive oil
salt
For the sauce:
1 onion, finely chopped
1 carrot, finely chopped
1 celery stalk, finely chopped
3 tablespoons extra-virgin olive oil
6 zucchini (courgettes), thinly sliced
1 tomato, peeled
1 garlic clove, chopped
pinch of oregano

pinch of marjoram
pinch of ground chili pepper
salt
½ cup (4 fl oz/125 ml) meat stock

SERVES 6

❡ Trim the leeks, wash well, cut in strips and cook in boiling water with a little salt for about 20 minutes.
❡ Meanwhile, in a mixing bowl, combine the ricotta, eggs, Parmesan and nutmeg.
❡ When the leeks are cooked, drain well. Add to the ricotta mixture and mix well. Transfer to a food processor and process, adding the olive oil in a thin stream, until the mixture is smooth.
❡ Scrape the purée into a buttered baking dish, adding salt if necessary. Bake at 325°F (150°C) for 20 minutes. Cover the dish with aluminum foil and continue baking for a further 20 minutes, or until a toothpick inserted into the center comes out dry.
❡ Prepare the sauce: Gently fry the onion, carrot and celery in the oil until golden. Add the zucchini, tomato, garlic, oregano, marjoram and chili pepper. Season with salt, moisten with the stock and cook for 15 minutes. Purée the mixture in a food processor.
❡ Invert the leek mold on a serving plate, cover with the sauce and serve at once.

Top: Apulian mammola artichoke; bottom: romanesco artichoke

ARTICHOKES

Known to the Greek and Latin worlds at least as far back as the sixth century BC, the artichoke has had an unusual place in the history of gastronomy. Appreciated in ancient times, it was then forgotten for centuries and reappeared only towards the end of the Middle Ages, apparently due to the enterprise of some merchant who took the risk of importing it from Ethiopia. Thus the *kinara* (Greek) or *cynara* (Latin) spread first of all within Italy, to Tuscany and the Veneto, and subsequently throughout Europe and the world under the name derived from the Arab *al kharshuf,* which became *carciofo* in Italian, *Artischocke* in German, artichoke in English, and so on. Today Italy is the major world producer of this unusual vegetable.

The artichoke is not a fruit, but a bud. If not picked, it blooms as a pale violet-colored flower tinged with lilac. This is how it appears, alternating with sprigs of rue (the herb of grace) on the insignia of the Order of the Thistle, which in England is second only to the Order of the Garter. The artichoke was created from a series of cross breedings from the original wild cardoon.

In Italy artichokes are grown mainly in Liguria, Sardinia, the country areas around Rome, and Apulia. There are two major families, one with spikes and one without. Of the former, the finest are the Albenga artichokes and, more generally, the ones grown throughout the Ligurian Riviera, followed by those from Sardinia. Both have tapered leaves pointing up towards the central peak. Another spiky variety, grown in Palermo, is rounder in shape. Among those without spikes, the most sought-after are definitely the *romanesco,* the Roman variety, and the Apulian *mammola,* which are both cooked in a variety of ways. In Rome, *carciofi alla romana,* stuffed artichokes, and *carciofi alla giudia,* flattened out and fried in olive oil, are famous.

Only the central tender portion of the artichoke is eaten, after the tough upper part of the leaves has been cut off; the top of the stalk is also eaten, and when peeled it has the same flavor as the heart. Once the artichoke has been cut it is plunged into water acidulated with lemon juice to prevent it from darkening.

Artichokes have a long season which varies according to the area where they are grown, the climate, and the techniques of cultivation that are used. In fact fresh artichokes can be found from November right through to the end of spring.

The most highly prized artichokes are those grown in Liguria, particularly sought-after by gourmets in the period between late November and mid-January, when they are at their peak.

These varieties are most popular served raw, very thinly sliced and dressed simply with olive oil, salt and pepper and lemon juice. However, there are those who prefer them *in pinzimonio* which means dipping the leaves one by one into the oil and other condiments presented in a small cup or bowl, and then scraping off, one bit at a time, the lower, more fleshly and flavorsome portions of each leaf.

Its appearance notwithstanding, the artichoke is a delicate vegetable. It will keep for no more than a few days in its raw state, and should be stood on its stalk in a vase filled with water, exactly like a flower.

Left: Carciofi alla Giudia; right: Carciofi alla Romana

CARCIOFI ALLA GIUDIA

JEWISH ARTICHOKES

Served above all in Rome, this dish used to be found only in the restaurants of the so-called Jewish ghetto area around Portico d'Ottavia, but now one can eat it in almost any restaurant.

8 Roman artichokes (large green globe variety)
juice of 1 lemon

salt and freshly ground pepper
abundant olive oil

SERVES *4*

❡ It is essential to choose very young artichokes of the type the Romans call *cimarolo* for this dish. Remove the tough outer leaves and trim the stems to about 1½ in (4 cm) long. Using a small, sharp knife, shape the artichokes one at a time by turning them with one hand as you cut to remove

artichokes when they are laid on the bottom. When the oil is hot (but at less than its maximum temperature), add the artichokes and cook, turning often, to cook evenly for 10 minutes. Turn the artichokes over and stand them, head down, in the pan. Turn up the heat to its highest and cook for 10 minutes. Remove the artichokes from the oil and drain on paper towels before serving.

CARCIOFI ALLA ROMANA

ROMAN ARTICHOKES

The Romans are very proud of this marvelous dish, which is very common both at homes and in restaurants. There are as many variations as there are people preparing it. For example, it is normally cooked in the oven, but there are some who prefer to cook it in a pan on the stovetop. Among other ingredients that may be included are anchovies and white wine. In short, this is a dish that lends itself to individual variations.

1 garlic clove
1 bunch flat-leafed parsley
½ cup mint leaves
olive oil
8 tender Roman artichokes (large globe variety)
salt

SERVES 4

❡ Finely chop the garlic, parsley and mint together. Put this mixture in a cup, stir in 3 tablespoons of olive oil and mix well. Preheat the oven to 325°F (160°C).
❡ Remove the tough outer leaves of the artichokes, trim the stalks to 1½ in (4 cm) long and trim off the external fibers. Shape the artichokes with a small knife to eliminate the remaining tough bits. Open each one by parting the leaves; insert a teaspoon at the center and take out the choke. Fill each artichoke with the prepared mixture, press closed with your hands and place upside-down in a deep terracotta casserole dish. (The casserole must be just big enough to contain the artichokes pressed closely against one another.) Sprinkle with salt and pour on sufficient liquid (two parts olive oil to one part water) to cover completely. Put a lid on the casserole.
❡ Bake in the oven for 1 hour. At the end of this time, drain the artichokes. Serve hot, as a vegetable accompaniment or appetizer, or allow to cool and serve as an antipasto.

the toughest parts of the remaining leaves. Discard the fibrous bits and external strings from the stems. As each artichoke is prepared, plunge it into a basin of water and lemon juice to prevent darkening.
❡ As soon as all the artichokes are prepared, remove from the water and dry well. Bang each artichoke against the table so it opens out like a sunburst. Dust the insides with salt and pepper.
❡ Put a wide, high-sided pan on to heat with sufficient olive oil to reach halfway up the

Various types of asparagus: thin wild asparagus; large, thick white-tipped asparagus from Tuscany and Liguria

Asparagus

The name is Greek in origin — *asparagos* — but derived from an Iranian term. Asparagus came from Iran or Iraq some time in the distant past, spreading first throughout the Mediterranean basin and later all over the world. Its existence has been known since the time of the Pharaohs; a fresco in an Egyptian tomb depicts pale pastel-green asparagus along with other foods being offered to the gods. In Cato the Elder's *De Agricoltura* an entire chapter is devoted to techniques of asparagus growing that are almost identical to those used today, and Pliny points in particular to the quality of the asparagus grown in Ravenna.

Asparagus' appearance on the table was not due to its gastronomic qualities, as normally happens, but rather to its medicinal properties. Always considered a beneficial food, it was classified by the *Scuola Salernitana* as an excellent diuretic.

Asparagus was also believed to be of value in stimulating the libido and restoring a waning sexual potency. True or false these theories may be, but it is a fact that this liliaceous plant has the seal of approval from modern science because of the wealth of minerals it contains.

In Italy the systematic cultivation of asparagus began in the sixteenth century.

Some of the best varieties are those from Albenga (in Liguria), from the area of Bassano del Grappa (in the Veneto) and from a few small towns in the plains by the River Po (between Milan, Pavia and Novara, in Lombardy). But the Tuscan town of Pescia is recognized to be "the asparagus capital of Italy" because the esculent plants growing there are taller, thicker — and according to the locals also tastier — than anywhere else.

Asparagus is generally served boiled or steamed, but care must be taken because the tips, the choicest part of the vegetable, are extremely delicate. Traditionally asparagus spears are tied together in bunches and stood upright in salted boiling water — reaching only halfway up their stalks — for 10 to 15 minutes, depending on the thickness. Possibly the best way to dress the asparagus is to lay the drained spears side by side on the plate, sprinkle them with freshly grated Parmesan cheese and finally top them with butter and with the eggs fried in the same. This simple but delicious preparation is particularly dear to the gourmets of the Lombardy region who traditionally celebrate it on outings aptly called *asparagiate*.

Left: Asparagi alla Milanese; right: Fagiolini alla Genovese (page 170)

ASPARAGI ALLA MILANESE

MILANESE ASPARAGUS

Asparagus is served throughout the Lombardy region as a light meal for spring and summer when it is in full season. The rather large, soft, white variety with purplish tips is the kind used in this recipe.

3 lb (1.5 kg) asparagus
salt
8 tablespoons (4 oz/125 g) butter
4 eggs
¾ cup (3 oz/90 g) freshly grated Parmesan cheese
SERVES 4

❡ Clean the asparagus thoroughly and trim the root ends to make them all the same length. Tie in a bundle with kitchen string. Stand the asparagus upright in a saucepan with water reaching halfway up the stems; this way the tips are cooked by steaming. Add a little salt to the water,

bring to a boil and cook for about 20 minutes.

❡ Melt 1 tablespoon (½ oz/15 g) of the butter in a skillet and add an egg. Cook it and set aside. Repeat the process for the remaining 3 eggs. Divide the asparagus among 4 serving plates, cover them generously with grated Parmesan and top each serving with an egg. Melt the remaining butter until boiling fast and pour over the asparagus.

SALSA PER ASPARAGI
Sauce for asparagus

Plain boiled asparagus can be served with this sauce from the Veneto region. Hard-cook 4 eggs and remove the shells; break them up with a fork and continue mashing until they become a fine, homogeneous mixture. Still working with the fork, add some extra-virgin olive oil, 1 teaspoon of vinegar and some salt and freshly ground pepper, a little at a time. Serve in a sauceboat with the asparagus, which should be very hot.

FAGIOLINI ALLA GENOVESE

GENOESE-STYLE GREEN BEANS WITH ANCHOVIES

The green beans used in this dish should be slender and stringless. They appear in many recipes in Liguria, including several for savory tarts, but their principal use is as a light and tasty accompaniment for meat dishes. In the version given here, the rather sweet taste of this vegetable and the contrasting distinct, sharp flavor of the anchovies are blended with butter.

1¼ lb (625 g) green beans, trimmed
1 sprig parsley
½ garlic clove
3 anchovy fillets
2 tablespoons olive oil
3 tablespoons (1½ oz/45 g) butter
salt and freshly ground pepper

SERVES 4

❡ Place the beans in a saucepan full of boiling salted water and drain when they are cooked al dente, after about 20 minutes. Finely chop the parsley with the garlic and anchovies. Combine this mixture in a wide, shallow skillet with the oil and butter. Fry gently for a few minutes, stirring with a wooden spoon until the anchovies disintegrate completely. Add the beans, mix well and season with salt and pepper. Cook for a further 2 or 3 minutes. Serve hot. (See photograph page 169.)

PUREA DI FAVE CON CICORIA SELVATICA

FAVA BEAN PURÉE WITH WILD CHICORY

This dish is common to all Sicily and Apulia, and the recipe is one of the oldest in Mediterranean gastronomy. Already in existence in Egypt at the time of the Pharaohs, it later was known in Roman plebeian cuisine as puls fabata, *and has come down to us with only minimal changes. Its Sicilian title is* maccu, *which comes from* ammaccare, *a dialect word meaning to crush. Some recipes advise cooking the onion with the beans as described here, others stay closer to the ancient formula and suggest adding the onion raw at the end of cooking. This purée is like a soup, but any that is left over will harden like polenta, and can be sliced and fried, or sautéed with vegetables. In Apulia it also is served to accompany a seafood soup.*

1 cup (6 oz/185 g) dried fava (broad) beans
2 potatoes, sliced

1 celery stalk
1 small onion, sliced
salt
9 oz (280 g) wild chicory
½ cup (4 fl oz/125 ml) olive oil
1 cup (8 fl oz/250 ml) extra-virgin olive oil

SERVES 4

❡ Soak the beans for about 2 hours. Drain and put in a saucepan, ideally terracotta. Lay the potato slices on top. Place the celery and onion slices over the potatoes. Add salt to taste and water to cover. Simmer over moderate heat for 1 hour, skimming from time to time.
❡ Meanwhile, clean the wild chicory and put it into a saucepan with just the water that remains from washing it. Cook over moderate heat, with salt to taste, for 20 to 25 minutes. Sauté in a skillet with the olive oil for 5 minutes to bring out the flavor.
❡ Check the progress of the beans as they cook, stirring them often so that the mixture becomes a purée. When they have absorbed all the water, add the extra-virgin olive oil, mix well and serve the beans and chicory together in small bowls.

SFORMATO DI CAVOLO

CABBAGE MOLD IN CHEESE SAUCE

This is a modern version of an old specialty from Val d'Aosta. The ancient soupe valpellinentze *is here transformed into an elegant example of a new cuisine. The original recipe has no cream, only a rich meat stock in which the cabbage and the rest of the ingredients are cooked. The boiling soup is then poured into bowls containing slices of toast, and topped with slices of Fontina cheese.*

½ green cabbage, trimmed and shredded
1 onion, chopped
2 tablespoons olive oil
2 bay leaves
salt and freshly ground pepper
½ cup (4 fl oz/125 ml) vegetable or veal stock
3 tablespoons basil leaves
4 eggs
¾ cup (6 fl oz/185 ml) heavy (double) cream
For the fondue:
5 oz (155 g) Fontina cheese, diced
2 tablespoons (1 oz/30 g) butter
⅓ cup (3 fl oz/90 ml) milk
1 egg yolk

SERVES 4

Left: Purea di Fave con Cicoria Selvatica; right: Sformato di Cavolo

❦ Blanch the cabbage several times, plunging it into cold water after each boiling.

❦ In a stewpan, brown the chopped onion with the olive oil and bay leaves. Add the cabbage and salt and pepper to taste. Add the stock, cover and cook for 20 minutes. Set aside to cool. In a food processor, purée the cabbage and vegetables with the basil. Push the purée through a sieve into a bowl. Using a whisk, beat in the eggs and cream.

❦ Preheat the oven to 325°F (160°C). Butter 4

small molds or ramekins. Fill the molds with the cabbage mixture. Set the molds in a roasting pan and add hot water to reach halfway up the sides of the molds. Bake in the oven for 30 minutes.

❦ Meanwhile, make the sauce: Melt the Fontina with the butter and milk in a pan set over simmering water. When the mixture is perfectly smooth, whisk in the egg yolk. Pour a pool of the sauce onto each plate and unmold the cabbage in the center.

Top: Parmigiana di Melanzane; bottom:
Melanzane Fritte al Pomodoro

MELANZANE FRITTE AL POMODORO

FRIED EGGPLANT AND TOMATO

A specialty from Calabria that is more often found in homes than in restaurants, this recipe is halfway between the classic fried vegetables and the Ligurian imbrogliata di carciofi. It is served as a main course.

3 eggplants (aubergines)
kosher (coarse) salt
1 cup (8 fl oz/250 ml) olive oil
4 or 5 tomatoes, chopped
2 tablespoons freshly grated Pecorino cheese
3 eggs, beaten
SERVES 4

❧ Cut the eggplants into medium-size cubes, sprinkle with kosher salt and set aside in a strainer for at least 1 hour to remove their bitter juices.
❧ Rinse the eggplant cubes under running water and dry with paper towels.
❧ Place the olive oil in a skillet over moderate heat. When the oil is very hot, add the eggplant cubes and fry until golden brown. Drain and reserve.
❧ Discard almost all the frying oil, return the pan to the heat and add the tomatoes. Stir well and add the eggplant. Season with salt. Stir the cheese into the eggs. Add to the pan and turn off the heat. Stir until the eggs have set. Serve.

PARMIGIANA DI MELANZANE

EGGPLANT PARMESAN

In spite of its name, this dish did not originate in Parma. Campania and Sicily both claim it as their own, but it is in Sicily, where it is known simply as parmigiana, *that it is most commonly found, both in homes and restaurants. Its resemblance to the moussaka of Greece and Turkey is interesting (a different type of cheese is used, and the ground [minced] meat and some oriental flavors such as cinnamon are missing).*

4 medium eggplants (aubergines)
salt
2 cups (16 fl oz/500 ml) olive oil
1 onion, finely diced
1 sprig basil
1 lb (500 g) ripe tomatoes, peeled, seeded and diced
all-purpose (plain) flour, for coating
¾ cup (3 oz/90 g) freshly grated Parmesan cheese
8 oz (250 g) mozzarella cheese, sliced
2 eggs, hard-cooked, shelled and thinly sliced
SERVES 4

❧ Cut the eggplants into thin slices, lay them on a cutting board, sprinkle with salt and place the board at a slant for at least 1 hour so that the bitter juices run off.
❧ Meanwhile, put a stewpan on the heat with 3 tablespoons of the oil. Add the onion and a few basil leaves. Fry gently for 3 or 4 minutes over low heat until the onion is golden. Add the tomatoes and salt to taste; cook for 30 minutes. Put the mixture through a food mill and reserve in a bowl.
❧ Rinse the eggplant slices to remove the salt and dry with paper towels. Coat the eggplant slices with flour. Fry them in a large skillet in the remaining oil, which should be very hot, until golden.
❧ Preheat the oven to 350°F (180°C). Oil a baking dish and arrange a layer of the eggplant slices on the bottom. Scatter Parmesan and slices of mozzarella on top. Add some thinly sliced hard-cooked egg and a few tablespoons of the tomato sauce. Cover with a second layer of eggplant slices, top with Parmesan, mozzarella and tomato sauce as before, and continue in this manner until all the ingredients have been used. Cover the last layer with tomato sauce and scatter with a few more basil leaves.
❧ Bake in the oven for 30 minutes. The *parmigiana* is considered to be perfect when it is just lukewarm, but it can also be served hot or cold.

Clockwise from left: "Florentine Violet"; "Black Beauty"; "Naples Violet"

EGGPLANTS

The ancient Romans called the eggplant (aubergine) *mala insana,* which appears to be why today in Italy this vegetable is called *melanzana* rather than retaining the Arab root *albadinjan,* which became *aubergine* in French and *alberengena* in Spanish. The origin of that *mala insana* ("unhealthy sickness"), according to some experts, goes back to when it first appeared, as the result of trading by the Italian maritime republics of Genoa, Pisa, Amalfi and Venice. At that time it was eaten in an unhealthy way. The leaves were consumed along with the rest of the eggplant, and they are rich in solanine, a poisonous substance that can lead to madness. The eggplant was therefore subject to a prejudice that was not dispelled for centuries. This is probably why the eggplant appeared relatively late in Italian recipe collections. Ignored by Maestro Martino and Platina, it was at last accepted by Bartolomeo Scappi, who proposed various methods of baking, stuffing and frying it.

Botanically speaking the eggplant is a fruit; in Italy it grows mainly in the south, and in family market gardens in Tuscany and Liguria. More than most plants, it likes the sun, and its ideal habitat is in Sicily, where the most famous variety, an oval-shaped hybrid known as "Black Beauty," can grow to a considerable size. A similar large variety from Florence is known as "Florentine Violet." It is a vegetable that requires careful preparation. Its liquid has a bitter taste and must be eliminated by slicing the eggplant and sprinkling the flesh with kosher (coarse) salt. The slices are then left for a couple of hours in a strainer or on a slanted wooden board so that the liquid drains away.

Although found in abundance in the markets throughout Italy, eggplants are mainly used in recipes from the areas where they are grown. In Sicily and all over the south, eggplants usually are boiled, diced and presented in one form or another of the *caponata,* or are sliced, broiled (grilled) and served cold on large trays as an antipasto or vegetable accompaniment, sprinkled with garlic and parsley and drizzled with olive oil. Typically Sicilian, in spite of its name, is *melanzane alla parmigiana,* eggplant slices fried and arranged in layers alternating with a tomato sauce and cheese. In Liguria, the elongated and rather small eggplants are often halved, scooped out and filled with the flesh mixed with eggs, cheese and herbs and then baked. A long slender variety from Naples called "Naples Violet" is especially suited to stuffing.

Left: Tortiera di Patate al Forno; right: Cuculli di Patate

TORTIERA DI PATATE AL FORNO

POTATOES BAKED WITH TOMATO AND ONION

This is one of the many baked vegetable dishes from Apulia, and is known locally by its dialect name, tiella, from the large baking dish in which it is cooked. Regularly made at home as well as in restaurants it is a classic example of Mediterranean cooking.

2 lb (1 kg) potatoes, sliced ¼ in (6 mm) thick
2 onions, thinly sliced
1 lb (500 g) ripe tomatoes, seeded and chopped
½ cup (4 fl oz/125 ml) olive oil
salt
2 tablespoons dried oregano
½ cup (2 oz/60 g) freshly grated Pecorino cheese
1 cup (8 fl oz/250 ml) water
SERVES 4

❦ Preheat the oven to 350°F (180°C). In a large bowl, combine the potatoes, onions and tomatoes, sprinkle with the olive oil, salt, oregano and Pecorino and mix. Add the water and combine well.
❦ Transfer the mixture to an oiled baking dish. Bake in the oven for 1 hour. Serve hot.

CUCULLI DI PATATE

POTATO FRITTERS

In a strictly traditional lunch in Genoa these cuculli, a kind of rough and tasty croquette of fried potatoes, are served as a hot antipasto, or as a vegetable with stewed rabbit or lamb. Other Italian regions have similar dishes, but what makes the Genoese cuculli special is the fine flavor imparted by the marjoram and pine nuts.

2 lb (1 kg) floury potatoes
7 tablespoons (3½ oz/105 g) butter
1 sprig marjoram
¼ cup (1 oz/30 g) pine nuts
salt
3 eggs, separated
2 tablespoons freshly grated Parmesan cheese
1 cup (4 oz/125 g) dry breadcrumbs
olive oil, for frying
SERVES 4

❦ Wash the potatoes thoroughly. Boil in plenty of salted water until cooked through. As soon as they have cooled enough to handle, peel the potatoes and mash them in a food mill, a potato ricer or with a fork. Add 4 tablespoons (2 oz/60 g) butter and beat vigorously until the potatoes are smooth and soft.
❦ Pound the marjoram and pine nuts in a mortar and place in a bowl with the potatoes and a pinch of salt. One at a time, beat in the egg yolks, making sure each one is absorbed before adding the next. Stir in 1 to 2 tablespoons of Parmesan, until the dough is soft but firm.
❦ In a shallow bowl beat 2 egg whites with a fork or whisk. Place the breadcrumbs in another shallow bowl. Take about 2 teaspoons of the potato mixture and form it with your hands into a little ball. Dip it in the egg white and then in the breadcrumbs. Continue until all the potato "dough" is used. Put a large skillet on to heat with enough olive oil to cover the fritters. When the olive oil starts to smoke, fry the potato balls until they swell up and are evenly browned. Drain on paper towels. Serve hot.

FIORI DI ZUCCA FARCITI ALLA RICOTTA

ZUCCHINI FLOWERS WITH RICOTTA FILLING

This is a particularly elegant example of an updated traditional Italian dish. It is found in Apulia, a region with a high level of vegetable production. Elsewhere zucchini (courgette) flowers are stuffed with more complicated mixtures — sometimes even with lobster mousse — and steamed, or they may be simply fried in batter.

This recipe follows the tradition of frying in oil but is tempered by the use of the simplest of fillings and a delicate sauce.

Left: Fiori di Zucca Farciti alla Ricotta; right: Zucchini a Scapece

12 zucchini (courgette) flowers
2 eggs
6 oz (185 g) ricotta
salt and freshly ground pepper
200 g zucchini (courgettes), trimmed
2 tablespoons freshly grated Parmesan cheese
1 teaspoon butter
2 cups (16 fl oz/500 ml) extra-virgin olive oil

SERVES 4

❡ Blanch the zucchini flowers in salted water. Drain and dry.
❡ Beat the eggs in a bowl. Mix in the ricotta; season with salt and pepper. Fill the zucchini flowers with the mixture.
❡ Meanwhile, cook the zucchini until soft in a small amount of salted water. Purée in a food processor. Transfer the purée to a small pan, stir in the Parmesan and butter and cook for 2 or 3 minutes. Coat the bottom of each plate with the purée.
❡ Fry the stuffed zucchini flowers in the olive oil for 3 minutes. (The oil should be just smoking and deep enough to cover the flowers.) Arrange the flowers over the sauce and serve at once.

ZUCCHINI A SCAPECE

MARINATED ZUCCHINI

This is a Neapolitan specialty served to accompany a main course.

6 zucchini (courgettes), trimmed and thinly sliced
1/4 cup mint leaves
2 garlic cloves, minced
1/2 cup (4 fl oz/125 ml) olive oil
white wine vinegar
salt

SERVES 4

❡ Spread out the zucchini slices on a large plate. Cover with a towel or napkin and leave in the sun for a couple of hours to dry.
❡ Heat the olive oil in a skillet. When it is very hot, fry the zucchini, turning constantly until dark golden. Place the fried zucchini in a bowl just large enough to contain them. Add the mint, garlic and a sprinkling of salt. Add enough vinegar to cover the zucchini. Cover the bowl and set aside to rest for several hours.

Cuscus

CUSCUS

COUSCOUS

The origin of this dish from the town of Carloforte on the island of San Pietro, off the south coast of Sardinia, is a curious one. It is a classic Arab couscous, but it is based exclusively on vegetables (the North African couscous includes fish, chicken and mutton). The people of Carloforte are of ancient Ligurian stock who have retained their ethnic integrity over centuries of migration, although they have acquired different culinary traditions since their ancestors moved first to Tunisia in the fifteenth century, and subsequently to this island.

1¼ cups (8 oz/250 g) chickpeas
1 lb (500 g) coarse semolina
2 cups (16 fl oz/500 ml) water
1 to 2 tablespoons extra-virgin olive oil
salt
1 onion, finely chopped
3½ lb (1.7 kg) vegetables in season, such as zucchini (courgettes), fava (broad) beans, artichokes, eggplants (aubergines), peas, carrots, cauliflower and cabbage
½ teaspoon mixed spices, either black or white pepper, or ground chili powder, mixed with a pinch of saffron powder or cinnamon

SERVES 4–5

❡ Soak the chickpeas overnight in water with a pinch of baking soda. Place them in a saucepan with plenty of water, bring to a boil and then simmer, covered, for 2 hours, until tender. Drain and set aside.
❡ Work the semolina with the water on a pastry board, keeping your hands unclenched so the mixture turns into even crumbs and no lumps are formed. A little extra water can be added if

necessary. Sprinkle with a little olive oil, to keep the crumbs separate. Steam the mixture in a perforated container over a saucepan of boiling salted water for 2 hours, until tender.
❡ Meanwhile in a large skillet, cook the onion in the olive oil for 2–3 minutes then add the vegetables, brown them a little, then cook, covered, in their own liquid, for about 15 minutes, until tender. Drain.
❡ When the couscous is cooked, transfer it to a large bowl and flavor with the spices. Then mix in the vegetables little by little, finish with the chickpeas, and serve.

LENTICCHIE IN UMIDO

LENTIL STEW

As a symbol of wealth and prosperity, lentils are obligatory at any Italian New Year's dinner. Traditionally they are served with the zampone of Modena, or with boiled cotechino, and everyone eats at least a spoonful to ensure that the year will be prosperous for them. Lentils are produced in many areas of Italy, but the most sought-after are the small, quick-cooking ones grown at Castelluccio in Umbria.

10 oz (315 g) lentils
2 tablespoons olive oil
1 onion, finely chopped
2 oz (60 g) pancetta, finely chopped
5 or 6 sage leaves
1 garlic clove, chopped
salt

SERVES 4

❡ Soak the lentils overnight in plenty of warm water. Drain and wash under running water. Drain well.
❡ In a stewpan, combine the olive oil, onion, *pancetta*, sage leaves and garlic and fry gently for 2 or 3 minutes. Do not let the garlic brown. Add the lentils and water to cover. Season with salt, cover and cook over low heat for 1 hour.
❡ Serve as an accompaniment to any kind of cooked pork product or with fresh polenta.

PECORINO FRESCO E MELANZANE

FRESH PECORINO AND EGGPLANT

This recipe, a unique example of a peasant dish from the Aeolian Islands, brings together two symbols of the gas-

Top: Lenticchie in Umido; bottom: Pecorino Fresco e Melanzane

tronomy of southern Italy: the eggplant (aubergine) and the primo sale, a tasty Sicilian cheese that is eaten fresh. The tradition of offering dairy products as an antipasto is common to all of southern Italy.

2 medium eggplants (aubergines) with firm flesh and
   tight skin, thinly sliced
salt
Sauce 1:
8 tablespoons olive oil
2 tablespoons white wine vinegar
1 garlic clove, finely chopped
1 sprig flat-leafed parsley, chopped
pinch of ground red chili pepper
pinch of black pepper
Sauce 2:
2 cups (16 fl oz/500 ml) extra-virgin olive oil
2 tablespoons red wine vinegar
1 teaspoon ground red chili pepper

1 teaspoon oregano
13 oz (410 g) primo sale (fresh Pecorino), sliced
SERVES 4

❡ Prepare the eggplants: Lay the slices on a cutting board, sprinkle with salt, and place the board at a slant for at least 1 hour, to allow the bitter juices to run off. Rinse the slices and pat dry with paper towels. Broil (grill) the eggplant on both sides, then arrange on a platter.
❡ Prepare Sauce 1: Combine the olive oil, white wine vinegar, garlic, parsley, chili pepper, black pepper and salt. Pour over the eggplant.
❡ Prepare Sauce 2: Combine the olive oil, red wine vinegar, salt, chili pepper and oregano, and beat well with a fork.
❡ Arrange the slices of *primo sale* neatly over the eggplant. Pour Sauce 2 over and serve.

Top: Piselli al Prosciutto; bottom: Spinaci alla Romana

PISELLI AL PROSCIUTTO

PEAS WITH PROSCIUTTO

This is another Roman dish that has entered the national Italian cuisine. In Rome, and especially in family homes and the more modest trattorie, it is considered a light and economical main course, but there is a tendency these days to serve it as an accompaniment to meat courses.

5 oz (155 g) prosciutto (or pancetta)
3 tablespoons (1½ oz/45 g) butter
1 onion, thinly sliced
2 lb (1 kg) small, tender green peas, shelled
1 cup (8 fl oz/250 ml) beef stock
salt

SERVES 4

❡ Chop the *prosciutto* finely, discarding the very fatty parts. (If a stronger flavor is desired, use *pancetta*.)
❡ In a skillet, melt half the butter. Add the *prosciutto* and onion. Cook over low heat until the onion is translucent. Add the peas with 2 or 3 tablespoons of the stock. Season with salt. Cover and cook for 10 minutes. Add more stock if the mixture dries out too much. Stir in the remaining butter and cook for a few more minutes before serving.

SPINACI ALLA ROMANA

ROMAN-STYLE SPINACH

A light, elegant vegetable dish from Roman cuisine, this is one of the most classic accompaniments to meat dishes and is found everywhere, sometimes with minor variations.

2 lb (1 kg) spinach (English spinach)
salt
3 tablespoons golden raisins (sultanas)
3 tablespoons (1½ oz/45 g) butter
¼ cup (2 fl oz/60 ml) olive oil
1 garlic clove, peeled and bruised
½ cup (2 oz/60 g) pine nuts

SERVES 4

❡ Clean the spinach thoroughly, washing it several times in running water to remove all the gritty soil. Put the spinach into a saucepan with the water that clings to the leaves. Add a pinch of salt and cook slowly until the spinach is wilted and quite soft. Drain, squeeze dry and set aside on a plate.
❡ Meanwhile, soak the golden raisins in lukewarm water for 10 minutes or so. Drain and squeeze dry.
❡ In a wide, shallow pan, melt the butter with the olive oil. When heated add the garlic and fry gently until colored. Remove the garlic and add the spinach, pine nuts and golden raisins. Cook for 5 or 6 minutes, stirring frequently. Taste for salt. Serve.

INVOLTINI DI VERZA

CABBAGE ROLLS

In a way this is a vegetable version of the various Italian stuffed pastas. Involtini are part of Italy's peasant tradition of using up all leftovers. The recipe originated in the northeastern Piedmont area (Novara/Lake Maggiore), but the dish also appears in Lombardy and other areas of the Po tablelands with similar fillings.

1 cabbage
2 tablespoons (1 oz/30 g) butter
¼ cup (1 oz/30 g) freshly grated Parmesan cheese
2 eggs
3 oz (90 g) prosciutto, finely chopped
1 sprig flat-leafed parsley, minced
pinch of nutmeg
salt

SERVES 4

Left: Involtini di Verza; right: Funghi Trifolati

❡ Core the cabbage, remove the largest leaves and blanch and reserve them. Blanch the smaller tender leaves, rinse and shred.

❡ Sauté the shredded cabbage in a skillet with half the butter for 4 or 5 minutes, until soft.

❡ Preheat the oven to 350°F (180°C). Turn the cabbage into a large bowl and add the Parmesan, eggs, *prosciutto*, parsley and nutmeg. Mix well; season with salt. Divide the mixture among the large cabbage leaves. Roll up and secure with toothpicks. Bake the rolls in the oven with the remaining butter, for 10 to 15 minutes, until browned.

FUNGHI TRIFOLATI

MUSHROOMS FRIED WITH GARLIC AND PARSLEY

A very popular dish from Lombardy, this is usually served with a main course of meat, but may also be served alone, particularly as a light luncheon dish. While the actual nutritive value of the mushrooms is almost zero, their flavor is extraordinary.

1¼ lb (625 g) porcini (boletus) mushrooms, cleaned and thinly sliced
3 tablespoons (1½ oz/45 g) butter
½ cup (4 fl oz/125 ml) olive oil
1 sprig flat-leafed parsley, minced
1 garlic clove, minced
salt

SERVES 4

❡ In a pan, melt the butter with the oil. Add the parsley and garlic and fry gently. When the garlic begins to brown, stir in the mushrooms. Season with salt. Cook over moderate heat for about 20 minutes, until the mushrooms are tender but firm and are mixed with the cooking liquid to form a sauce.

GREEN SALAD LEAVES

The salad par excellence in Italy is a green one, and, at most, it may extend to the three colors of the Italian flag. This results, for example, when white Belgian endive (witloof), red radicchio and green lettuce are placed together on the plate. A different color scheme is produced by combining other kinds of equally common vegetables: cos (romaine) lettuce, the green of its elongated leaves gradually lightening until it fades into the white of the ribs, or the ruffled pale yellowish leaves of the escarole (Batavian endive), or the heads of green endive concealing a heart that is almost completely white.

These are just a few of the so-called green salads in Italian cuisine. To them we must add the different kinds of seasonal salad greens — most of them appearing in spring — which vary according to the area where they are grown and the time they are picked. Then there are other types of salad that are not cultivated but grow wild, and we shall learn more about these later.

In Italy, the salad is rarely served as a separate course. It comes to the table as an accompaniment to more important dishes, or immediately following them when there is a need to refresh the palate with something light and cool, for example after eating a rich meat sauce.

HISTORY OF SALADS

The first appearance of the salad in the literature of Italian gastronomy was in 1627, when a Venetian published *L'Archidipno, Ovvero della Insalata*, by Salvatore Massonio, a doctor, scholar and man of letters from Abruzzo. The book is nothing less than a treatise on edible plants, with sixty-eight chapters covering the nature of salads and dressings and the times of the season when each is available to the cook. The writer starts from the basic consideration that salads are beneficial to the poor, who at very little expense can achieve a feeling of hunger satisfied, but equally so to the rich because a salad will lighten their dinners "so that the stomach is not offended by too much food."

It was the poor who discovered the benefits of many wild herbs that are difficult to find on the market today but are still present in the daily diet of country folk — the cuckoo flower, the slender and delicious wild asparagus and the different types of chicory that are picked in fields and by rivers and streams.

Historically the salad is probably the oldest food in existence. It is common to all known gastronomic cultures and varies only in the methods used to flavor it. Today in Italy the main dressing is olive oil, used alone or mixed with vinegar or lemon juice, but this has not always been the case. In the past the fat component added to the vegetables to make them more palatable was related to what the local soil had to offer. In Piedmont, for example, where there are no olive groves but plenty of walnut trees, salads used to be dressed with walnut oil, and the same was true for Lombardy, where linseed oil was also widely used, whereas in the Veneto the oil produced from grape seeds was preferred. Still further north, on the Austrian border, some types of salad were, and still are, dressed with hot animal fats. This is the case with the cabbage salad typical of Alto Adige: the raw cabbage is shredded very finely and flavored with a sauce made from pieces of speck melted over heat and sprinkled at the last minute with a little vinegar.

VARIANTS

A luxurious variant of the humble green salad — of longstanding origins — is the *insalata coi tartufi* (salad with truffles) from Turin. Over the tender and still pale green leaves white truffles are finely sliced and then topped with a sauce comprising hard-cooked egg yolks, olive oil, vinegar, mild mustard and anchovy paste (a concoction not dissimilar to a "Cambridge sauce"). An extravagant touch is sometimes added by topping this salad with the brightly colored sepals of nasturtium and balsam flowers.

Another highly palatable preparation — introduced in the last few years — is *pizza alla rucola*: a square of warm white pizza (with oil and salt) is topped with red *prosciutto* and a generous quantity of puny, green, fragrant and tasty leaves of *rucola*, or *rughetta*, (arugula/rocket lettuce). It could be a mere coincidence, but it is also a fact that once again a tantalizing treat comes to us dressed in the colors of the national flag!

There is a variety of Easter salads and dishes especially associated with this festive occasion. The springtime greens used in salads are known as *pasqualina*. The tenderest leaves and heart of the artichoke are used in a dish which is called *torta pasqualina* (Easter Pie). This pie consists of artichokes, cooked in olive oil and garlic, borage and marjoram, mixed with a rich sauce of fresh cheese.

Valerianella, or lamb's lettuce, is an early salad green which heralds the beginning of spring. It is eaten for lunch on Easter Sunday after the *agnello pasquale* (Easter lamb). *Valerianella* has a slightly lemony taste, most pleasing and delicate. It is dressed with olive oil and lemon juice or vinegar.

Crescione (watercress) is a leafy plant of the mustard family. It is native to the Mediterranean region and has been eaten in Italy since Roman times. It is a popular salad vegetable in Italian cooking.

1. *lattuga romana;*
2. *& 3. butter lettuce;*
4. *Belgian endive (witloof);*
5. *radicchio; 6. &*
9. *pasqualina; 7. arugula (rocket lettuce); 8. crescione*

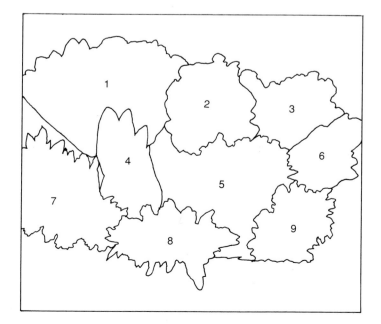

Left: Insalata di Lattuga e Finocchi; right: Scarola Ripiena

INSALATA DI LATTUGA E FINOCCHI

LETTUCE AND FENNEL SALAD

What makes this dish special is not the flair of the cook, but simply the extraordinary quality of the ingredients brought together intelligently.

1 head of lettuce, separated
2 small, tender fennel bulbs
5 tablespoons extra-virgin olive oil
juice of 1 lemon
salt

SERVES 4

❡ Wash each lettuce leaf separately, cut it into strips and put it into a large salad bowl. Wash the fennel, halve lengthwise and then cut into paper-thin slices. Add to the lettuce. Dress with olive oil, lemon juice and salt to taste. Serve with any meat or fish course.

SCAROLA RIPIENA

STUFFED ESCAROLE

The Neapolitans came rather late to spaghetti; pasta entered their cuisine only at the beginning of the last century. In the eighteenth century people from Naples were referred to disdainfully as mangiafoglia (leaf-eaters) because they consumed so many vegetables. This stuffed escarole (Batavian endive), served as a first course, belongs to this period.

4 escarole (Batavian endive) heads, trimmed
1 garlic clove, peeled
12 black olives, pitted
1 tablespoon golden raisins (sultanas)
¼ cup (1 oz/30 g) pine nuts
½ cup (2 oz/60 g) freshly grated Romano
    (Pecorino) cheese
¼ cup (2 fl oz/60 ml) olive oil

SERVES 4

❡ Cook the escarole in boiling salted water with the garlic for 7 to 10 minutes. Drain while still fairly compact; gently squeeze out the excess liquid. Put them on a chopping board and spread the leaves. Divide the olives, golden raisins, pine nuts and half the Romano among the 4 heads of escarole and mound them together in the center of each head. Close up the leaves and press well to form a roll. Brown the rolls in the olive oil in a skillet. As soon as they color, transfer them to an oiled baking dish, sprinkle with the remaining Romano and finish cooking in a preheated 400°F (200°C) oven for 15 minutes.

FUNGHI IN FRICASSEA

FRICASSÉED MUSHROOMS

This Tuscan dish is usually made with fresh porcini (boletus) mushrooms and served as a light main course.

⅓ cup (3 fl oz/90 ml) olive oil
3 garlic cloves, peeled and lightly bruised
1 sprig marjoram
1¼ lb (625 g) porcini (boletus) mushrooms,
    thinly sliced
salt and freshly ground pepper
2 tablespoons light stock (optional)
2 egg yolks
juice of ½ lemon

SERVES 4

❡ In a terracotta pan or skillet, heat the olive oil, garlic and marjoram. Remove the garlic when it begins to color. Add the mushrooms, season with salt and pepper and cook over low heat, stirring from time to time, for 15 or 20 minutes. If necessary, add a little hot stock. Adjust the salt, if required.
❡ Beat the egg yolks with the lemon juice. When the mushrooms are tender, add the egg yolk mixture and mix quickly but gently. Serve at once.

FUNGHI ALLA GENOVESE

GENOESE MUSHROOMS WITH POTATOES AND BASIL

This is the most widespread method of preparing mushrooms in the Liguria region and probably resulted from the desire to intensify the flavor of the mushrooms through the neutral support provided by the potatoes.

¾ cup (6 fl oz/185 ml) olive oil
3 or 4 potatoes, thinly sliced
salt
4 garlic cloves, peeled and lightly bruised
1 bunch basil, washed and dried
13 oz (410 g) porcini (boletus) mushrooms,
    thinly sliced

SERVES 4

❡ Preheat the oven to 350°F (180°C). Pour ½ cup (4 fl oz/125 ml) olive oil into a baking dish and tilt the dish to evenly coat the bottom and sides. Make a layer of potato slices on the bottom, sprinkle with salt and add the garlic cloves and a handful of basil leaves. Cover with a layer of mushrooms, scatter with more basil leaves and sprinkle generously with the remaining olive oil. Season again with salt.
❡ Bake in the oven for about 45 minutes.

Left: Funghi in Fricassea; right: Funghi alla Genovese

MUSHROOMS

Almost all of Italy's regional cuisines contain many mushroom dishes, and there are even specialist mushroom markets. In Trento, capital of one of the major mountain regions, a daily mushroom market has existed for centuries in a small square in the historic city center. The stalls display only mushrooms — no less than 200 different species of edible mushroom can be found.

In each of the places where mushrooms are marketed there are experts who keep close watch, checking every delivery, ensuring that there are no poisonous specimens.

The prize for quality, as well as the preference of the gourmet, goes to two mushrooms in particular — the *porcino* (*Boletus edulis*) and the *ovolo* (*Amanita caesarea*). These are followed by the *porcinello*, the *chiodino*, the

trombetta, the *finferlo*, and others.

One of the great joys of autumn, especially in the north, is to go out scouring the fields and woods to fill your basket with wild mushrooms. Those that grow in the woods are more highly prized and nowadays so many people go collecting that weight limits have been placed on how much each person can gather.

The nutritive value of mushrooms is practically

nil, but they are particularly appreciated for their fragrance and flavor, foundations for some of the most famous dishes in Italian gastronomy. The Genoese mushroom *tocco*, for example, is a rich sauce made from *porcini* mushrooms that is used with lasagne or fet-tuccine: *funghi trifolati*, chopped mushrooms cooked with oil, garlic and parsley, are used to crown a plate of fresh

to two different types of fungus, similar in appearance and taste but which grow in different places in the woodlands. One is found on tree-trunks and the other, with a detectably sweeter flavor, grows in the ground. Both are used in the making of sauces or for *frittata* and are also enjoyed as a dish on their own, cooked in olive oil with perhaps some garlic and parsley.

Because Italians have a preference for mushrooms that come from the woods, some tend to look down on those, like *prataioli* (field mushrooms), that don't. Nevertheless, they have a restrained, sweetish taste and are delicious eaten raw, finely sliced with a light dressing. This is a pleasant way of eating most mushrooms, provided they have been picked young and are firm. A common addition is some tasty cheese such as Parmesan, lightly flaked over them. Alternatively, a marinade consisting of olive oil, lemon juice, garlic, basil, salt and pepper can be prepared and the mushrooms are left in it for about two hours before being eaten. Marinated mushrooms can also be bottled and kept and *prataioli* and *russole* are good for preserving in oil, when young.

Dried mushrooms are greatly appreciated too, but appear as an ingredient in a variety of recipes, never as a dish on their own. They are usually *porcini,* sliced and

spread out to dry in a sunny place and then packed in small boxes or cellophane bags. If your trip to the country to pick mushrooms has gone well and yielded a good quantity, you might try drying them at home. They must be thoroughly cleaned, using a knife, if need be, to remove the greenish part under the cap. They are then cut into slices ¼ inch (5 millimeters) thick and laid out on wooden boards in the sun, covered with cheesecloth to protect them from dust and insects. Turn the slices every three or four hours, and take them indoors at night. After four or five days they will be perfectly dry and ready to pack in small bags or jars.

Mushrooms are simple to use in cooking. Ideally they should not be washed, merely cleaned with a soft brush, and if necessary with a sharp knife to remove all traces of soil. They are highly perishable and must be eaten within a couple of days of picking, and kept in the bottom vegetable section of the refrigerator. In addition to drying, they can be preserved in oil, vinegar or brine.

As we have seen mushrooms are used in a wide range of Italian specialties. Today some of these recipes are well known and appreciated all around the world, like the famous Neapolitan *pizza ai funghi* (mushroom pizza), whilst some others are still in the realm of the gourmets. For example there is the luxurious type of home made pasta, that derives its dark color and delicious taste from the generous quantity of *porcini* minced and added to this dough. One of the two best varieties we know is produced near Pisa, in a village called Molina di Quosa, and the other by a "cottage industry" — run by the descendants of one of Italy's oldest families — in the picturesque medieval village of Artena, near Rome.

1. *chiodini;* 2. *russola;*
3. *ararici;* 4. *porcini;*
5. *prataioli;* 6. *ovoli*

polenta or may serve as the perfect accompaniment for a majestic roast or any baked meat. Fresh young *porcini* and *ovoli* are sublime served as a salad. Sliced wafer-thin, mixed with equally thin slivers of *Grana* cheese, and dressed with a drizzle of olive oil, very little salt, a grinding of pepper and a few drops of lemon juice, they make an antipasto of outstanding elegance.

Chiodino actually refers

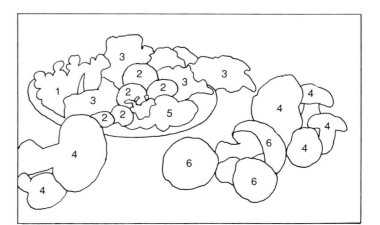

Onions

Italian cuisine exists because onions do. At least 80 per cent of the dishes that make up the country's gastronomic inheritance would be impossible to imagine without this precious vegetable. It is an indispensable element of the *soffritto*, the essential and distinctive flavor base of so many Italian dishes.

A *soffritto* is made by combining cooking fat (usually olive oil and butter, sometimes lard) with a *trito* of onion, to which may be added garlic, parsley, carrot, celery and other herbs depending on the recipe in question (a *trito* means the components are finely chopped together). These ingredients are fried gently to release their flavor, and the resulting *soffritto* forms the base for pasta sauces, risottos,

meat stews and even vegetable soups.

Apart from this fundamental use, the onion in its own right is a star of the Italian table — the larger white onion can be stuffed and baked in the oven, cooked with sugar and vinegar as a sweet–sour vegetable accompaniment, or boiled for serving with meat dishes or with other boiled vegetables such as potatoes and greens. The small white onion is used to create a delicious sweet–sour vegetable dish, *cipolline in agrodolce*, cooked in sugar and vinegar, or can just be used raw like the long, bulbed salad onions. The onion is also a main ingredient of *frittatas*, pies and other baked dishes, not to mention salads. Onions feature in some typically Italian

combinations that everyone should try: tuna in oil with raw onion and boiled beans, a simple and superb Tuscan main dish, and onions sliced wafer-thin and mixed with tomatoes in a salad.

SPECIES

Various species of onion are found throughout the country, with the fragrant sweet white onion grown more or less everywhere. The red one typical of the Tropea area in Calabria, with its particularly delicate flavor, is eaten raw with various kinds of salad vegetables. Also belonging to the same lily (Lilaceae) family are the ever-popular leeks.

The onion entered the history of Italian cooking a few thousand years ago. The plant was initially developed in western central Asia and was first known to the Assyrian and Babylonian civilizations. Subsequently it was cultivated by the Egyptians, the Greeks and the Romans. Later it spread from the Mediterranean basin throughout the world. The claim that the onion existed in America before Christopher Columbus is unfounded, since all the species of the vegetable cultivated in America are of European origin.

In Piedmont there is a mouthwatering dish, called simply *siule piene* (stuffed onions). Part of a traditional festive meal prepared in Settimo (a small town near Torino) on the last Sunday of August, this specialty is prepared by half-boiling large, white onions, filling

them with a mixture of their own chopped "hearts" with eggs, cheese and butter, seasoning them with freshly ground pepper and with a potent spirit distilled locally from peaches, and finally by baking them.

Other recipes devoted to the humble onion are to be found in many of the Italian regions. In Naples (Campania) they bake them — after sticking two cloves in each — with olive oil, thyme and Marsala wine. In Lecce (Apulia) they proudly prepare *pizza rustica*, an onion pie with tomatoes, anchovy fillets and black olives. The regions of Tuscany and Calabria both boast a variant of onion soup; both versions are as good as, or better than, the more celebrated one prepared in France (which is also based, by the way, on a recipe brought to France by the Florentine cooks of Caterina de Medici in the first half of the sixteenth century).

1. white onions; 2. red Tropea onion; 3. small white onions for cooking in vinegar and sugar or using raw; 4. green (spring) onions for use in salads

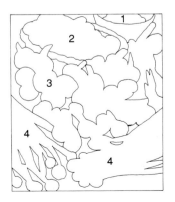

CIPOLLE RIPIENE

STUFFED ONIONS

At lunch in Piedmont, these onions may be served hot as a whole meal, since they make a rich and complete dish on their own, as a vegetable accompaniment or, if they are not too large, cold, as an antipasto.

6 tablespoons (3 oz/90 g) butter
7 oz (220 g) ground (minced) lean veal
4 large onions, peeled
¾ cup (3 oz/90 g) freshly grated Grana cheese
salt and freshly ground pepper
1 egg
2 tablespoons grappa

SERVES 4

❡ In a wide, shallow pan, melt 2 tablespoons (1 oz/30 g) butter over moderate heat. Add the veal and cook until lightly browned. Set aside.
❡ Meanwhile, boil the onions until half-cooked. Cut in half horizontally and scoop out the centers. Mince the scooped out onion.
❡ In a bowl, combine the onion, veal, cheese and salt and pepper. Add the egg and mix well.
❡ Preheat the oven to 400°F (200°C). Stuff the onions with the mixture and place a teaspoon of butter on top of each one.
❡ Grease a baking dish with the remaining butter. Stand the onions in the dish and sprinkle with a few drops of grappa. Bake in the oven for 50 to 60 minutes, until the onions are tender.

CIPOLLINE IN AGRODOLCE

SWEET AND SOUR ONIONS

This dish is an excellent accompaniment for roasts and meat dishes and may be served cold as an antipasto.

2 oz (60 g) prosciutto fat, finely chopped
2 teaspoons butter
3 tablespoons sugar
½ cup (4 fl oz/125 ml) white wine vinegar
1½ lb (750 g) cipolline (small onions), trimmed and soaked for 30 minutes in cold water
salt and freshly ground pepper

SERVES 4

❡ In a large, wide pan over gentle heat, combine the *prosciutto* fat and butter and melt without burning. Stir in the sugar and continue stirring for 4 or 5 minutes.

Top: Cipolline in Agrodolce; bottom: Cipolle Ripiene

❡ Meanwhile, drain the onions.
❡ Add the vinegar to the pan, mix and add the drained onions. Season with salt and pepper. Cover the pan and cook over moderate heat for 20 minutes or so, until the onions are soft and pale gold.

PEPERONI IN PADELLA

PAN-FRIED BELL PEPPERS

This very simple dish can serve either as a cold antipasto or as a hot or warm vegetable to accompany meat dishes. It is common throughout southern Italy.

½ cup (4 fl oz/125 ml) olive oil, for frying
4 lb (2 kg) large, sweet bell peppers (capsicums)
1 garlic clove, minced
3 tablespoons capers, drained
3 oz (90 g) black Gaeta olives, pitted
salt and ground chili pepper
1 sprig flat-leafed parsley, chopped

SERVES 4

❡ Heat the olive oil in a skillet until very hot. Add the bell peppers and fry over moderate heat until soft but not colored. Reserve.
❡ Drain most of the oil from the skillet and return it to the heat with the garlic, capers and olives. Mix well. Add the bell peppers and cook, stirring, for 5–6 minutes. Taste and season with salt, if required, and a pinch of chili pepper. Sprinkle with parsley just before serving. (See photograph page 188.)

Left: Melanzane alla Genovese; right: Peperoni in Padella (page 187)

MELANZANE ALLA GENOVESE

GENOESE EGGPLANT WITH EGGS

Unlike the famous eggplants (aubergines) grown in the south of Italy, the ones produced in Liguria are small and elongated, with a particularly delicate flavor.

The first part of the following recipe, typical of the cuisine of Genoa, is in some ways similar to the one for Sicilian caponata, *but here the dish is finished with eggs in a classic fricassée of the type used with lamb or chicken. This is generally served hot to accompany roasted white meats.*

8 long, thin eggplants (aubergines)
1 cup (8 fl oz/250 ml) olive oil
1 onion, sliced
2 large, ripe tomatoes, peeled, seeded and chopped
salt

2 eggs
1 sprig marjoram

SERVES 4

❧ Wash the eggplants. Slice them into rounds with the skin on, and immerse in cold water.
❧ Heat the oil in a wide skillet. Add the onion and fry until it begins to color. Drain the eggplant slices and pat dry. Add to the onion and fry gently to let the flavors blend. Add the tomatoes and salt to taste, cover and cook over moderate heat for about 20 minutes, or until tender.
❧ When the eggplant is cooked, break the eggs into a bowl, add the marjoram and a pinch of salt and beat quickly with a fork. Pour the beaten eggs over the eggplant and stir away from the heat (there is sufficient heat from the eggplant to cook them). They will form a soft cream. Transfer to a serving plate and take to the table.

Left: white truffles; right: black truffles

TRUFFLES

The first person to write about truffles was Theophrastus, more than two thousand years ago. Because he classified the truffle as a vegetable, he imagined it was reproduced via seeds, but as these seeds were absolutely impossible to find, a mystery grew up around the truffle, leading ancient scholars to attribute obscure origins to it. Pliny thought the truffle was a "callous" of the Earth, and since it appeared in autumn after the summer storms, he opined that truffles developed where lightning had struck. Only much later, in the eighteenth century, did botanical studies employ the microscope to establish the real nature of the truffle, placing it within the family of underground fungi propagated by means of mycelium.

Although several species of truffle are known, only two are considered to be of high gastronomic standing. The most important is the white truffle of Alba (capital of the Langhe in Piedmont), which also grows in many other parts of Italy, notably the Monferrato hills adjacent to the Langhe, and all along the Piedmontese strip of the Apennines, from the Pavia side of the Po River to the Marches. Thus, in addition to Alba, major crops are produced in Piedmont at Nizza Monferrato, and in the Marches at Acqualagna and at Sant'Angelo in Vado inland from Pesaro.

Then there is the black truffle, which grows mainly in the Nerina Valley in Umbria around the town of Norcia and is similar to the Périgord truffle.

There are notable differences between the two types. The white truffle is always eaten raw, so as not to dissipate its very delicate perfume and even more delicate taste. The black one may be eaten raw, especially in salads or grated over richly sauced pasta dishes, but it is mainly used cooked and in this role it enriches many sauces. Although truffles — white ones in particular — are found in restricted areas elsewhere in the world, they are a characteristic feature of Italian gastronomy. They are gathered in the woods from the beginning of autumn and through December, with the help of specially trained dogs endowed with particularly sensitive noses.

Once the truffle has been sniffed out, the hunter removes the dog from the spot and uses a small hoe to dig out his precious loot. As the truffle is a fungus, it is essential not to destroy the invisible and delicate mycelium network destined to produce further crops in future seasons. Every truffle gatherer has his own area and goes there before dawn so as not to reveal the route to others.

In great demand among gourmets and sold at incredible prices, truffles raise many dishes to the height of the sublime. A plate of *taglierini all'uovo* with melted butter and Parmesan cheese is one of the year-round specialties of the Langhe in Piedmont, but topped with shavings of truffle, cut with a special tool, it becomes something exceptional. The same is true of a plain risotto with Parmesan.

The truffle is not washed but simply brushed with care to remove any soil or impurities, and then kept in a cool place wrapped in porous paper to let it breathe, or covered in rice.

This latter method keeps the truffle in good condition and at the same time the truffle flavors the rice, which then makes a magnificent risotto without anything else being added to it.

Balsamic vinegar

BALSAMIC VINEGAR

Although known as vinegar, *aceto balsamico* might more appropriately be called a wine sauce. It is made only in the Modena area, at Spilamberto. Here the *Consorteria degli Assaggiatori di Aceto Balsamico* (Balsamic Vinegar Tasters'

Cooperative) meets periodically to confer the right to use the title of balsamic vinegar on the small annual production of the authentic product, which has been aged for at least 15 years.

The story of this vinegar has its roots in a centuries-old tradition linked to the "must culture" that was practiced in Emilia from the time of the Romans. The Modena area used to produce a weak wine for on-the-spot consumption. It was never drunk on a large scale but had other uses — as vinegar and as boiled must and in very

concentrated form it became sweet enough to use in place of honey. The vinegar was used for preserving or seasoning foods, and for treating wounds. Mixed with water, it became the daily drink for peasants, soldiers and slaves. It was also used as a medicine, in the form of a gargle to cure sore throats or to reawaken dormant passions in lovemaking.

Balsamic vinegar, as we know it today, prospered thanks to the favor of the Grand Ducal court, where it was produced from 1800 onwards. It is obtained from grape must slowly boiled to reduce it to one-third of its original volume. The cooked must is strained and left to cool, and then put into a 12½ gallon (50 liter) cask. Every year the vinegar is transferred into smaller casks of a different wood — oak, chestnut, cherry, ash, mulberry — which are stored in the attics of old buildings. As the years pass the vinegar condenses, takes on the fragrance of each of the woods, mellows and finally reduces to an intense brown liquid that is almost a sauce. An initial 25 gallons (100 liters) of must will become, after 20 years or more, just 5 or 6 quarts (liters) of balsamic vinegar.

Balsamic vinegar should be used, drop by drop, to flavor a salad or to impart a particular character to a sauce for calf's liver, fillet of beef or trout.

CONDIGLIONE ALLA LIGURE

LIGURIAN MIXED SALAD

The ingredients in this salad may be varied according to the season. The recipe arose largely out of a need to combine all the requirements for a summer meal into a single dish, but these days it is no longer served in large quantities and has become an antipasto served in small portions. Along with fresh vegetables it invariably includes various types of preserved fish, and hard-cooked eggs. It is always presented on a base of boiled potatoes or lightly moistened toasted bread slices.

2 lb (1 kg) potatoes, cooked, peeled and sliced thickly
3 large tomatoes, seeded and sliced or coarsely chopped
1 fennel bulb, trimmed and sliced
1 bell pepper (capsicum), trimmed and cut into strips
1 onion, thinly sliced
1 bunch of celery
3 or 4 anchovy fillets, chopped
6 eggs, hard-cooked and cut into wedges
5 oz (155 g) mosciamme *(dried dolphin, tuna or swordfish), sliced paper-thin*
3 oz (90 g) tuna in oil, drained and crumbled
1 cup (8 fl oz/250 ml) olive oil
vinegar
salt
1 sprig marjoram

SERVES 6

Top: Condiglione alla Ligure; bottom: Insalata di Melanzane alla Griglia

❡ Arrange the sliced potatoes over the bottom of a large platter. Arrange the tomatoes, fennel, bell pepper, onion and celery on top. Scatter the anchovies over all. Tuck the wedges of egg among the vegetables and dot with the dried fish and crumbled tuna. Drizzle on the olive oil, sprinkle with vinegar and season with salt to taste. Sprinkle the leaves from the sprig of marjoram on top.

❡ Present the dish at the table in its arranged state, but before serving toss all the ingredients together.

INSALATA DI MELANZANE ALLA GRIGLIA

SALAD OF GRILLED EGGPLANT

In the restaurants of Apulia this salad always occupies the place of honor in the large selection of vegetable antipasti displayed near the entrance.

1 garlic clove, minced
½ cup (4 fl oz/125 ml) olive oil
salt and freshly ground pepper, or ground red chili pepper
2 medium eggplants (aubergines)
2 tablespoons red or white wine vinegar

SERVES 4

❡ Stir the garlic into the olive oil and add a pinch of salt and a little pepper (or better still, chili pepper). Stir and set aside to infuse.

❡ Wash the eggplants; cut lengthwise into slices no more than ¼ in (5 mm) thick. Sprinkle with salt and set aside to drain on a sloping board or in a strainer for at least 1 hour so they will lose their bitter juices.

❡ Rinse the eggplant under running water to wash off the salt, and dry carefully. Brush each slice with the oil and garlic mixture and grill (barbecue) or broil (grill) for a few minutes on each side. Transfer to a serving plate to cool.

❡ When the eggplant is cool, sprinkle with vinegar. Treated in this way the eggplants will keep well for some days. They are served cold as an antipasto.

*From right: extra-virgin olive oil from Lake Garda; Ligurian
extra-virgin olive oil; Tuscan extra-virgin olive oil*

OLIVE OIL

With the exception of just a few specific areas of particular regions, Italy is virtually one vast olive grove, with about 100 million trees extending almost uniformly from the north to the south in the areas where the climate allows this very ancient tree to flourish. There are groves in Liguria all along the coast and inland to where the hills begin; there are groves in Tuscany, Latium, Umbria, Campania, Sardinia, Calabria, and Sicily; there are some immense groves in Apulia, and on the Adriatic side olives grow up as far as the hills of Emilia Romagna. There are none on the Po plains, where environmental conditions are unsuitable, but olive trees flourish around the lakes, particularly Lake Garda.

The reasons behind this diffusion are not merely commercial, for since ancient times, the olive has been considered a sacred tree. Spread throughout the Mediterranean by the Greeks, it is easy to graft, which has led to numerous hybrids multiplying the varieties of olive, and hence the varieties of oil, available to consumers.

Theophrastus tells us that the Romans in the third century BC already had ten different types, classified according to precise commercial regulations that took into account not only the quality of the olive but also the degree of ripeness of the olives and the type of pressing.

The olive is a very delicate fruit that must be in flawless condition if it is to produce a perfect oil. Olives that are immature or overripe, have been left too long after picking waiting to be pressed, or have been subject to attack by parasites or bad weather, will never give top-quality oil, and this is the main reason why oil has always remained a highly valued product that represents good sales for the grower. The Republic of Venice was aware of this when it ordered olive-planting in its domains to ensure that the Serenissima would have wealthy provinces capable of paying their taxes to the central government. This is why several million olive trees were planted to cover the islands of Corfu and Cephalonia in the Ionian archipelago between Italy and Greece.

The olive grows very slowly. "You plant olives for your children," say the country folk of Tuscany.

Serving olives symbolizes hospitality in country areas of southern central Italy, where guests are offered bread and olives or bread and oil. The practice is the distant origin of the *bruschetta* or Tuscan *fettunta* served as an antipasto in restaurants today. The flavor of the simple bread and oil has been enriched by rubbing garlic over the bread or adding tomato slices and leaves of basil, but it remains substantially the same as it was a thousand years ago.

The law governing the production of olive oil in Italy is extremely strict, and establishes the acidity index for the various categories. Close attention must be paid to the label, remembering that if you want absolutely the best oil, you must buy one with the words *olio extravergine d'oliva* marked clearly on the label. Extra-virgin oil can contain no more than 1.1 per cent oleic acid, and it is the best one for using uncooked on salads and for flavoring soups, pasta or meats at the end of cooking. A classic example is the drizzle of extra-virgin olive oil that elevates *pasta e fagioli alla veneta* to perfection. Next there is *olio d'oliva vergine*

(virgin olive oil), slightly inferior in quality, with a maximum acidity of 2 per cent, followed by other types of oil obtained by refining and mixing oils of different origins.

In Italy, there are three types of extra-virgin oil, all very highly esteemed. The Ligurian oil, mainly produced in Imperia on the coast between Genoa and the French border, is considered the lightest and most refined. It is a clear pale yellow, its perfume is intense, and its flavor very delicate. Alongside the Ligurian oil the connoisseurs class the oil from Lake Garda, also light yellow in color with some brighter reflections, and with a fine, intense flavor. Equally good oil is produced in Tuscany and in Umbria, but here the color is usually more pronounced and has greenish tinges, there is much greater intensity in the fragrance and the flavor is stronger. Similar features are found in the olive oils produced in the south, especially in Apulia. The Umbrian, Tuscan and southern oils, given their very definite flavor, are the best ones to use in salads with stronger greens and herbs. A salad where arugula (rocket) is used, for example, marries better with a Tuscan oil than with a Ligurian one.

HISTORY

The beautiful olive tree bears a grand ancestry due to its prized produce.

Throughout history nobles and kings of cultures all over the world have been anointed

with olive oil. Today the Roman Catholic Church still uses it to anoint children and the dying. The Romans had many uses for olive oil. Athletes oiled themselves to make their muscles supple, while noble ladies maintained the freshness of their skin with it. Olive oil was also used to light lamps.

Even the Roman breakfast was a kind of porridge doused in olive oil. Records tell of rich patricians that dined on fish from the Black Sea preserved in olive oil and on sweet dumplings of fried ricotta. As it was such a major part of their lives, the Romans had an olive press in every courtyard.

Olive oil remained prominent all through the Middle Ages, and was still being used for a variety of functions. During the Renaissance food was fried and of course cooked in oil. However the poorer regions of Italy may not have used olive oil as it was a quality commodity.

Only in the last 50 years has it been used in regions like the North of Italy. Before then it was only a special additive to salad dressings. At this time Tuscan restaurateurs opened eateries in the North. After this, olive oil became generally accepted as an essential ingredient of Italian cuisine.

Italy now produces one third of the world's total, with great demands for it on the export market. To meet ever-growing demands which are difficult to satisfy,

olive oils from other countries are now imported and mixed with the Italian oil.

The most effective type of olive tree grown is the *Olea sativa*, which includes over 30 varieties, which are grown in different areas. An intriguing feature of the olive tree is that it can reproduce itself from the underground stump, even when the tree is apparently dead. This was proven in Chianti in the early 1980s when frost driven trees apparently bore new shoots within 12 months. The process of growing an olive oil tree is however quite lengthy and takes about ten to twelve years to reach full development.

Olives are harvested in November and December. Green olives are picked before they are fully ripe, while purple and black olives are picked when they are ripe or overripe. Methods of picking the olives and producing the oil have scarcely changed over centuries. The olives are collected by pickers with large wicker baskets, or by spreading large nets around the base of each tree and shaking it. As soon as they have harvested, they are taken to the *olivicio* — olive mill — where the oil must be extracted within a week. The best oil is produced in one or two days. The whole process takes place without any use of heat or chemicals, so that the end result is the pure juice of the olive with the nutritional value of the fruit still in it.

PUNTARELLE ALLA ROMANA

ROMAN PUNTARELLE

In the picturesque markets of the old quarter of Rome, and especially the most famous of them all, the one in Campo dei Fiori, you often will see old women behind the fruit and vegetable stalls cutting tiny bunches of greens in a special way and then throwing them into a container of cold water. They are preparing puntarelle, *the most typical of all Roman salad greens. Picked from autumn through late winter, they come from a particular kind of chicory known as* Catalogna *(Catalonia). Only the more tender inner leaves are used, and the special cutting and immersion in cold water makes the leaves curl.*

2 lb (1 kg) curly endive (chicory)
4 garlic cloves, peeled
8 anchovy fillets
3 tablespoons red or white wine vinegar
½ cup (4 fl oz/125 ml) olive oil
salt and freshly ground pepper, or ground red chili pepper

SERVES 4

❡ Discard the outer leaves of the endive and the fibrous parts of the interior section. Pull the leaves off the stalks and cut into thin strips about 4 in (10 cm) long and no more than ¼ in (5 mm) wide. Submerge in cold water for 1 hour so they acquire the curly appearance characteristic of *puntarelle*.

❡ Meanwhile, make the dressing: Put the garlic, anchovy fillets and vinegar into a mortar or food processor and pound or process to a creamy paste. Gradually mix in the olive oil. Taste and add salt, if necessary, and a little pepper (or better still, some chili pepper).

❡ Drain the endive well and dry as thoroughly as possible. Put in a salad bowl and toss with the dressing. (To add a different flavor, a few leaves of mint may be included in the dressing.)

INDIVIA STRASCINATA IN PADELLA

PAN-FRIED ENDIVES WITH ANCHOVIES AND GARLIC

The custom of boosting the flavor of vegetables with a second cooking after they have been boiled in water is quite widespread in Italy. The only difference is that butter is used in the north and oil in the center and the south. This

Top: Puntarelle alla Romana; bottom: Indivia Strascinata in Padella

endive dish, belonging to popular Roman tradition, is usually served with baked or boiled white meats.

4 Belgian endives (witloofs)
3 tablespoons olive oil
2 garlic cloves, peeled
2 anchovy fillets, minced
1 sprig mint
salt

SERVES 4

❡ Trim the endives, removing the outer leaves and retaining only the hearts. Put into boiling salted water and remove after 2 or 3 minutes, when half-cooked. Drain well and let cool to lukewarm.

❡ In a skillet, heat the oil and garlic over low heat. When they begin to brown, add the anchovies and cook – still over low heat – stirring continuously until the anchovies have completely disintegrated.

❡ Add the endives to the pan, mix, and cook for approximately 10 minutes. Taste for seasoning. Stir in the mint leaves then remove from heat. Serve immediately.

Spices

With regard to spices, Italians are divided into two basic schools of thought. One was started by the Venetians who, once pepper was being transported on their ships and sold in the Rialto markets, began to adopt it in their cooking; then its use spread throughout the Veneto region. The Genoese, who also traded in Oriental spices, remained faithful to their traditional local herbs, and added only hot chili pepper, which was and still is the only real major Italian spice. Hot chili peppers, known as *diavolillo*, may be used in cooking either fresh, dried or ground.

Nothing remains in today's Italian gastronomy of the elaborate cuisine of those times. So, whenever spices are mentioned, an Italian will immediately think of chilies, found everywhere in the center and the south, and much favored for their beneficial properties.

Other spices associated with Italian cooking include nutmeg, cloves, white and black pepper and cinnamon.

1. & 3. fresh red pepper (diavolillo); 2. dried diavolillo; 4. ground red pepper; 5. cherry sized red peppers; 6. white peppercorns; 7. black peppercorns

From left: orto; fiori; erbe; spezie; fresco

Vinegar

An indispensable component of many salads, vinegar is most useful in the kitchen for any number of other purposes. It is used to preserve all manner of foods, from capers to mushrooms, to bake certain types of fish in the Neapolitan manner, and to touch up the flavor of sauces. It even finds a place in fruit dishes.

Wine is transformed into vinegar through fermentation caused by specific bacteria. The process occurs at a temperature between 68° and 86°F (20° and 30°C) in well-ventilated wooden vessels. Making vinegar at home is simple, as long as you have a warm place for the container. Find a 5-gallon (20 liter) keg with a tap at the bottom and a fairly wide opening in the top half (at least 4 inches/10 centimeters across) to ensure aeration. The opening should be protected from insects by very fine netting. Half-fill the keg with white or red wine with an alcohol content that is less than 12 per cent. Drop a few beechwood chips soaked in vinegar into the wine, and the bacteria required for the transformation will develop within a few weeks.

All you need to do when the quantity of vinegar needs replenishing is to add more wine carefully.

Italian vinegars include *orto*, with an onion and garlic flavor; *fiori* and *erbe* which include basil, oregano and marjoram; *spezie*, made from red or black pepper; and *fresco*, a light-tasting vinegar made from young wine.

Herbs

Much Italian cooking owes its fame to the substantial contribution of the herbs used in its dishes. Italian cuisine is based on the *soffritto*, a base of oil or butter or both (and occasionally lard or other animal fat) that sizzles gently in the pan with a few herbs or aromatic vegetables, chopped or whole (such as onion, garlic, parsley and celery) at the start of every cooking process. The various dishes are then built on this foundation with the addition of the herbs that grow wild throughout the land.

WILD HERBS
A most striking example of regional wild herbs is found in the small fruit and vegetable markets of Genoa, where the stallholders sell bunches of the famous *preboggion*. This dialect word refers to a collection of wild herbs which varies according to location and season, but basically consisting of wild beet (beetroot), sow thistle, parsley, pimpernel, dogtooth violet and borage. All the major dishes in Genoese cooking include this most refined combination of flavors and fragrances.

Because of the favorable climate, most of the herbs commonly used in cooking are found fresh, supplied by the markets in the regions where they can be cultivated or gathered wild all year round.

The following are the herbs that are most commonly used in Italian cooking:

PARSLEY
In Italy the parsley most widely used is the flat-leafed variety. Without question it is the most popular herb of all. Often it is not even mentioned in recipes because it is assumed everybody uses it. Parsley is generally used fresh, but if it must be kept it is better to put it into plastic containers or small bags and store it in the freezer, to be added at the moment of cooking when it will thaw immediately. Together with garlic, it is used in frying meats, with fish and with mushrooms, and forms the base of most pasta sauces. Chopped parsley is used to finish risottos and other dishes as they are sent to the table.

BASIL
Used especially in Genoese cuisine, basil is often grown on balconies in small pots so there will always be a supply of fresh leaves on hand. Basil can be frozen, but it loses a great deal of flavor when dried. It is the main ingredient of Genoese pesto and numerous other dishes.

There is another variety of basil in Italy with large leaves and a predominant scent of mint, but only the small-leafed Genoese variety possesses the delicate perfume that has made this herb famous. One of its main uses raw is to enhance the flavor of tomato salads. The leaves must be used whole or torn by hand, because cutting or chopping basil with a metallic instrument alters its fragrance considerably.

OREGANO
Oregano grows wild everywhere in the countryside close to the sea, and is the most popular herb that is used dried. The little plants are gathered into bunches and hung in shady, well-ventilated areas and finally shaken into a large container so that the dried leaves and seeds are collected. These keep in a jar until the following summer when the new oregano arrives. An essential ingredient of many salads, oregano also features in certain sauces for fish and in pizzas.

CHIVES
While they are grown in many parts of Italy, chives are used especially in the cuisine of Alto Adige. The slender stalks, with their delicate flavor tinged with garlic, are added raw to many soups and meat stews.

MARJORAM
Mainly used in Liguria, marjoram features in a number of fillings for pasta (ravioli, cannelloni), savory pies (*torta pasqualina*, beet pie) and meat dishes (*cima alla genovese*), and also provides a perfect finish for a *frittata* or an egg and vegetable dish, such as scrambled eggs with artichokes. The leaves are used both fresh and dried.

SAGE
Sage grows easily in Italy and is used widely in cooking, especially in the North. In many dishes dressed with melted butter, the butter is heated with a few leaves of sage. It is essential to the delicious *fagiolo all' uccelletto* of Tuscany. In Tuscany, large sage leaves are coated in a light batter and deep fried in oil.

CALAMINT
Wild mint of *nepitella* is used in Roman cooking to stuff *carciofi* (artichokes) together with bread crumbs, garlic, parsley and olive oil. It also appears in a dish of tripe, cooked in meat juices with celery, bay leaf and grated Pecorino. The mint is added right at the end of the process and counteracts the slight sweetness of the tripe. In Naples, mint leaves are used to dress fried eggplants (aubergines) and zucchini (courgettes).

ROSEMARY
Rosemary is a perennial bush that grows wild near the sea. Its name actually means "sea dew." The best use for rosemary is in roasting meat. A bird or red meat may be brushed with a sprig of rosemary dipped in olive oil. In northern and central Italy, where it is more popular than in the south, it is always present with meat and roast potatoes.

In addition to these, other herbs that are widely used include savory,

various kinds of mint, tarragon, dill, marjoram, laurel and coriander.

WILD FENNEL

The bulbous part at the base of the plant's stalk is one of Italy's most popular vegetables. As a salad additive it is thinly sliced, with lemon juice and olive oil. It is also most refreshing as an antipasto which is lightly mixed with some flakes of good Grana cheese. Sicilian salad mixes include fennel with oranges, chicory and black olives. There are many recipes for cooked fennel including *finocchi fritti* — blanched fennel, coated in egg and breadcrumbs and fried.

THYME

The best thyme or *timo* is the wild variety native to the Ligurian mountains. The other common kind, also called *serpillo* or *pepolino*, is also good and used in cooking. Thyme is used in a variety of meat and fish dishes, which goes into most marinades and is one of the essential herbs in a bouquet garni.

1. marjoram; 2. oregano;
3. thyme; 4. chives; 5. sage;
6. flat-leafed parsley;
7. laurel; 8. dried fennel;
9. basil; 10. rosemary

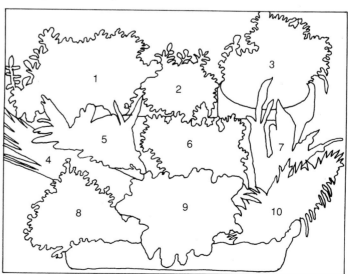

Top: Cardi Trippati alla Fiorentina; bottom: Cavolfiore Fritto

CAVOLFIORE FRITTO

FRIED CAULIFLOWER

Small cauliflower florets are included in almost all Italian mixed fried vegetable dishes. In the Marches, a region with a great vegetable tradition, cauliflower has a place in its own right as a vegetarian meal or as an accompaniment to main dishes.

⅔ cup (3 oz/90 g) all-purpose (plain) flour
salt
1 egg, beaten
1 cup (8 fl oz/250 ml) dry white wine
1 cauliflower, about 2 lb (1 kg)
olive oil, for frying
SERVES *4*

❡ Combine the flour with a little salt and add the egg and enough wine to make a soft, smooth batter. Take care that no lumps form. Cover and set aside to rest.
❡ Trim the cauliflower and put in a saucepan full of boiling salted water. Cook until tender but still al dente, drain. When cool, cut into florets.
❡ Dip the cauliflower florets into the batter and deep-fry in very hot oil. Drain on paper towels. Serve hot.

CARDI TRIPPATI ALLA FIORENTINA

FLORENTINE-STYLE CARDOONS

This rich winter meal belongs to the culinary tradition of Tuscany and is best made with cardoons that have been exposed to the first night frosts in the fields, for this helps to soften the fibers. While this dish can still be found in Tuscan homes, it is served mainly in trattorie *because of the long and complicated four-stage preparation involved.*

1 cardoon, about 1½ lb (750 g)
1 lemon, halved
1 teaspoon all-purpose (plain) flour
10 tablespoons (5 oz/155 g) butter
1 onion, thinly sliced
1 cup (8 fl oz/250 ml) meat stock, boiling
¼ cup (1 oz/30 g) grated Parmesan cheese
pinch of ground cinnamon
3 cups (12 oz/375 g) dry breadcrumbs
3 tablespoons freshly grated Parmesan cheese, mixed
  with 2 tablespoons dry breadcrumbs, for topping
SERVES *4*

❡ Clean and trim the cardoon, discarding the green leaves. Cut into 3 in (8 cm) lengths. Remove the exterior fibrous bits. Rub the pieces with half the lemon and place in a bowl of water. Squeeze the lemon half into the water.
❡ Bring a saucepan of salted water to a boil. Add the juice of the remaining half lemon. Take a ladleful of water and mix in the flour, stirring briskly to prevent lumps from forming. Add the flour mixture to the saucepan of water. Add the cardoon and cook for at least 30 minutes, until tender. Drain, remove any remaining fibrous bits and spread out on a kitchen towel to dry and cool.
❡ Melt 3 tablespoons (1½ oz/45 g) butter in a wide, shallow pan, add the onion and wilt over very low heat. Add the cardoon, lining the pieces up close together. Turn up the heat a little and pour in the stock. Cook for 15 minutes. Sprinkle on half the Parmesan and the cinnamon. Remove the cardoon from the pan.
❡ Roll the cardoon pieces in the breadcrumbs, then fry them in 5 tablespoons (2½ oz/75 g) of butter.
❡ Transfer the cardoon to a baking dish and arrange in layers. Scatter the remaining butter, in curls, and grated cheese on top. Finish with a layer of Parmesan mixed with breadcrumbs, cover the dish with foil and bake in a slow oven for about 20 minutes. Serve hot.

Garlic

GARLIC

Garlic has always occupied an important place among the flavorings used in Italian cooking.

Known since ancient times, this bulb is believed by some scholars to have originated in India, but according to the eighteenth-century botanist Linnaeus it comes from Sicily. This would make it one of the few vegetables to have originated in Italy rather than coming in via migration or sea trading. Garlic's success lies both in its gastronomic and beneficial properties, known to popular lore for centuries. It is a powerful antiseptic, capable of inhibiting the action of bacteria. Mashed garlic cloves were applied to wounds before the discovery of antibiotics, and we know that medieval doctors wore masks stuffed with garlic in times of plague. Rich in vitamins and minerals, garlic is considered excellent for the treatment of blood pressure problems. Hippocrates considered garlic to be both a laxative and a diuretic.

These beneficial properties have contributed to the widespread use of garlic in cooking, notwithstanding its smell, which not everyone finds agreeable. Though garlic is the main ingredient in only two recipes, *agliata* and the famous *spaghetti aglio e olio,* it is used in any number of dishes — almost every *soffritto,* for example (and particularly the ones used as a base for cooking fish and mushrooms), marinades and aromatic bases for stews, braises and roasts. Raw, it lifts a salad (it can be used whole to boost the flavor, and then removed, or rubbed over the base of the bowl), and features in the making of pork products. In Norcia, where the most typical Italian salamis are made, it is customary to rub the hands with garlic before mixing the meat to go into its sausage casing.

In general use, garlic cloves are cut in half lengthwise and the green piece in the center is removed. Or they may be cooked with the skin left on. There are some who prefer to scald garlic in milk before using it, while others cook it in butter rather than oil to achieve a milder result.

It is important not to burn garlic when cooking it as garlic takes on an unpleasantly strong flavor when burnt.

Fresh garlic comes to the markets in Italy in late spring, and remains throughout the summer. Gathered in braids, it will keep at home in a cool place for months. Use only perfect cloves, discarding any that are marked or soft.

MUSTARDS AND SAUCES

The most complete Italian cookbooks list no fewer than thirty typical sauces and mustards to accompany given dishes to the table. Of these only two, béchamel and mayonnaise, have been borrowed from French cuisine and one, probably, from the English. This latter is the *salsa del povr'om* of Piedmont, which is exactly like the English "poor man's sauce" (and the name is the Piedmontese dialect equivalent of the English). It is made with chopped shallots (onions in the English version), meat stock, gravy from a roast, breadcrumbs, cucumber, vinegar, parsley and pepper, all mixed together while the liquids are still boiling and served with boiled meats.

Another seasonal Piedmontese sauce is the *salsa d'uva* used with boiled or roast meats. Grape-must is put in a saucepan (this is a sauce for grape-picking time) and cooked for a long time with pears, quinces, figs, walnuts and hazelnuts. The same sauce is used in Emilia Romagna, while in Tuscany there are some home cooks and a few typical restaurants still making the very old *salsa d'agresto*, a mixture of sour grapes, walnuts, almonds, sugar, garlic, onion and parsley. This is a seasonal sauce which does not keep; it is served hot and freshly made to accompany boiled or roast meats.

From Tuscany to Sicily the popular *salsa di pomo-doro* (tomato sauce) is used on a variety of provincial dishes. But of all the Italian sauces, *salsa verde* (green sauce) is the best known outside Italy. It is a relish from northern Italy best used on *bollito misto* (boiled meat), boiled fish and hard-cooked eggs.

When boiled meats are mentioned in Italy the first thing that comes to mind is *mostarda di Cremona* which, along with *torrone*, is the gastronomic symbol of the town of Stradivari. A rich mixture of candied fruit enveloped in a sweet syrup spiced with mustard seeds, this speciality of Cremona is difficult to make at home. It is bought ready-made, the product of a couple of commercial firms or of the odd artisan pork butcher. The chief characteristic of Cremona mustard is that the fruit is left whole, and its appearance on the table never fails to impress.

In Liguria, home of the famous pesto, also worth mentioning is *agliata*, a simply prepared sauce suited to hearty appetites, which is served with boiled meat or fish. In a mortar or food processor, combine one skinned clove of garlic per person, then add olive oil (about a cupful) until you have a thick cream. Add a pinch each of salt and pepper and a roll with the crust removed, which has been soaked in vinegar and squeezed out, and mix well. This sauce is made as required and served immediately.

Pesto genovese is made with basil, olive oil, Pecorino, Parmesan and pine nuts.

Garlic is also heavily present in a famous Piedmontese sauce that is itself a main dish to be enjoyed in convivial company. This is *bagna cauda*, a winter dish traditionally made in a large terracotta dish and brought to the table over a small spirit lamp so it is kept simmering. To make *bagna cauda* you need the following ingredients: a large amount of olive oil, butter, crushed garlic cloves (at least one per diner) and anchovies chopped up and dissolved in the mixture. The dish is placed in the center of the table and diners dip raw vegetables into it.

These days *bagna cauda* is served in restaurants in little individual terracotta pans. The most common accompaniment is cardoons, and to be really good they must have had their fibers softened by the first night frosts in the fields. The same sauce, served cold, is used in Piedmont to coat bell pepper (capsicum) slices, raw or roasted in the oven, which are served with pickles and all the other numerous antipasto dishes that tradition dictates.

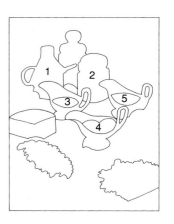

1. olive oil; 2. salsa di pomodoro; 3. salsa verde; 4. mostarda di Cremona; 5. pesto genovese

BREADS, PIZZA AND FOCACCIA

BREADS, PIZZA AND FOCACCIA

I TALIANS ARE CONSIDERED THE WORLD'S GREATEST BREAD EATERS, BUT IT WOULD BE MORE ACCURATE TO EXTEND THE CLAIM TO THE whole of the Mediterranean basin.

❡ Many of the types of bread now eaten in Italy were first made in ancient times. Among them are the large loaves that are prepared at home in certain towns in Apulia and Basilicata, and taken to the village oven to bake, each identified by a wooden stamp used by the family to imprint their initials or a rustic design on the dough. Of ancient origin, too, are the Sicilian breads enriched with saffron and sesame seeds, similar to those made in Asia Minor and along the North African Mediterranean coast. The paper-thin Sardinian *carta da musica* (music paper) and the *piadina* of Romagna are both similar to the unleavened matzoh that Jewish people eat once a year to commemorate the journey of the chosen people across the Red Sea.

❡ It is a very short step from bread to pizza, not least because no pizza can be made without using bread dough as a start.

❡ Pizza is an ancient food, born of the need to find a simple way of enriching bread to make it tastier and more substantial. The oldest example is a plain pizza the Neapolitans call *alla Mastu Nicola*, probably in honor of a pizza-maker by the name of Nicola who made it famous. The circle of dough is spread with a little pork fat and topped with slices of cheese, some salt and pepper and basil leaves.

❡ The pizza is a complete food, from the nutritional point of view, and an ideal example of dietary balance: a little flour, water, a pinch of yeast, oil, tomato and cheese, all blended perfectly together through rapid cooking. The universal success of the pizza is contained within this simple formula, and in the many transformations accomplished by simply adding or replacing one or more components. The variations are endless. Spread your ingredients over a circle of rolled-out dough, and you have a pizza. Gather the ingredients in the center of the dough and fold it in half and you have a *calzone* (or if it is smaller, a *panzerotto*), to be either baked in the oven or fried in a pan.

❡ Focaccia (meaning "cake" or "bun") is similar to pizza in that they are both flat breads topped with savory ingredients. Focaccia is usually more simply topped, perhaps with just a little olive oil, herbs, onions or olives. The Venetian variety, *fugazza*, includes egg, sugar and alcohol in the mixture.

❡ The recipes included in this chapter start from the basic instructions for making bread dough, and represent a summary of the breads that are best known and most widely consumed in Italy.

Previous pages: There are over a thousand different shapes of bread in Italy. It has also been calculated that Italians eat half a pound (250 g) of bread per person a day. Bread is served with every meal and is eaten plain, without butter. CARLO CANTINI

Opposite: It is estimated that there are approximately 35,000 bakers in Italy. There is a panetterie *in almost every street in every large city and it will usually specialize in the local favorites.* APL/OLYMPIA/LEONARDI AND VITALE

PAN DE FRIZZE

PORK-FLAVORED LOAF

This is a rare and rather curious pane condito — bread with added fat. The recipe, which is from the Friuli region, probably came into being because of the need to enrich the daily peasant diet without incurring any added expense. The traditional Friuli version of this recipe uses pork scratchings — scraps of rendered fat left over after the making of lard, which would normally be discarded. This richer version of the recipe is made with the lard or pork fat itself.

7 cups (1¾ lb/305 g) all-purpose (plain) flour
6½ oz (200 g) pork fat, ground (minced)
5 eggs, beaten
pinch of salt

SERVES 4

❡ Preheat oven to 400°F (200°C). Mound the flour on a pastry board and make a well in the center. Add the pork fat, eggs and salt. Knead vigorously for about 10 minutes until you have a soft, well-mixed dough. Shape the dough into a dome, place it on a buttered baking sheet and make small cuts all over the surface with the point of a knife. Bake in the oven for about 1 hour. When cool, serve sliced as a snack with a glass of wine, or to accompany antipasti, stewed meat or vegetable dishes.

PANINI AL ROSMARINO

ROSEMARY AND GOLDEN RAISIN ROLLS

These small flavorsome rolls are made in Tuscan family kitchens, especially in the country where it is easier to find authentic wood stoves for breadmaking. They are one of the best examples of delicious cooking with just a few very simple ingredients.

1 batch Pasta da Pane (see page 208), prepared to the
    first rising
3–4 tablespoons olive oil
1 sprig rosemary
1 tablespoon golden raisins (sultanas)

MAKES 8 SMALL ROLLS

❡ Place the dough on a lightly floured board and make a small hole in the center. Heat the oil in a

Back: Pan de Frizze; front: Panini al Rosmarino

small skillet over very low heat and add the rosemary leaves; fry gently for about 10 minutes. Strain the oil and pour it into the hole in the dough. Knead the dough with care so the oil does not spill out. When the oil has been completely absorbed, cut a cross in the top of the dough with a knife, put it into a bowl and cover it with a cloth. Set aside in a warm place to rise for at least 1 hour.

✿ Meanwhile, soften the raisins in lukewarm water. Squeeze dry.

✿ When the dough has risen, knead on the board, adding the raisins.

✿ Preheat the oven to 400°F (200°C).

✿ Divide the dough into 8 small pieces, oil your hands and shape the dough into rolls. Put them on a lightly oiled baking sheet, cut a cross into each one and set aside, covered with a cloth, to rise for 30 minutes. Bake in the oven for 10 minutes.

Top: Panzerotti alla Pugliese; bottom: Focaccia al Formaggio

PANZEROTTI ALLA PUGLIESE

APULIAN FRIED CHEESE AND TOMATO PASTRIES

Deeply rooted in the tradition of Bari, these tasty little morsels have now taken their place as a snack food and a leading light among hot antipasti dishes all over central and southern Italy. Although they share the same features as calzoni, *they are fried rather than baked in the oven, and they are eaten hot.*

9 oz (280 g) cherry tomatoes
salt
8 oz (250 g) mozzarella cheese, diced
1 batch Pasta da Pane *(see page 208), prepared through the first rising and divided into 4 pieces*
oil, for deep-frying

SERVES 4

✿ Make the tomato sauce: Scald the tomatoes in boiling water so the skins come away easily, then push them through a strainer over a small saucepan. Add a pinch of salt and cook over moderate heat for 10 minutes.

✿ Roll out each piece of dough to form three 4 in (10 cm) circles. In the center of each, spread a little of the tomato sauce and a few pieces of mozzarella. Sprinkle with salt, fold the dough over and press the edges together to seal.

✿ Deep-fry the pastries in plenty of very hot oil for 10 minutes or until golden, drain on paper towels and serve piping hot.

FOCACCIA AL FORMAGGIO

CHEESE FOCACCIA

This Ligurian speciality is the pride of the little town of Recco, between Genoa and Portofino. It is relatively recent in origin, the creation of a tavern owner in the late nineteenth century who was looking for a snack to offer her customers that would stimulate their thirst. It was certainly a success as all the bakers in Recco make this focaccia each day and it is served in restaurants as a hot antipasto.

9½ oz (300 g) whole wheat (wholemeal) flour
salt
1 lb (500 g) Stracchino, or other soft melting cheese, cubed
½ cup (4 fl oz/125 ml) lukewarm water

SERVES 4

✿ Preheat the oven to 400°F (200°C). Work the flour with lukewarm water, adding a little more water if necessary, and a pinch of salt. Knead until smooth and dense. Divide in half. Roll out the pieces to form 2 circles, one about 1 in (2.5 cm) bigger than the baking pan you plan to use. The baking pan should be no more than ¾ in (2 cm) deep and 12–16 in (30–40 cm) in diameter.

✿ Oil the pan and line the base and sides with the larger circle of dough. Distribute the cheese over it. Cover with the second circle of dough, pressing the edges together with your fingers to seal. Bake in the oven for about 20 minutes, or until the surface of the focaccia is a uniform golden brown.

PASTA DA PANE

BASIC RECIPE FOR YEAST DOUGH

However simple it may seem, the making of yeast dough requires patience, skill and experience. Many cooks in Italy prefer to buy it ready prepared from the baker. Using this recipe, however, you can try it with a good chance of success. It provides the base for baking not only homemade bread but also pizza and a whole series of savory pies with a variety of fillings that belong to the classic Italian gastronomic tradition. Much depends on your oven, however, and to achieve a good result it must be heated to a high temperature — in the case of a domestic oven not less than 500°F (260°C).

Another basic recommendation as far as pizza is concerned is that it must on no account be put into a pie plate or pan, but is simply laid on a capacious baking sheet in order to reproduce as closely as possible the conditions of the big wood ovens in the pizzerie of Naples. As they say in Naples, "the pizza must be born on the marble bench naked as Venus, amid the clouds of flour created by the kneader, and must slither dry and intact from the baker's shovel to bake in the soft blazing heat of the brick oven." This, of course, is the classic pizza. But it should also be said that along the Sorrento peninsula in particular, as well as in Naples, the art of the so-called "pizza by the yard" made in long, narrow baking pans has emerged.

This is the basic recipe for bread dough. This quantity yields 14 oz (440 g).

½ oz (15 g) dried or 1 oz (30 g) fresh yeast
2⅔ cups (9½ oz/300 g) all-purpose (plain) flour
pinch of salt
3 tablespoons lukewarm water

MAKES 6 ROLLS OR PIZZAS

❡ In a cup, soak the yeast with the water — no hotter than 86°F (30°C) or the yeast will die. Add about ½ cup (2 oz/60 g) of the flour, knead rapidly and shape the dough into a ball. Put it into a floured bowl, cover with a kitchen towel and set aside in a warm place to rise until doubled in volume.

❡ Punch down the dough and work in the remaining flour and a pinch of salt, adding just enough lukewarm water until all the flour is absorbed and the dough is smooth and elastic. (Be sure to work away from drafts and air conditioning.) The formation of tiny bubbles on the surface is a sign that the dough is ready.

❡ Put the dough on a floured plate, cut a cross in the top with a knife, and cover with a cloth. Set aside in a warm place for about 2 hours until doubled in volume.

❡ To make rolls: Preheat the oven to 500°F (260°C). Divide the dough into 6 pieces and shape each into a round or elongated roll. Make a cross in the top with the point of a small knife. Set aside, covered, to rise once more. Place on a lightly oiled baking sheet and bake in the oven for about 20 minutes.

❡ To make pizzas: Divide the dough into 6 pieces. Smooth each piece of dough like a skilled pizza-maker does, stretching the dough with the fingers or rolling it out on a floured board. Using the ingredients given in the recipes that follow, it is also possible to make little 2 in (5 cm) pizzas for serving hot with drinks.

PIZZA BIANCA

PLAIN PIZZA

This is the forerunner of all pizzas. In Naples it is also called pizza alla Mastu Nicola (pizza in the style of Maestro Nicola), which suggests that it was first made by a pizzaiolo of that name. In any event it is the oldest known pizza, made with basic ingredients such as lard (much favored in Neapolitan cuisine in the nineteenth century and earlier), Pecorino cheese and basil. The fact that no tomato is used means that the recipe may well predate the arrival of the tomato in Europe.

1 batch Pasta da Pane *(see recipe this page)*,
   divided into 4 pieces
3 tablespoons (1½ oz/45 g) lard
¾ cup (3 oz/90 g) grated Pecorino cheese
4 bunches fresh basil, washed and dried

SERVES 4

❡ Roll out each piece of dough into a 12 in (30 cm) circle. Spread with a little of the lard, cover each pizza with one-quarter of the grated cheese and scatter 1 bunch of basil leaves on top. Place on a lightly oiled baking sheet and bake in a preheated 500°F (260°C) oven for about 20 minutes.

PIZZA MARGHERITA

QUEEN MARGARET'S PIZZA

This is the simplest and best known of all Neapolitan pizzas. Unlike its peers, created at some unspecified time in the dim distant past, the Margherita has a known

Top: Pizza Bianca; bottom: Pizza Margherita

date of birth — 9 June 1889. On that day King Umberto and Queen Margherita of Italy, holidaying in the Royal Palace at Capodimonte, decided they would like to taste the pizza they had been hearing about. As the royal cooks did not know how to make it, the most famous of the town's pizzaioli was called in, Don Raffaele Esposito, who owned a pizzeria in the center of via Chiaia. In honor of the queen he made a pizza using mozzarella, tomato and basil to represent the white, red and green of the Italian flag.

1 batch Pasta da Pane (see page 208), divided into 4 pieces
1 cup (8 oz/250 g) peeled, seeded and chopped or puréed tomatoes
8 oz (250 g) mozzarella cheese, thinly sliced
4 bunches fresh basil, washed and dried
salt
2 tablespoons olive oil

SERVES 4

§ Preheat the oven to 500°F (260°C). Roll out each piece of dough into a 12 in (30 cm) circle. Place them on a lightly oiled baking sheet (with a true pizza oven they are put in using the special wooden baker's "peel" and cooked directly on the brick floor of the oven). Cover with the tomato pulp, leaving a ½ in (1 cm) border around the edges. Arrange very thin slices of mozzarella on top and scatter on whole basil leaves. Sprinkle with a pinch of salt and drizzle with olive oil.
§ Bake for about 20 minutes, until browned but soft. Take care that the crusts do not burn.

Left: Pizza Napoletana; right: Pizza Marinara

PIZZA NAPOLETANA

NEAPOLITAN PIZZA

This is the same as the pizza Margherita, with one extra ingredient — anchovies — and oregano instead of basil. This one too is one of the most common and most famous pizzas. It can be made as one large pizza or four smaller pizzas.

1 batch Pasta da Pane (see page 208)
1 cup (8 oz/250 g) tomato pulp, puréed
2 mozzarella cheeses (each 4 oz/125 g), thinly sliced
8 anchovy fillets in oil
4 teaspoons oregano
2 tablespoons olive oil

SERVES 4

❡ Preheat the oven to 500°F (260°C). Roll out the dough into a large circle. Cover with the tomato pulp and arrange the thinly sliced mozzarella and the anchovies, whole or cut into small pieces, on top. Sprinkle with oregano and olive oil.
❡ Place on a lightly oiled baking sheet and bake in the oven for about 20 minutes.

PIZZA MARINARA

NEAPOLITAN MARINARA PIZZA

This famous and rather curious pizza is one of the family of classic Neapolitan pizzas. In spite of its name, it actually has nothing in it that comes from the sea. The ingredients are exclusively those of peasant cuisine.

1 batch Pasta da Pane (see page 208), divided
    into 4 pieces (optional)
1 cup (8 oz/250 g) tomato pulp, puréed
4 garlic cloves, thinly sliced
4 teaspoons oregano
2 tablespoons olive oil
salt

SERVES 4

❡ Preheat the oven to 500°F (260°C). Roll out each piece of dough into a 12 in (30 cm) circle. Spread some of the tomato on each and top with 1 thinly sliced garlic clove. Scatter the oregano and salt over and add a generous sprinkling of olive oil. Place on a lightly oiled baking sheet and bake in the oven for at least 20 minutes.

CALZONI AL PROSCIUTTO

HAM-FILLED ROLLED PIZZAS

The calzone derives directly from the pizza, being in fact a circle of pizza dough folded in two to enclose a filling. It is another example of a simple and complete food that is offered in every pizzeria.

6½ oz (200 g) ricotta, pushed through a strainer
6½ oz (200 g) mozzarella cheese, diced
3½ oz (100 g) cooked ham
1 cup (4 oz/125 g) grated Parmesan cheese
4 sprigs flat-leafed parsley
2 eggs
salt
1 batch Pasta da Pane (see page 208),
    divided into 4 equal pieces
2 tablespoons olive oil

SERVES 4

℘ In a bowl, combine the ricotta, mozzarella, ham, Parmesan and parsley. Beat 1 egg lightly with a fork; add to the cheese mixture with salt to taste.
℘ Preheat the oven to 500°F (260°C). Roll out each piece of dough into a 12 in (30 cm) circle. Brush the surface of each with half the oil. Spoon one-quarter of the prepared filling in the center. Brush the edges of the dough with the remaining beaten egg. Fold each circle in half over the filling, pressing the edges to seal well. Brush the surface of the dough with the remaining oil. Set on an oiled baking sheet. Bake in the oven for at least 20 minutes.

CALZONE ALLE CIPOLLE

ONION-FILLED PIZZA PIE

Found in Apulia, this calzone differs in shape from the classic Neapolitan one, being in fact a filled pie (very large ones are made in some restaurants) rather than a circle of pizza dough folded in two.

For the dough:
¾ oz (20 g) dried or 1½ oz (45 g) fresh yeast
1 cup (8 fl oz/250 ml) lukewarm water
3¼ cups (13 oz/410 g) all-purpose (plain) flour
2 tablespoons olive oil
For the filling:
1 lb (500 g) onions, sliced
⅔ cup (5 fl oz/ 155 ml) olive oil
12 little tomatoes, coarsely chopped
6½ oz (200 g) black olives, pitted

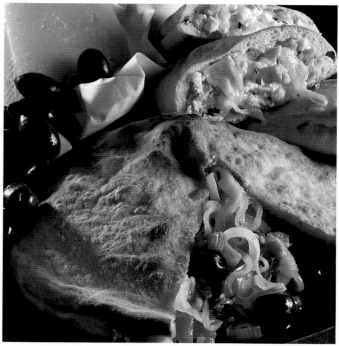

Top: Calzoni al Prosciutto; bottom: Calzone alle Cipolle

⅓ cup (1½ oz/45 g) capers
3 anchovy fillets, chopped
1 sprig flat-leafed parsley, chopped
salt
¾ cup (3 oz/90 g) grated Pecorino cheese

SERVES 4

℘ If you prefer not to make the dough you can use a yeast dough purchased from your local bakery. Otherwise, mix the yeast with the lukewarm water. Set aside to foam. Heap the flour in a mound on a pastry board and make a well in the center. When the yeast is foamy, add it to the flour along with the olive oil. Knead, adding sufficient lukewarm water to make a smooth, soft dough.
℘ Divide the dough in half. Roll out one half into a sheet and line an oiled 14 in (35 cm) pie dish with it. Cover with a cloth and set aside to rest for 30 minutes. Cover the other piece of dough and set aside to rise. Meanwhile, in a wide shallow pan, sauté the onions in half the oil until soft but not colored. Add the tomatoes and the olives and fry gently for a few minutes to blend the flavors. Add the capers, anchovies and parsley. Mix well and season with salt. Cook for about 10 minutes. Set aside to cool to lukewarm.
℘ Preheat the oven to 475°F (250°C). Stir the cheese into the onion mixture. Fill the pie shell with this mixture. Roll out the second sheet of dough. Cover the filling with it and seal the edges well. Brush the top crust with the remaining olive oil and bake in the oven for 30 minutes. Serve hot.

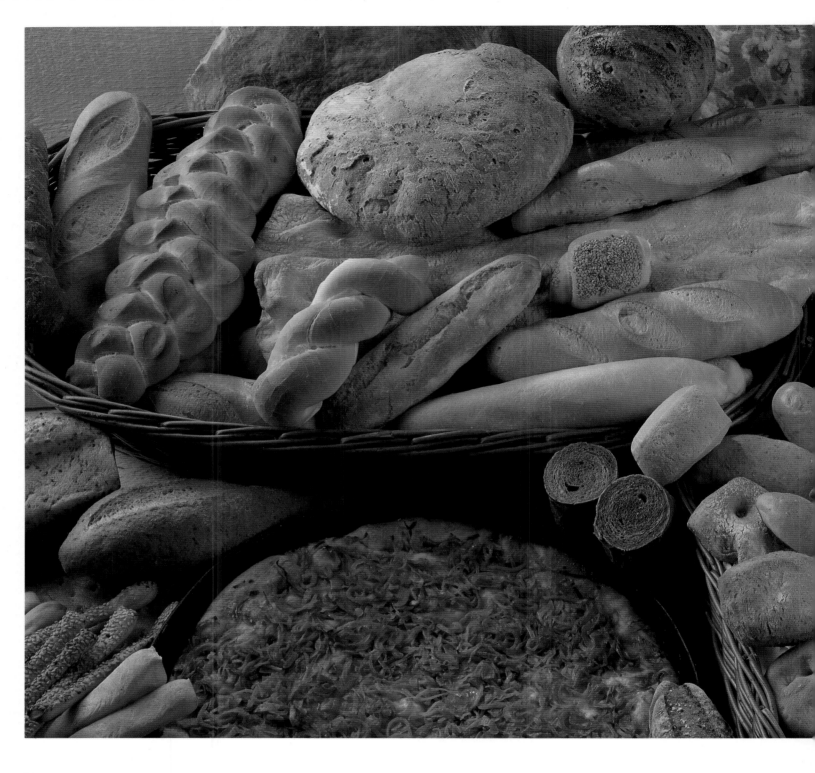

BREADS

In modern times, and
with more refined
techniques of bread-
making, bread has
changed to the point
where we now have
areas of consumption
characterized by different
types and shapes of
bread. In the north, the
traditional Milanese
rosetta and the *biova* of
Piedmont are made using

forced fermentation and
are often just an air
bubble enclosed within a
thin, tasty crust. Larger
loaves are produced in
central Italy and in the
south, for eating in slices.

The most typical
Italian breads today,
apart from the *rosetta*
and the *biova* already
mentioned, are the long
bastone or *filone* of Liguria,

distant relatives of the
famous French *baguette*;
a loaf from Ferrara
consisting of two circles
of dough made with oil
which are rolled up and
knotted together to form
a sort of elongated cross;
the Roman *ciriola*, similar
to the *rosetta*, and the
large homemade loaves,
pani casarecci, which are
made for slicing and

eating over several days.
All Italian bread has
salt added, with the
exception of the Tuscan
loaf, which has none at
all. Tradition has it that
as a protest against an
exorbitant tax imposed
on salt by the Papal tax
collectors, Tuscany's
bakers decided to make
bread that was totally
without flavor. This is

symbols of good luck or good wishes. Even today, in regions with rich cultural traditions, many ritual breads survive, made in special shapes according to a symbolism that has its roots in local custom or popular superstition. In Sicily a loaf in the shape of a woman with three breasts is a symbol of prosperity. In Sardinia there is more or less a bread for every town or village celebrating its patron saint, and a bread museum has been set up at the University of Cagliari.

It is customary to have a special form of bread made for a wedding, christening or other family celebration, and on these occasions the baker's imagination makes use of ingenious figures, flowers or rustic symbols to interpret not only the significance of the celebration but also the status of the family or guests of honor.

Also belonging to the bread family, but having a history of their own, are the Torinese *grissini*, slender crunchy breadsticks which, according to legend, were created in the seventeenth century on the prescription of a doctor who is supposed to have suggested to a baker that he make some very thin, crisp bread to feed a young Savoy duke who was ill. The name comes from the dialect term *ghersa*, meaning elongated bread. Commercial machine-made grissini have now spread throughout the world, all of them identical, but the true Torinese *grissino*

supposed to be one reason why all the things that traditionally go with bread in the region, from *prosciutto* and salami to Pecorino cheese, are decidedly saltier in Tuscany than anywhere else in Italy.

Over the ages, certain types of bread have been invested with celebratory significance or used as

(which is also made elsewhere by craftsmen) is the one called *rubata*, a dialect name meaning "rolled," which conveys the action of the baker who rolls out the pieces of dough by hand on his floured table, until they are like pencils, sometimes over 18 inches (45 centimeters) long.

Making an attractive display alongside the traditional shapes are some modern varieties with a range of added ingredients. There is walnut bread, olive bread, raisin bread, pine nut bread, onion bread, and breads made with white or whole wheat (wholemeal) flours which may be mixed with exotic flours or other ingredients.

In the best restaurants bread is baked twice a day just before it is to be served, with some serving a different type of bread with each course.

Focaccia is like a thick pizza but its texture is more like bread. It can be savory (topped with herbs or olive oil, or stuffed with ingredients such as cheese, tomatoes or salt cod), or it can be sweet.

Of course pizza is one of the most famous of Italian foods. Early versions of pizza were just dough drizzled with olive oil, herbs or perhaps honey. The pizza was undoubtedly born in Naples and it achieved its immense popularity when it was topped with two of the region's best products — tomatoes and mozzarella.

1. Milanese plaited treccia;
2. ciabatta; 3. Tuscan homemade loaf; 4. cumin bread; 5. bread with almonds;
6. long white bread loaves;
7. Genoese focaccia;
8. Sardinian bread; 9. cereal bread; 10. bread with fennel seeds; 11. rye bread;
12. Apulian durum-wheat bread; 13. French bread;
14. milk roll; 15. mattonella;
16. montasù; 17. biova from Piedmont; 18. Milanese michetta; 19. durum wheat roll with olive oil; 20. roll with olive oil; 21. grissini with cumin seeds; 22. plain grissini; 23. pizza topped with onion

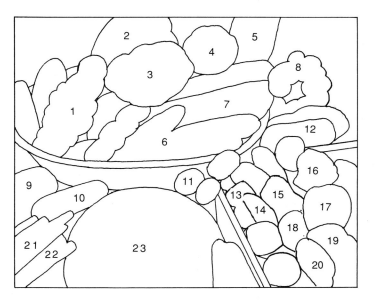

PIZZA QUATTRO STAGIONI ALLA NAPOLETANA

NEAPOLITAN FOUR SEASONS PIZZA

Here is a pizza for the lean times, when there are no fresh ingredients available and the cook turns to whatever the pantry might offer in the way of preserves. Thus we have olives, artichokes in oil, the small tomatoes that are traditionally hung in cellars or the shady corners of courtyards once summer is over, and anchovies preserved with salt. Only the mozzarella is fresh.

1 batch Pasta da Pane *(see page 208)*
3½ oz (105 g) green olives in brine, washed, pitted and sliced
3½ oz (105 g) small artichokes in oil, thinly sliced
⅔ cup (6 oz/185 g) tomato pulp, puréed
6 anchovy fillets, halved
8 oz (250 g) mozzarella cheese, thinly sliced
2 tablespoons olive oil
salt

SERVES 4

❡ Preheat the oven to 500°F (260°C). Roll out the dough into a large circle. Divide it into 4 sections by marking a cross with the point of a knife, but do not cut through. Scatter the olives in a thick layer over one of the sections of the pizza. Arrange the artichokes over the second section. Cover the other 2 sections with the tomato pulp. On one of them, layer the mozzarella and on the other scatter the anchovies. Scatter salt over all but the anchovy sections. Sprinkle with the oil and place on a lightly oiled baking sheet. Bake for approximately 20 minutes.

PIZZA ALL'ANDREA

THE ADMIRAL'S PIZZA

A richer version of the classic Genoese focaccia, this pizza also goes under the name of sardenaira, *and on the French coast in the vicinity of Nice it is called* pissaladière. *The name* pizza all'Andrea *is supposed to have come from the special fondness that the Genoese Admiral Andrea Doria is said to have shown for it. It is typical of western Liguria, and in particular of the Tyrrhenian coastal strip from Imperia to the border at Ventimiglia.*

For the dough:
4⅓ cups (1 lb/500 g) all-purpose (plain) flour
2 tablespoons (1 oz/30 g) dried or 4 tablespoons (2 oz/60 g) fresh yeast

6 tablespoons lukewarm milk
olive oil
salt
For the filling:
2 onions, thinly sliced
⅓ cup (3 fl oz/90 ml) olive oil
1 sprig fresh basil
2¼ lb (1 kg) fresh tomatoes, peeled, seeded and coarsely chopped
16 anchovy fillets preserved in salt, minced
4 garlic cloves
2 oz (60 g) black olives in brine, drained and pitted

SERVES 4

❡ Soak the yeast in the lukewarm milk — no hotter than 86°F (30°C) or the yeast will die. Add half the flour, knead rapidly and shape the dough into a ball, slowly adding the oil as you knead. Put it into a floured bowl, cover with a cloth and set aside in a warm place to rise until it has doubled in volume.

❡ Punch down the dough and work in the remaining flour and oil and the salt. Knead until all the flour is absorbed and the dough is smooth and elastic and tiny bubbles form on the surface.

❡ Put the dough on a floured plate, cut a cross in the top with a knife and cover with a cloth. Set aside in a warm place, for about 2 hours, until doubled in volume.

❡ In a wide, shallow pan, combine the onions with ⅓ cup (3 fl oz/90 ml) of the olive oil. Sauté until the onions begin to color. Add the basil leaves and tomatoes. Cook over moderate heat until a fairly thick sauce forms. Stir in the anchovies until they dissolve. Remove from heat.

❡ Preheat the oven to 400°F (200°C). Oil a large round or rectangular shallow baking dish about 14 in (35 cm) in diameter. Roll out the dough about ⅜ in (1 cm) thick. Lay the dough in the dish. Pour the tomato and anchovy sauce over the dough and push the garlic cloves and black olives into the dough. Bake for at least 40 minutes.

THE GENOESE FOCACCIA

The famous Genoese focaccia can be made at home using the dough described for pizza all'Andrea. Once the dough is rolled out and spread in the baking dish, it must be pinched with the fingertips to make little uneven dimples all over it, then scattered with kosher (coarse) cooking salt and sprinkled generously with the best quality olive oil. It is baked for 30 minutes or more in a preheated 475°F (250°C) oven, watching to make sure a golden brown crust is formed.

Top: Pizza Quattro Stagioni alla Napoletana; left: Pizza all'Andrea; bottom: Pizza Quattro Stagioni

PIZZA QUATTRO STAGIONI

FOUR SEASONS PIZZA

All over the world pizzas are made under this name, with the most varied ingredients imaginable. The best-known version is a pizza divided into four sections, each containing an ingredient that is related to one of the four seasons (tomato for summer, mushrooms for autumn, and so on), but there is no precise rule. This is the recipe most commonly used.

1 lb (500 g) mussels
1 batch Pasta da Pane *(see page 208)*
6½ oz (200 g) cultivated mushrooms, very thinly sliced
3½ oz (105 g) cooked ham, diced
¾ cup (6 oz/185 g) tomato pulp, puréed
8 oz (250 g) mozzarella cheese, thinly sliced
salt
2 tablespoons olive oil
pepper

SERVES *4*

❡ Scrub the mussel shells thoroughly, then wash them several times under running water. Heat the mussels in a large skillet until they open. Take the mussels out of the shells and reserve.

❡ Preheat the oven to 500°F (260°C).

❡ Roll out the dough to form a large circle. Divide the circle into 4 sections by marking a cross with the point of a knife, but do not cut through the dough.

❡ Cover one quarter with the mushrooms, another with the diced ham, the third with a little of the tomato pulp and the slices of mozzarella, and the fourth with tomato alone. Scatter salt over, and sprinkle generously with olive oil. Add a grinding of pepper if desired.

❡ Place on a lightly oiled baking sheet and bake in the oven for 10 minutes.

❡ Add the mussels to the last section — the one simply covered with tomato — and bake for a further 10 minutes.

TORTA VERDE

SPINACH PIE

In the southern part of Piedmont where this pie originated, it is made at home as a first course, and also plays an important role in the Easter Day meal. Given its proximity and the considerable exchange of experiences between the two areas, this torta verde has also become a classic of the cuisine of western Liguria between Imperia and the border at Ventimiglia, with a few variations. Whereas in Piedmont the basic ingredient is spinach along with the rice, in Liguria beet (beetroot) greens are used, and the animal fats (butter and salt pork) are replaced by olive oil. Also, the Piedmontese bake this pie without a crust, while the Ligurians place it between two thin layers of yeast dough.

¼ cup (2 fl oz/60 ml) olive oil
6 tablespoons (3 oz/90 g) butter
1 onion, finely chopped
3 tablespoons pork fat, chopped
1 garlic clove, chopped
2 lb (1 kg) spinach (English spinach), coarsely chopped
salt
1 cup (5 oz/155 g) rice
4 cups (1 qt/1 l) light beef stock, boiling
4 eggs, beaten
⅓ cup (1½ oz/45 g) freshly grated Parmesan cheese
2 tablespoons dried breadcrumbs

SERVES 4–6

❦ In a flameproof earthenware casserole, heat 3 tablespoons of the olive oil and half the butter. Add the onion and fry gently until it begins to color. Stir in the pork fat and garlic. Add the spinach and salt to taste. Cover the casserole and cook on low heat for about 15 minutes.
❦ Add the rice and cook for 10 minutes, adding a ladleful of stock from time to time. Remove the casserole from the heat and spread the contents out on a platter to cool quickly. Make sure that the mixture is fairly fluid.
❦ As soon as the rice and spinach are cool, transfer them to a bowl and add the eggs, Parmesan and a little more salt, if necessary. Mix.
❦ Preheat the oven to 350°F (180°C). Grease a rectangular or round 12 in (30 cm) baking dish with some of the oil and butter and sprinkle evenly with some of the breadcrumbs. Add the filling and even the top with the back of a spoon. Scatter the remaining breadcrumbs, oil and butter on top. Bake in the oven for 1 hour.
❦ Let the pie cool to lukewarm on a rack. Unmold the pie and serve.

ERBAZZONE

SPINACH AND CHEESE PIE

This is a typical dish from the Reggio Emilia area that has been adopted by neighboring Modena, with a few variations added. It is a vegetable pie that uses lard in the dough. This is linked to the tradition of Emilia, which has many large pig farms and hence is a major user of pork fat in all its forms.

For the filling:
3 lb (1.5 kg) beet (beetroot) leaves or spinach (English spinach)
salt
6½ oz (200 g) pancetta, chopped
2 garlic cloves, chopped
1 sprig flat-leafed parsley, chopped
6 large onions, finely chopped
¾ cup (3 oz/90 g) freshly grated Parmesan cheese
For the dough:
3¼ cups (13 oz/410 g) all-purpose (plain) flour
salt
5 tablespoons (2½ oz/75 g) lard

SERVES 6

❦ Wash the beet greens (with the central ribs removed) or spinach thoroughly. In a saucepan combine the greens with only the water that clings to them and a pinch of salt. Cook for about 20 minutes until tender. Drain and squeeze well; chop roughly.
❦ Chop the *pancetta*, garlic and parsley together. Reserve 1 tablespoon of the mixture and place the rest in a skillet with the onions. Cook until the mixture begins to turn golden. Turn off the heat, add the spinach, cheese and a pinch of salt, stirring until all of the ingredients are well mixed.
❦ Knead the flour with a pinch of salt and 4 tablespoons of the lard, adding lukewarm water until the dough is soft but firm and can be easily molded. Divide the dough in half. Roll out one half to about 13 in (33 cm).
❦ Preheat the oven to 400°F (200°C).
❦ With the remaining lard, grease the base and sides of a 12 in (30 cm) baking dish. Line it with the dough, leaving the excess dough to hang over the edge. Spread the filling over the pastry. Roll out the second piece of dough so that it is a slightly smaller size than the dish and cover the filling with it. Seal the pie by folding the overhanging edges of dough in towards the center. Sprinkle the surface with the reserved *pancetta*, garlic and parsley. Bake in the oven for 30 minutes. Serve hot or warm as a first course.

Top: Torta Verde; bottom: Erbazzone

TORTA DI PASQUA

EASTER BREAD

Unlike the Ligurian pasqualina *and other similar dishes, this one from Umbria is not a true filled pie but rather a kind of bread enriched with eggs and cheeses. At home it is made like a normal cake, but the bakers of Perugia present it in the form of a cylinder, as tall as the Milanese* panettone. *It is eaten hot or cold, accompanied by salami and hard-cooked eggs.*

5 eggs
salt
³/4 cup (3 oz/90 g) fresh Pecorino cheese, diced
³/4 cup (3 oz/90 g) freshly grated Parmesan cheese
¹/3 cup (3 fl oz/90 ml) olive oil
8 oz (250 g) Pasta da Pane, prepared to the first
  rising (see page 208)
1¹/4 cups (5 oz/155 g) all-purpose (plain) flour
lard

SERVES 6

❡ Break 3 whole eggs and 2 egg yolks into a bowl and add a pinch of salt, the Pecorino and Parmesan. Mix well and stir while adding the oil in a thin stream. Set aside to rest for 3 to 4 hours.
❡ Flour a pastry board and put the dough on it. Add the flour and knead until fully incorporated. Make a cavity in the center of the dough and put the egg and cheese mixture into it. Knead again, until the mixture is fully absorbed. Cover the dough with a cloth and set aside to rise for 2 hours in a warm place away from drafts.
❡ Preheat the oven to 350°F (180°C). Using lard, grease a cake pan 10 in (25 cm) in diameter, with 6 in (15 cm) high sides. Place the dough in the pan, cover it with a cloth and set aside to rise for 1 hour.
❡ Bake in the oven for 30 minutes, or until the bread becomes a lovely brown color.

TORTA PASQUALINA

SAVORY EASTER PIE

Certainly the most famous of the savory pies in Italian cuisine, this one takes its name from the Easter celebration because it is made mainly for this occasion. This is also the reason why the classic recipe requires the filling to be enclosed in 33 wafer-thin sheets of pastry: Christ was 33 years old when he ascended the cross. Nowadays however, even in the most strictly religious families the number is reduced to 18. Very complicated and time-consuming to make, it is superbly done in the characteristic little fried-food shops of the narrow streets surrounding the port in Genoa, its birthplace, as well as in all the Ligurian rosticcerie. *Usually made with a filling of beet (beetroot) leaves, during the month of February the beet is replaced by the superb artichokes grown in the Albenga area of western Liguria.*

9¹/2 cups (2¹/4 lb/1.1 kg) all-purpose (plain) flour
salt
³/4 cup (6¹/2 fl oz/200 ml) olive oil (1 cup/8 fl oz/250 ml
  if artichokes used)
2 lb (1 kg) beet (beetroot) greens, or 12 artichokes
¹/3 cup (1¹/2 oz/45 g) freshly grated Parmesan cheese
2 sprigs marjoram (if beet greens used)
1 onion, chopped (if artichokes used)
juice of ¹/2 lemon (if artichokes used)
2 bread rolls, crusts removed
1 cup (8 fl oz/250 ml) milk
10 eggs
1¹/4 lb (625 g) ricotta cheese
7 tablespoons (3¹/2 oz/105 g) butter

SERVES 6–8

❡ Heap 8²/3 cups (2 lb/1 kg) flour on a board and make a well in the center. Add ¹/2 teaspoon salt and ¹/4 cup (2 fl oz/60 ml) of the oil, and work into a smooth soft dough, adding water (about 1 cup/8 fl oz/250 ml) as required. Knead vigorously for 10 minutes.
❡ Divide the dough into 18 pieces, cover with a damp cloth and set aside on a floured board for at least 1 hour.
❡ Meanwhile, wash and trim the beet greens, discarding the ribs. Drain well, roll up tightly and cut into thin strips. Put into a pan with only the water remaining on the leaves after washing, and cook on low heat with a pinch of salt for 15 to 20 minutes, until tender. Drain and squeeze well; spread out on a plate. Sprinkle with a little Parmesan, salt to taste, and the marjoram leaves. (If you are using artichokes instead of the beet greens: Cut off the spiky tips and remove the tough outer leaves. Very thinly slice the artichokes and put them into a wide, shallow pan with 3 tablespoons oil, onion, the lemon juice and a pinch of salt. Cook for 10 minutes.)
❡ Soften the bread rolls in the milk. In a bowl, beat 4 of the eggs with 3 tablespoons Parmesan. Squeeze out the bread and add to the eggs and cheese, mix thoroughly. Add the beet greens (or artichokes). Stir in the ricotta.
❡ One at a time, take the pieces of dough and roll out thin. This is a very delicate operation, because

Left: Torta di Pasqua; right: Torta Pasqualina

the dough must then be made even thinner by holding it on the back of one hand while gently pulling the edges with the other.

❡ Grease a 12 in (30 cm) high-sided pie dish with 1 tablespoon of oil. Lay the first sheet of pasta on the bottom so that it lines the base and hangs over the side of the dish. Brush the dough with oil. Roll out the other pieces of dough in the same manner and lay 10 of the sheets on top of one another, oiling all except the last one (use 2 tablespoons of oil for this). Add the filling and drizzle 3 tablespoons oil over it. Make 6 hollows in the filling with a spoon. Put about 1 tablespoon of butter in each hollow and crack an egg into each. Sprinkle each of the eggs with the

remaining Parmesan and salt.

❡ Preheat the oven to 400°F (200°C). Roll out the remaining 8 pieces of dough and cover the pie with these, brushing the sheets with oil as before (using 1 tablespoon) and dotting the overlapping edges of each one with the remaining butter. Each sheet of dough must overlap the sides of the dish by about ⅜ in (1 cm). Cut off any excess. Gather up the edges of the dough with your fingers and fold them in toward the center, pressing gently. Brush the surface of the pie with 2 tablespoons oil and prick with a fork. Bake in the oven for about 45 minutes.

❡ This pie is served lukewarm, or even cold.

DESSERTS, CAKES AND BISCUITS

DESSERTS, CAKES AND BISCUITS

ASIMPLE RECIPE FOR AN ATHENIAN DESSERT HANDED DOWN TO POSTERITY BY THE STOIC PHILOSOPHER CHRYSIPPUS AROUND 250 BC goes like this: "Take some walnuts, almonds and toasted poppyseeds and pound them together, bind them with honey and a pinch of pepper, and place the mixture between two wafers." The basic idea is the forerunner of some varieties of dense cake still widely made in Italy, such as the Siennese *panforte* and the *spongata* of Sarzana.

❧ Italy's sweet tradition should be viewed first and foremost through the filter of its two main historic phases: the age of honey, which ran from antiquity to the Renaissance, and the modern age of sugar. Belonging to the former we have, for example, the hot fritters stuffed with fresh cheese and coated in honey known as *sebadas*, which conclude every major lunch or dinner in Sardinia. Just as ancient are the Apulian *cartellate*, ribbons of pastry made into spirals and served with honey, especially at the end of Christmas lunch.

❧ The arrival of cane sugar in ever-increasing quantities, initially from Asia and later from America, gave the cook what the Crusaders called "sweet salt." Hence the birth of modern pastrymaking, first in Italy, thanks to the Arabs, and later emerging in the northern regions under the influence of the French, Swiss and Middle European schools.

❧ In the south, almonds are processed to a paste which is then transformed under the fingertips of the pastrycook into those extraordinary sweet creations, veritable gastronomic *trompes l'oeil*, that reproduce pieces of fruit in unbelievably true colors. Alongside them the Sicilian table presents sensational cakes, layers of sponge coated in colored icings and decorated in oriental splendor with marzipan, ricotta, cherries and candied citron and orange peel.

❧ From Turin, French ways of baking spread quickly throughout the rest of Italy, especially the French art of making *mignon* cakes and *cannoli*, sweet fritters, little morsels that could be gracefully eaten in a single mouthful.

❧ In the midst of these schools of pastrycooking, the tradition of homebaked cakes took shape as an attempt to enrich the daily bread with sweet ingredients. Initially honey was added, and later sugar, after the process of refining the sugar beet had brought it within reach of everyone's purse, plus dried raisins, fruit, walnuts, hazelnuts and whatever else could be found in country larders. This is how the rich yeast cakes came into being. Then with experience, the sweet tart with a covering of sliced fruit or jam emerged, while the *biscotto*, a typical Italian sweet, of which almost every region has its special version, was moved from its place as dessert to breakfast or children's afternoon tea.

Previous pages: A pasticceria *(pastry shop) in Florence.* Pasticcerie *are always open on Sundays when families traditionally buy their* torta *(cake) for the Sunday lunch.* JOHN CALLANAN

Opposite: Little cakes called dolcetti *are popular throughout Italy and each region has its specialties. However, Sicily has the widest and most tempting array.* APL/OLYMPIA/WALTER LEONARDI

CALZONCELLI AI CECI

SWEET CHICKPEA PASTRIES

Chickpeas (or garbanzo beans as they are sometimes called) feature prominently in Mediterranean cuisine. However, they are considered to be rather a lowly ingredient. Due to the fact that they are highly suitable for blending with other flavors, they are found in many kinds of dishes from pasta sauces, soups, stews and meat dishes to sweet pastries such as this recipe.

Some maintain that pastries of this kind represent the starting point from which the large family of Italian stuffed pastas and pastries developed over the centuries. This sweet was imported into Sicily by the Arabs, and from there spread throughout southern Italy. The only modern ingredient is the chocolate — two kinds, cocoa and bar chocolate. These cannot have been used any earlier than the seventeenth century, the time when it was discovered that the fatty part of the cocoa bean could be extracted as cocoa butter, leaving the dry part.

For the filling:
10 oz (315 g) chickpeas, soaked overnight in water
2 tablespoons sugar
5 oz (155g) semisweet (dark) chocolate
1 tablespoon unsweetened cocoa powder
zest (rind) of ¼ orange, grated
zest (rind) of ¼ lemon, grated
½ cup (4 fl oz/125 ml) rum or maraschino liqueur
¼ teaspoon ground cinnamon
¼ teaspoon ground cloves
1 egg
For the pastry:
1¾ cups (7 oz/200 g) whole wheat (wholemeal) flour
1¼ cups (5 oz/155 g) all-purpose (plain) flour
salt
1 egg
2–3 tablespoons dry white wine
oil, for deep-frying
powdered (icing) sugar, for dusting

SERVES 4–6

❡ Make the filling: Boil the chickpeas in fresh unsalted water until they are very soft. Drain, reserving the cooking water. Push the chickpeas through a sieve into a saucepan. Dry out the purée by stirring over heat for a few minutes. Add the sugar, chocolate and cocoa and stir until the mixture is an even dark brown. Add the lemon zest, orange zest, rum, cinnamon and cloves. Bind the filling with the egg.
❡ Make the pastry: Mix the flours together and add a pinch of salt, the egg, wine and enough of the reserved cooking water to make a firm dough.

Roll out thinly (about ⅟₁₆ in/1 mm thick) and cut it into circles about 3 in (7.5 cm) in diameter. Place 1 teaspoon of the filling on each one and fold over; crimp the sides together.
❡ Deep-fry the *calzoncelli* in oil until golden, drain and place on a paper towel. Serve cold, dusted with icing sugar.

PICONI MARCHIGIANI

STUFFED PASTRIES FROM THE MARCHES

In the ranks of Italian filled sweet pastries the piconi marchigiani *have a place of their own as dessert, breakfast food and treat for afternoon tea. In some versions the ricotta used for the filling is flavored with a little rum.*

For the pastry:
4⅓ cups (1 lb/500 g) all-purpose (plain) flour
5 egg yolks, beaten
1 cup (8 oz/250 g) butter, softened
1¼ cups (8 oz/250 g) sugar
grated zest (rind) of lemon
For the filling:
3 egg yolks
1¼ cups (8 oz/250 g) sugar
pinch of ground cinnamon
grated zest (rind) of 1 lemon
1 cup (8 fl oz/250 ml) rum
3 oz (90 g) semisweet (dark) chocolate, grated
3 oz (90 g) shelled almonds, ground
1 lb (500 g) ricotta

SERVES 6

❡ Make the pastry: Heap the flour on a board and make a well in the center. Put in the egg yolks, butter, sugar and a little lemon zest. Knead quickly to obtain medium-soft dough. Roll into a ball, wrap in plastic and chill for 1 hour.
❡ Meanwhile, make the filling: In a bowl, beat the egg yolks (reserving a little for brushing the pastries), sugar, cinnamon, lemon zest, rum, chocolate and almonds into the ricotta. The mixture should be thick.
❡ Roll the dough out thinly (⅟₁₆ in/1 mm). Cut into 3 in (8 cm) circles. Put 1 teaspoon of the filling in the center of each circle and fold the dough over into a half-moon shape, pressing with your fingers to seal the edges well. Preheat the oven to 300°F (150°C).
❡ Put the pastries onto a buttered baking sheet and brush them with the reserved beaten egg. Bake in the oven until a toothpick inserted into one of them comes out dry, about 20 minutes.

Top: Piconi Marchigiani; bottom: Calzoncelli ai Ceci

Panettone and Traditional Christmas Food

There have been numerous stories about the origin of the *panettone di Milano*, the cake that symbolizes Christmas in Italy. One that is as appealing as it is improbable suggests that the name derives from a baker named Antonio (Tony) who, worried about his poor sales, had the idea of adding small candied fruits and sugar to his bread dough. Thus was born "*pan del Toni*," Tony's bread, which later became *panettone*.

Another popular belief attributes the origin of *panettone* to a story of thwarted love. In the fourteenth century — according to this legend — a young nobleman fell in love with the daughter of a very strict and protective baker and, to be close to the object of his desires, he sought employment as an apprentice in the same shop. Whilst practicing and experimenting, and thinking of ways to steal a kiss from his beloved Nelita, Ughetto prepared a prototype of *panettone* which, needless to say, quickly became a bestseller in Milan. The baker — his disposition mellowed by the new-found riches — consented to the natural conclusion of the love story he previously opposed . . . and the most famous of Lombardy's cakes has made people happy ever since.

In an important book published in 1650 by a doctor from Bologna named Vincenzo Tanara, we read that "the peasants mix flour with yeast, salt and water and add honey, and into this they work raisins and pumpkin that have been dressed with honey." This is the real origin of the *panettone*: the simple and spontaneous evolution of a traditionally "poor" food which, in some cases at least, had to function as the rich reward for the

sacrifice of working long and hard in the fields. And what better occasion than Christmas, the celebration that is certainly closest to the hearts of Italians?

Sociologists and students of marketing have attributed the success of the *panettone* to the moment at the end of Christmas dinner when the head of the family slices it and hands it out to the diners, thus renewing almost in a priestly manner the religious ritual of the Communion.

In recent times many producers have added different variants to the classical *panettone*, to extend the already flourishing market. Some are encrusted with almonds, some enriched with chocolate or with crumbed "marrons glacés" (candied chestnuts), whilst others have "pockets" filled with *zabaglione allo champagne* (a bain marie-cooked mixture of egg yolks, sugar, vanilla and spumante — or champagne — wine). Whilst many "purists" prefer to remain faithful to the traditional product, shunning all the commercial elaborations, others have come up with their own delicious "stuffings," such as the one blending the flavor of *torroncino* (nougat) and chocolate gelati with rum and *alchermes* liqueurs. A few boutique bakeries in Milan are still producing the flatter *panettone artigianale*, meticulously following the centuries-old method, and proudly lauding the excellent results of their labor.

The original recipe is very simple: flour, sugar, eggs, golden raisins (sultanas), candied fruits and butter. This does not mean, however, that it is easy to make. Quite the opposite. The process is so complex that it can be tackled only by an expert baker with an appropriate laboratory at his disposal, or commercially where there is an army of specialists capable of following the lengthy preparation and cooking procedure.

Nearly all Italian regions and cities have a traditional cake, or sweet, to celebrate Christmas and many of these are now available throughout the year. In Genoa it is *pandolce*, a sort of sweet loaf rich in golden raisins (sultanas) and pine nuts and only lightly leavened. In Verona it is the highly leavened and very light star-shaped *pandoro*, prepared without fruits and sprinkled with finely ground vanilla sugar. In Sicily they use ricotta cheese, candied fruits, chocolate and an orange liqueur to prepare the *cassata* cake. In the country villages to the south of Rome, walnuts and honey are the base of the festive *nociata* sweets and in Ferrara cocoa and honey are used to flavor a traditional light and yeasty rolled cake called *pan pepato al cioccolato*.

The delicious *torrone* is a brittle bar sweetened with honey, flavored with almonds or hazelnuts and enclosed in two paper-thin layers of rice paper. Already known and highly praised by the ancient Romans, *torrone* is a specialty shared by many regions: Piedmont, Lombardy, Sicily, Campania, Abruzzi — famous for the softer chocolate-flavored variety made in Sulmona — and Tuscany. Siena, in Tuscany (renowned for the horse races held every year in the center of the city) is also well known for a flat cake with an intriguing spicy taste, called *panforte*. Made primarily with cane sugar, almonds and candied fruits, *panforte* is flavored with a secret blend of spices that includes coriander, cinnamon, cloves and nutmeg. Its origins can be traced back to the thirteenth century. Today, this specialty is exported worldwide.

1. commercially made Milanese panettone;
2. Veronese pandoro;
3. panettone with almonds;
4. special pastrycook's Milanese panettone;
5. Sienese panforte;
6. Genoese pandolce

BIANCO MANGIARE CON CREMA AL CARAMELLO

ALMOND BLANCMANGE WITH CARAMEL CREAM

There are two varieties of almonds — mandorle dolci (sweet almonds) and mandorle amare (bitter almonds). This recipe uses both types.

Almonds have for centuries been a popular ingredient in Italy used for making cakes, candy, marzipan and other desserts. However it was the Arabs who originally experimented with the almonds in cooking and through the Arabs in Sicily the almond passed into Italian cuisine.

This ancient dessert, based on ground almonds or almond milk, has been in use all over Europe since medieval times. In Italy it exists in several regional cuisines, but above all in the culinary tradition of Mantua, where the recipe was used at the court of the Gonzagas.

For the blancmange:
⅓ cup (2 oz/60 g) blanched almonds
2 teaspoons chopped, skinned bitter almonds
¾ cup (6 fl oz/185 ml) milk
1⅔ cups (13½ fl oz/410 ml) cream
2 teaspoons plain unflavored gelatin
1 cup (5 oz/155 g) powdered (icing) sugar
3 tablespoons cherry liqueur
For the caramel cream (makes 2 cups/16 fl oz/
*   500 ml):*
5 egg yolks
1¼ cups (8 oz/250 g) sugar
2 teaspoons all-purpose (plain) flour
1 teaspoon vanilla extract (essence)
2 cups (16 fl oz/500 ml) milk

SERVES 6

¶ To make the blancmange: In a food processor process both types of almonds. Add the milk and blend. Whip the cream. Dissolve the gelatin in ¾ tablespoon cold water. Strain the milk and almonds through dampened cheesecloth or muslin into a bowl, pressing on the nuts to squeeze out as much liquid as possible. Stir in the powdered sugar, cherry liqueur and dissolved gelatin. Fold in the whipped cream with care.

¶ Put the blancmange in a 10 in (25 cm) diameter mold and chill in the refrigerator.

¶ Make the caramel cream: Beat the egg yolks with ½ cup (4 oz/125 g) of the sugar. Add the flour and vanilla.

¶ Put the milk on medium heat. In another pan, caramelize the remaining sugar with 3 to 4 tablespoons water (heat until the sugar liquifies

and becomes a clear syrup). Stir the boiling milk and the caramel into the eggs and sugar. Set aside to cool.

¶ Pour the cold caramel cream over the base of each plate. Put a layer of blancmange on top, and decorate with a few toasted almonds, if desired.

GELO DI MELONE

WATERMELON ICE

The range of sweet dishes in the Sicilian repertoire is endless, but this simple sorbet is looked upon not only as a great dessert, but as a proving ground for every housewife. There are pasticcerie and even major restaurants on the island where this gelo is made, but it is also a source of pride in the homes of traditional Sicilian families. Watermelon here is known as melone, while elsewhere in Italy it is called either anguria or cocomero. The skill in making this ice consists in knowing exactly how much of the delicately flavored rose water to add and not overdoing the dark chocolate drops that represent the seeds of the watermelon.

juice of 1 ripe watermelon
⅔ cup (3 oz/90 g) rice starch or cornstarch (cornflour)
1½ cups (11 oz/345 g) sugar
rose water
chocolate drops, for garnish

SERVES 8

¶ In a saucepan, cook the watermelon juice, starch, sugar and a few drops of rose water. At the first hint of boiling, turn off the heat. Divide the mixture among 8 glass goblets and refrigerate for a few hours, until the ice thickens.

¶ Garnish with the chocolate drops and serve.

BONET

BONET

A traditional dessert from Piedmont, this one is made in the Langhe with cream from the top of the milk, while in other areas of the region whole milk is used. Both produce equally good results, but the second (this recipe) is a little lighter.

3 egg yolks
½ cup (4 oz/125 g) sugar
1 cup (4 oz/125 g) amaretti cookies, crushed
1 tablespoon unsweetened cocoa powder

Top left: Bianco Mangiare con Crema al Caramello; top right: Gelo di Melone; bottom: Bonet

2 cups (16 fl oz/500 ml) milk
1 tablespoon rum
3 egg whites, stiffly beaten
SERVES 4

❡ Preheat the oven to 300°F (150°C). Beat the egg yolks with the sugar until smooth. In a food processor, combine the egg yolk mixture with the amaretti, cocoa, milk and rum. Process for a couple of minutes until very well mixed. Strain the mixture into a bowl. Gently fold in the egg whites. Pour into four 2 in (5 cm) individual molds or a single large 10 in (25 cm) ring-mold.
❡ Set the mold(s) in a roasting pan and add hot water to reach halfway up the sides of the molds. Bake in the oven for about 30 minutes, or until set. Let cool. Turn out onto a plate and serve.

(Back row) Left: small chocolate Easter eggs; center: hand-decorated chocolate Easter egg; right: colomba pasquale; (front row) marzipan fruits and marzipan lambs

TRADITIONAL EASTER FOOD

Just as the *panettone* symbolizes Christmas in Italy, so the *colomba* is the symbol of Easter. Again this is a yeast dough, shaped into the form of a dove using a special metal or paper mold. It is a soft dough with citron, golden raisins (sultanas) and candied orange peel added, topped with a sugar glaze and whole almonds. The image of the dove is used in this case because of its symbolic significance as a bearer of peace and serenity.

The tradition of the chocolate Easter egg, which is just as typical but not exclusively Italian, has a different origin. During Lent, Catholics used to be strictly forbidden to eat not only meat, but eggs as well. The ban began on Ash Wednesday and ended on the morning of Easter Day. According to other theories of pagan origin, the egg as a symbol of fertility has a propitiatory value for the harvest, and in a wider sense is seen as the emblem of fertility and life itself. Hence the custom of exchanging eggs with a gift inside. Eggs are marketed containing gifts of varying degrees of interest, but it is customary in cases of importance to ask the trusted local pastrycook to make a special egg and put into it a more valuable gift, an item of jewelry for example.

In addition to the dove and the egg, there are other culinary Easter traditions — including both savory and sweet specialties — that are observed in various parts of Italy.

From Genoa comes the *torta pasqualina*, an Easter pie filled with a mixture of hard-cooked eggs, spinach, artichokes and a slightly sour cheese produced in the surrounding hills.

In Siena the classic *panforte* is eaten and given as a gift, while the neighboring Umbrians make a cake of wheat and almond flours mixed with eggs, in the shape of a twisted serpent. Here again the custom has obviously grown out of popular beliefs: the serpent is the symbol of evil, but a serpent biting its tail and thus forming a circle is also a symbol of continuing life. Eating therefore takes on the value of exorcism and propitiatory rites. This interpretation holds for all the ring-shaped cakes that appear on Italian family tables on Easter Day, some of them even made with real eggs inserted in specially made hollows in the batter and cooked as part of the cake.

In the country around Rome a full traditional Easter breakfast will include hard-cooked eggs and salami — washed down with a sweet white vermouth — a sliced *colomba* cake and chocolate eggs. The inhabitants of Rome could not celebrate Easter without an outing to a *trattoria* in the Castelli — the hills surrounding the eternal city — where they will feast on *agnello pasquale* — suckling lamb marinated in oil, lemon juice and rosemary before it is roasted in the oven.

In many regions of Italy — but more so in the south and in the islands — it is common practice to prepare and give as presents sweets or marzipan, shaped like fruit and lambs to symbolize the concept of new life associated with the spring season and with the celebration of Easter.

Another typical and very old custom is to give painted hen's eggs. Some say the tradition goes back as far as the Rome of Alexander Severus, where eggs painted purple and gold were believed to bring good luck. Nowadays artificial food colors, dissolved in boiling water, are used to color the eggs, which are then given a luster by rubbing them with oil.

STRUDEL DI FRUTTI DI BOSCO

WILD BERRY STRUDEL

The use of whipped cream, wild berries, strudel pastry and yogurt brings together the dessert traditions of an area that once belonged to a single empire, whose borders extended to the Orient.

This elegant, rich dessert is typical of the cuisine of Upper Adige, and in particular of the city of Bressanone.

For the pastry:
2½ cups (10 oz/315 g) all-purpose (plain) flour
2 tablespoons olive oil
pinch of salt
2 cups (16 fl oz/500 ml) water
For the fruit cream:
3 oz (90 g) raspberries
¾ cup (6 oz/185 g) plain yogurt
1 cup (2 oz/60 g) sugar
juice of ½ lemon
1 cup (8 fl oz/250 ml) heavy (double) cream, whipped
For the filling:
5 oz (155 g) raspberries
5 oz (155 g) blackberries
5 oz (155 g) wild strawberries
¾ cup (6 oz/185 g) superfine (caster) sugar

SERVES 6

❡ Make the pastry: Make a soft, smooth dough with the flour, oil, salt and water. Set aside to rest for 2 hours.
❡ Preheat the oven to 350°F (180°C).
❡ Roll out the dough very thinly (about ¹⁄₃₂ in/ 0.5 mm) and cut into 24 x 2 in (6 cm) circles. Arrange the pastry rounds on an oiled baking sheet. Bake in the oven for 10 minutes, until golden and crisp. Set aside to cool.
❡ Make the fruit cream: Mix the raspberries with ⅓ cup (3 oz/90 g) of the yogurt, the superfine sugar and the lemon juice. Stir until the sugar has completely dissolved. Fold in the whipped cream. Do not chill.
❡ Place a sheet of pastry in the center of the serving plate. Spread a layer of the fruit cream and superfine sugar over it. Cover with the raspberries and more superfine sugar. Add another pastry sheet, more fruit cream, superfine sugar and the blackberries. Continue in this manner, forming 3 layers of filling using each type of berries.
❡ Garnish with remaining yogurt, sweetened with 1 tablespoon of sugar if desired.

Top: Strudel di Frutti di Bosco; bottom: Budino di Pere Martine

BUDINO DI PERE MARTINE

PEAR MOLDS

This is an elegant version of the classic Piedmontese bonet, with the added flavor of Martine pears — so named because they are the last pears of the season and are eaten around the time of the feast of San Martino in early November.

6 small firm cooking pears, peeled and thinly sliced
1 tablespoon sugar
8 amaretti cookies, crushed
2 cups (16 fl oz/500 ml) dry white wine
1 teaspoon plain unflavored gelatin, dissolved in ⅓ cup (3 fl oz/90 ml) dry white wine

SERVES 6

❡ Layer the pears in a wide, shallow skillet. Sprinkle on the sugar, add wine to cover, and cook over low heat until the pears are cooked and the wine is completely absorbed. Set aside to cool.
❡ Push the pears through a sieve together with the cookie crumbs. To the resulting purée add the gelatin and stir. Pour the mixture into 6 small molds and chill.
❡ At serving time, immerse the molds in hot water for a moment or 2 until the puddings come away from the sides. Unmold onto the center of each plate.

Left to right: Sicilian orange liqueur; nocino; figs in alcohol; apricots in alcohol; cherries in alcohol

SPIRITS

The earliest mention of the distillation process in Italy actually describes the birth of grappa. This spirit is obtained by distilling what is left over from the winemaking process. Grappa used to be rather rough because the must from all the grapes finished up in the recipe without any selection being made. But over the past twenty years grappas made from single species have begun to appear such as Tocai, Sauvignon, Picolit and Cabernet.

Nocino is a spirit made mainly in the Modena area in the northern regions of Emilia, and in Sorrento. It is made from walnuts picked when the shell has not yet hardened. The walnuts are left for one month, still enclosed in their green husk, in an infusion of alcohol, spices, water and sugar.

The home production of fruit and herbal liqueurs spread throughout Italy in the middle of the nineteenth century, due to a fall in sugar prices. The best examples of Sicilian orange liqueur are homemade and individual recipes are closely guarded.

These elixirs of oranges or mandarins have an intense bouquet and are proudly displayed in crystal-clear decanters, to allow guests to admire the rich colors of the sun-burnt fruits used to prepare them.

The preparation of liqueured fruits, including figs, apricots and cherries, similar to that of home-made liqueurs, is also enjoying renewed popularity in Italy. Some of the procedures are quite demanding, requiring the fruits to be partly candied before being gently covered with a blend of their own sugary syrup and distilled alcohol, then flavored with sugar-cane spirit and vanilla beans.

TIRAMISU'

TIRAMISU'

This is a unique and enjoyable dessert that is so simple to make that it has met with tremendous success worldwide and already figures among the dishes typical of Italy. Tiramisu' means "pick me up" which is appropriate as the dessert is absolutely delicious and contains a shot of Marsala and strong coffee. There are several different versions of this recipe in existence.

It is not known who created the recipe, but very likely it was a cook somewhere between Venice and Treviso, because this is where tiramisu' *spread like wildfire from restaurant to restaurant before taking over the whole country.*

4 egg yolks
1¼ cups (5 oz/155 g) sugar
¼ cup (2 fl oz/60 ml) dry marsala
8 oz (250 g) mascarpone
1 cup (8 fl oz/250 ml) heavy (double) cream
30 ladyfingers (sponge finger biscuits/savoiardi)
6 cups (1½ qt/1.5 l) strong espresso coffee, cooled to room temperature
3 tablespoons unsweetened cocoa powder
1½ oz (45 g) semisweet (dark) chocolate

SERVES 6

❡ Make the zabaglione. Stir the egg yolks in a double boiler adding the sugar and marsala until the sugar dissolves, about 10 minutes. Take off heat and stir continuously until cool.

❡ Beat the mascarpone and the cream together until thick. Fold into the cold zabaglione until smooth and well mixed.

❡ On the base of a 12×8×2 in (30×20×5 cm) rectangular baking dish put a layer of ladyfingers lightly soaked in coffee, and sprinkle with unsweetened cocoa powder pushed through a sieve that is held over the dish. Add a second layer of coffee-soaked ladyfingers and more cocoa, and cover with the remaining zabaglione cream. Tap the dish lightly to settle the contents, then coat with a further layer of cocoa and some shavings of dark chocolate. Chill for a few hours in the refrigerator.

FOGLIE DI CIOCCOLATO ALLA MOUSSE DI CASTAGNE

CHOCOLATE LEAVES FILLED WITH CHESTNUT MOUSSE

A sophisticated modern version of the classic monte-bianco, made with strictly local ingredients, this dish comes from the hills of Romagnola, inland from Rimini, where there are rich chestnut groves. The recipe has quickly become part of the new Italian cuisine.

12 medium-size chestnut leaves
6 oz (185 g) semisweet (dark) chocolate
2½ lb (1.2 kg) chestnuts, unshelled
2 cups (16 fl oz/500 ml) milk
¾ cup (6 oz/185 g) sugar
1 vanilla bean (pod)
¾ cup (6 fl oz/185 ml) heavy (double) cream, whipped
For the custard:
2 cups (16 fl oz/500 ml) milk
4 egg yolks
⅔ cup (5 oz/155 g) sugar
½ vanilla bean (pod)

SERVES 4

❧ Clean the chestnut leaves using a cotton tip dipped in alcohol. Melt the chocolate over very low heat and paint one side of each leaf with the melted chocolate. Put the leaves in the refrigerator to set.

❧ Cook the chestnuts in boiling water for 45 minutes, peel and remove the inner skins. Return the chestnuts to the heat in a pan along with the milk, sugar and vanilla bean. Boil slowly until nearly all the milk has disappeared. Discard the vanilla bean.

❧ In a food processor, purée the chestnuts until smooth. Cover and chill. When cold, fold in the whipped cream.

❧ Take the chocolate leaves from the refrigerator and carefully peel the leaves away from the chocolate. Coat each chocolate leaf with some of the chestnut mousse. Return to the refrigerator.

❧ Combine all the custard ingredients in a double boiler. Cook, stirring constantly, without letting the mixture come to the boil, until it coats the back of the wooden spoon. Cover and chill.

❧ When the custard is cold, cover the bottom of each plate with it, lay the chocolate leaves on top and serve.

Left: Tiramisu'; right: Foglie di Cioccolato alla Mousse di Castagne

DRIED FRUIT AND NUTS

A wide variety of nuts and dried fruit can be found on the Italian table. Nuts such as walnuts, almonds and hazelnuts are commonplace, as are dried fruit such as figs, apricots, prunes and peaches. These foods are eaten mainly in winter, and are traditional fare for Christmas and end-of-year festivities. An attractively packed basket of dried fruit and nuts is always a welcome gift, and these are seven of the 13 desserts presented at the New Year's Eve dinner table, to symbolize Christ and the 12 Apostles.

Of special importance in Italy are hazelnuts, walnuts, figs and almonds. Hazelnuts, which grow on a shrub common to the entire Mediterranean area, are a major crop both for direct consumption and for the making of *torrone*, a nougat typical of various areas of Italy. The best quality walnuts are the *noci de Sorrento*, so called because crops flourish on the Sorrento peninsula south of Naples. (The species has spread far and wide and has also been found to grow very well in some parts of the United States.) These walnuts are eaten as is and used in a variety of sweet and savory dishes, including *panforte di Siena* and the sauce that is served in Genoa with *pansoti*, the local pasta stuffed with vegetables and cheese.

Figs grow only in the South. Dried figs are fruit that are left on the tree until fully ripe and then picked and dried in the sun. These small, very tasty figs, covered in a light-colored, flour-like film, are sold loose, by weight. They are also prepared in a number of ways: threaded onto wooden skewers alternately with almonds, or cut open and stuffed with an almond and then packed in clear cellophane, or flavored with small pieces of bay leaf and fennel seeds.

Known for thousands of years, the almond grows widely in the Mediterranean region. Almonds are of great importance in Mediterranean confections of all sorts, particularly in Sicily. *Frutti di Marturana*, marzipan delights shaped and colored to look like miniature pieces of fruit, are among the jewels of Sicilian sweetmaking. *Pignoli* (pine nuts) are the seeds found in the cones of some species of pine trees: the kernels used in Italy come from the majestic Mediterranean pine trees, also called parasol pines because of their umbrella shape.

Many dishes in Italian cuisine require the use of these exquisite resinous nuts, the most famous being the Ligurian *pesto alla genovese*, a green sauce blending the creamy flavor of the pine nuts with the pungent aroma of fresh basil, garlic and olive oil. This sauce is used for pasta dishes and to enrich soups.

Pine nuts are also widely used in the preparation of sweets and desserts.

Originally from Palestine, Persia and Syria, pistachio nuts (*pistacchi*) were exported to many parts of the world. In Italy, pistachios are grown in Apulia and Sicily to be used mainly in the preparation of ice creams and cakes. Sometimes they are used to give an exotic touch to mortadella. Pistachios are also popular salted and served with aperitifs and cocktails.

1. packaged dried figs;
2. walnuts; 3. pistachio nuts;
4. raisins; 5. dried figs;
6. almonds; 7. hazelnuts;
8. pine nuts

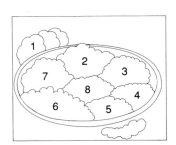

Left: Semifreddo alle Nocciole con Zabaione al Miele (page 236); right: Budino di Papavero

BUDINO DI PAPAVERO

POPPYSEED PUDDING

Poppyseeds are a distinguishing feature of the cuisine of Upper Adige. In some areas — the Val Senales, for example — children are given big sweet fritters filled with poppyseeds and chestnut jam for afternoon tea. This pudding is from the Val d'Ultimo in the mountains behind the Stelvio massif, on the border with the Valtellina. Valtellina is Italy's major buckwheat-producing area.

1 cup (8 fl oz/250 ml) milk
3 tablespoons sugar
7 tablespoons (3½ oz/100 g) butter, softened
1¼ cups (5 oz/155 g) buckwheat flour
4 eggs, separated
3 tablespoons poppyseeds, ground
SERVES 4

❡ Preheat the oven to 350°F (180°C). Place the milk and sugar in a saucepan and bring to a boil. Beat the butter and add the flour. Off the heat, add to the milk and mix well.
❡ Beat the egg yolks with the poppyseeds. Beat the egg whites until stiff.
❡ Stir the egg yolk mixture into the milk mixture.
❡ Pour the mixture into 4 individual molds. Set the molds in a roasting pan and add hot water to reach halfway up the sides. Bake in the oven for 30 minutes until the puddings are evenly browned. Chill and serve.

SEMIFREDDO ALLE NOCCIOLE CON ZABAIONE AL MIELE

CHILLED HAZELNUT PUDDING WITH HONEY ZABAGLIONE

This is one of the most important desserts in the modern cuisine of Emilia-Romagna. Butter is not used in this recipe, beaten egg whites provide a lighter touch, but this is still a very rich dessert. The honey zabaglione is similar to an ancient dish from Friuli, sufrit, made with eggs, honey, milk and wine.

For the pudding:
2 eggs, separated
⅔ cup (5 oz/155 g) or ⅔ cup (5 oz/155 g) superfine (caster) sugar mixed with ½ tablespoon vanilla extract (essence)
8 oz (250 g) hazelnuts, shelled and processed to a pulp
1 oz (30 g) hazelnuts, shelled and chopped
⅓ cup (3 fl oz/90 ml) heavy (double) cream
For the sauce:
¼ cup (2 oz/60 g) sugar
½ cup (4 fl oz/125 ml) water
3 oz (90 g) semisweet (dark) chocolate
⅓ cup (3 fl oz/90 ml) heavy (double) cream
For the honey zabaglione:
3 tablespoons liquid honey
1 egg yolk
2 tablespoons brandy
⅓ cup (3 fl oz/90 ml) heavy (double) cream, whipped
3 tablespoons shaved white chocolate

SERVES 4

❧ Mix the hazelnut pulp with 1 egg white then add the chopped hazelnuts (reserving some for garnish), 2 egg yolks, vanilla sugar and cream.
❧ Fill 4 individual molds with the mixture. Refrigerate for a few hours.
❧ Make the chocolate sauce: Dissolve the sugar in the water in a saucepan. Add the chocolate and stir to melt. Set aside to cool.
❧ Whip cream. Fold into the chocolate mixture.
❧ Make the honey zabaglione: Beat the honey with the egg yolk and brandy in a double boiler over simmering water for about 10 minutes — it should be a dense creamy consistency. Remove from the heat. Fold in the whipped cream.
❧ Spread the chocolate sauce over half of each well-chilled plate. Pour the zabaglione onto the other half. Place the unmolded pudding in the center and decorate with the reserved chopped hazelnuts and the shavings of white chocolate. (See photograph page 235.)

PASTIERA DI GRANO

RICOTTA FRUIT PIE

At one time this Neapolitan sweet was prepared only from January to Easter, the best time of year for wheat and ricotta. These days, though, it is eaten all the year round.

For the dough:
4⅓ cups (1 lb/500 g) all-purpose (plain) flour
3 eggs
¾ cup (6 oz/185 g) sugar
¾ cup (6 oz/185 g) butter, softened
powdered (icing) sugar, for dusting
For the filling:
1¼ cups (8 oz/250 g) wheat
1 lb 6 oz (685 g) ricotta
3 cups (1¼ lb/625 g) sugar
2 tablespoons hot milk
2 tablespoons (1 oz/30 g) butter
2 tablespoons vanilla extract (essence)
5 whole eggs plus 2 egg yolks
½ tablespoon orange flower water
⅓ cup (3 oz/90 g) diced candied fruit

SERVES 12

❧ Put the wheat in a saucepan, cover it with cold water and set aside to soak for 8 days, changing the water every day.
❧ Prepare the dough: Heap the flour into a mound and make a well in the center. Add the eggs, sugar and butter and knead vigorously to make a smooth dough. Wrap in plastic and refrigerate for 2 hours.
❧ Prepare the filling: Stir the ricotta and sugar together. Push the mixture through a sieve and set aside for about 18 hours. Drain the wheat, cover with fresh water and boil over medium heat for 15 minutes. Add the milk, butter and vanilla extract. Simmer for 2 hours, until the wheat has absorbed all the liquid. Cover and chill. When cold, mix in the ricotta, eggs, orange flower water and candied fruit.
❧ Preheat the oven to 350°F (180°C). Roll out the dough to ⅛ in (2 mm). Cut out a circle large enough to line the base and sides of a 14–16 in (35–40 cm) cake pan.
❧ Pour the filling into the pastry, cover with a lattice of pastry strips.
❧ Bake in the oven for about 1 hour. Turn off the heat and leave the *pastiera* to dry out in the oven for 15 minutes. Cover and cool to room temperature. Dust with powdered sugar, serve. (See photograph page 238.)

From left: caffé espresso in bicchiere piccolo; caffé espresso in tazza piccola; cappuccino senza schiuma; cappuccino con schiuma; caffé e latte

COFFEE

The daily coffee is a ritual no Italian can do without. As soon as Italians wake up in the morning they drink a cup of piping hot black coffee, made in a home *espresso* maker or in the old *napoletana* coffee pot, which is more traditional but now fast disappearing. At the coffee bar near the office they drink an extra-strong and fragrant *espresso ristretto,* or maybe a *cappuccino,* with a brioche, and so on through the day. On a working day it is nothing for a well-patronized bar to serve as many as 5,000 cups of coffee.

Coffee used to be made by the infusion method, with the coffee grounds suspended in hot water and allowed to fall to the bottom. *Caffé all'italiana,* as we know it, was the result of later attempts at filtering and the triumph of *la caffettiera napoletana,* the Neapolitan coffee pot which consists of two parts separated by a container full of finely ground dark-roasted coffee. Water is poured into the bottom chamber and the pot is put on to boil, then turned upside-down so that the coffee filters through the coffee grounds and drips into the bottom chamber.

Later came sophisticated methods such as the moka, where the same process is achieved through the water vaporizing in the bottom chamber and condensing in the upper part of the pot, after passing through the coffee grounds.

It was the Italian invention of the *espresso* coffee machine that brought this drink to international fame. True *espresso* must be brewed under pressure so that the steam is forced through the finely ground coffee.

There are several types of *espresso* coffee specialties include *caffé espresso in tazza piccola* and *in bicchiere piccolo,* literally in a small cup. The *ristretto* is a very short black coffee that less than half fills the cup. The *lungo* is made with the same quantity of ground coffee as the *ristretto,* but with more water. A *macchiato* is a *ristretto* with a few drops of milk. A *cappuccino* is served in a larger cup, half filled with *espresso* and then topped up with milk heated with pressurized steam from the *espresso* machine, which gives the drink a creamy, frothy topping. There are two types: *cappucino senza schiuma* (without froth) and *cappuccino con schiuma* (with froth). Sometimes this is sprinkled with a small amount of cocoa powder. Then there is *caffé e latte,* a combination of coffee and milk which is served in either a cup or a glass.

CASTAGNACCIO

CHESTNUT CAKE

There are chestnut forests in many regions of Italy, and this autumn fruit provides the raw material for sweet confections that have passed into international cuisine. Montebianco, for example, is a delicious treat made with boiled chestnuts put through a sieve and mixed with whipped cream. This castagnaccio, however, is made only in Tuscany, and is an example of the old unleavened cakes known as stiacciate, among the earliest foods consumed by humans. The castagnaccio is served in slices as a dessert or sometimes is cut into small squares and eaten at the end of the meal.

2 cups (16 fl oz/500 ml) water
3¼ cups (13 oz/410 g) chestnut flour
salt
¼ cup (2 fl oz/60 ml) extra-virgin olive oil
2 tablespoons golden raisins (sultanas)
2 tablespoons small thin strips of orange zest (rind)
¼ cup (1 oz/30 g) walnut pieces
¼ cup (1 oz/30 g) pine nuts
1 tablespoon rosemary leaves

SERVES 4

❡ Preheat the oven to 400°F (200°C). Whisk the water into the chestnut flour until smooth and without lumps. The mixture should be fairly liquid. Add a pinch of salt, olive oil, golden raisins, orange zest and walnuts. Mix thoroughly.
❡ Pour the batter into a round cake pan about 14–16 in (35–40 cm) in diameter. Sprinkle the surface with a little oil and scatter the pine nuts and rosemary leaves on top.
❡ Bake in the oven for 35 to 40 minutes, or until the surface is covered by a dark crunchy crust. Serve cold, molded or unmolded.

Top: Pastiera di Grano (page 236); bottom: Castagnaccio

GELATO AND SORBET

The art of making gelato (ice cream) and sorbet was introduced into Sicily by the Arabs, and we could say it is thanks to them that modern gelato was born. But even in ancient Rome it was customary to preserve the winter's snow in the cool of a cave, pressed and protected between layers of straw, to be used for making iced drinks and fruit juice mixtures in summer.

According to some experts, we owe today's gelato to the invention of a sixteenth-century Florentine architect by the name of Bernardo Buontalenti, who successfully experimented with ways of transforming the snow that remained in the grottoes of the Boboli Gardens into a soft cream by adding various ingredients — cream in particular.

Others credit one of Charles I of England's pastrycooks with inventing the orginal formula, after which it spread throughout Europe. In any event, the true initiator of the modern gelato was a Sicilian, Francesco Procopio di' Coltelli, who in 1686 moved to Paris to open a shop serving coffee, chocolate and ice creams. This was the Café Procope, destined to go down in literary history as a meeting place for the followers of the Enlightenment and the scene of historic disputes between such intellectuals as Diderot and D'Alembert.

Although the creation of the gelato industry was due to an American named Fussell, a milkman from Baltimore who had the idea of turning unsold milk into ice cream, from the time of the Café Procope, the image of gelato-making as a craft has remained linked to Italy and its artisans.

From places like Longarone, a mountain village near Belluno, legions of roving *gelatai* (ice cream vendors) set out with their carts to travel all the roads of Europe. The descendants of those *gelatai* still come to Longarone every year from all over the world for a memorable celebration.

There are two kinds of gelato: the *grasso* "fat" type made by beating milk and egg yolks with sugar, and the *magro* or "lean" variety made with fresh fruit and water, or milk if a thicker, creamier texture is desired. As far as the taste of gelato is concerned, the imagination knows no limits: from powdered chocolate to crushed hazelnuts, from mandarin to apricot, from coffee to a *zabaglione* mixture, almost anything can be made into gelato.

These days several companies offer small machines for making perfect gelato at home. But for the classic Italian gelato, the creamy variety, the basic mixture remains the same: 8 egg yolks, 1½ cups (10 oz/315 g) sugar and 4 cups (1 quart/1 liter) milk. Beat the yolks thoroughly with the sugar, then mix them with the milk and heat, stirring constantly, until the mixture becomes thick. Allow to cool. Transfer the mixture to an ice-cream maker and churn until a thick, soft, cold cream forms.

Chocolate and wafers, strawberry and kiwifruit make mouth-watering combinations, as do the special black and white *tartufo*. Nothing is more delectable than gelato of hazelnut or mushroom-shaped vanilla with white chocolate — not to mention chestnut.

Sumptuous sorbets come in orange, grape-fruit and lemon. Tempting they may sit alone while gelato rests in chocolate, vanilla, strawberry or *stracciatella* cones.

Zuccotto is a delightful Florentine pudding. The top consists of alternate brown and white segments made from cocoa powder and confectioners' (icing) sugar. Some gourmets fill the *zuccotto* with chocolate pieces, hazelnuts and almonds instead of the candied citron and orange peel included in the original recipe.

1. zuccotto; 2. stracciatella gelato; 3. vanilla–chocolate gelato; 4. strawberry gelato; 5. chocolate and stracciatella gelato; 6. strawberry and kiwifruit gelato; 7. orange sorbet; 8. grapefruit sorbet; 9. lemon sorbet; 10. coffee gelato; 11. hazelnut gelato; 12. vanilla and white chocolate mushroom-shaped gelato; 13. chestnut gelato; 14. white tartufo; 15. black tartufo

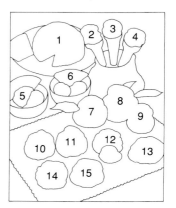

Zaleti (on plate, left); Biscottini di Prato (on plate, right); right: Torta di Mele

ZALETI

CORNMEAL COOKIES

These cookies, found throughout the Veneto region, are made from ordinary wheat flour mixed with cornmeal, which gives them a pale yellow color. Zaleti are sold in bakeries and cake shops, but they have a strong family tradition and every housewife has her own secret formula.

3 egg yolks, beaten
1/3 cup (3 oz/90 g) sugar
1/2 teaspoon baking soda (bicarbonate of soda)
1 cup (5 oz/155 g) cornmeal
1 1/4 cups (5 oz/155 g) all-purpose (plain) flour
pinch of salt
grated zest (rind) of 1 lemon

10 tablespoons (5 oz/155 g) butter
1/2 cup (3 oz/90 g) golden raisins (sultanas), soaked and squeezed dry
powdered (icing) sugar

SERVES 6–8

❡ Preheat the oven to 375°F (190°C). Beat the egg yolks, sugar and baking soda.
❡ Mix the cornmeal and flour on a pastry board. Add the salt and lemon zest.
❡ Melt the butter on low heat. Pour over the flour mixture and begin to knead the dough. Add the egg yolk mixture and the golden raisins. Knead until the dough is soft but dense, adding a little lukewarm water or milk if necessary.
❡ Form the dough into two rolls about 1 1/2 in

tom is to dip the cookies in the Vin Santo. The recipe is very simple, and the cookies will keep in an airtight container for several months.

8²⁄₃ cups (2 lb/1 kg) all-purpose (plain) flour
8 eggs, beaten
5 cups (2 lb/1 kg) superfine (caster) sugar
½ teaspoon baking soda (bicarbonate of soda)
salt
8 oz (250 g) blanched almonds, finely chopped

SERVES 6

❡ Preheat the oven to 300°F (150°C). Heap the flour in a mound on a pastry board. Make a well in the center and add the eggs, sugar, baking soda and a pinch of salt. Knead briefly. Add the almonds and knead again to mix thoroughly.
❡ Roll the dough into lengths about 1½ in (4 cm) in diameter (2 in/5 cm long). Flatten slightly. Arrange the cookies on a buttered and floured baking sheet.
❡ Bake in the oven for 7 to 8 minutes, or until golden. Remove from the oven, cut into diagonal slices about ⅜ in (1 cm) thick. Return to the oven to finish cooking until perfectly browned, about 7 to 10 minutes.

TORTA DI MELE

APPLE CAKE

Soft and fragrant, this recipe incorporates the apples in the mixture rather than having them arranged on top.

2 egg yolks
⅓ cup (1½ oz/45 g) all-purpose (plain) flour
1 tablespoon sugar
pinch of salt
⅙ oz (5 g) dried yeast
¼ cup (2 fl oz/60 ml) milk
2 lb (1 kg) apples, peeled and thinly sliced
2 egg whites, beaten until stiff
2 tablespoons (1 oz/30 g) butter

SERVES 6–8

❡ Preheat the oven to 325°F (170°C). Beat the egg yolks. Add the flour, sugar, salt, yeast and milk. Mix well. Add the apples and mix. Fold in the beaten egg whites.
❡ Pour the mixture into a buttered 10 in (25 cm) cake pan. Bake in the oven for about 45 minutes, until a skewer inserted in the center of the cake comes out dry.
❡ Allow to cool before serving.

(4 cm) in diameter. Slice and press lightly into oval shapes about 3 in (8 cm) long. Arrange the cookies on a lightly buttered baking sheet.
❡ Bake in the oven until evenly golden.
❡ Dust with powdered sugar and serve warm or cold.

BISCOTTINI DI PRATO

TUSCAN ALMOND COOKIES

In Tuscany these are the obligatory ending to any lunch. Small, dense-textured and dry, they are served with Vin Santo, a sweet and strongly perfumed wine made from grapes that have been left to dry in the cellars. The cus-

CHEESE AND WINE

CHEESE AND WINE

ATTEMPTING TO COMPILE A CHEESE MAP OF ITALY IS A HIGHLY COMPLEX UNDERTAKING. IN A COUNTRY WITH A DEEP-ROOTED agricultural and pastoral tradition like Italy's, wherever there is pasture every isolated cottage and every Alpine hut houses cheesemaking equipment and a cool cellar with rows of soft cheeses set out on wooden planks: *caciotta, Robiola, scamorza* and *Provola* of all sizes and descriptions. So widespread is cheesemaking that the making of pork products, impressive though it is, fades into second place beside it.

¶ There are, however, a few Italian cheeses which, by virtue of their special qualities and the environment in which they are produced, can provide a profound experience for the gourmet traveling in Italy. Described below are the most characteristic and best known of the more than 400 different types of cheese the country produces.

¶ *Parmigiano Reggiano*: Parmesan is certainly the most famous and oldest of all Italian cheeses. It has been known at least since the fourteenth century, and is mentioned not only in old recipe collections but also in the works of such

illustrious writers as Giovanni Boccaccio. It is chiefly a grating cheese, but is also incomparable served in slivers at the end of a meal, or with a fine wine. It is produced in a defined area of the provinces around Parma, Reggio Emilia, Modena, Bologna and Mantua. Once formed, the cheeses must be aged for some time. (*Fresco* is aged under 18 months, *vecchio* is aged 18 to 24 months, and *stravecchio* is aged 24 to 36 months.) One hundred and twenty-five gallons (500 liters) of milk are required to make a cheese of 70 pounds (32 kilograms) average weight. Protected by a seal of quality granted according to the strictest of controls, *Parmigiano Reggiano* is not commercially produced but actually comes from a multitude of small cheesemakers who collect the milk from a small number of cows and produce at most five or six cheeses a day. Parmesan is produced only from May to September using milk from cows that are fed on fresh pasture.

¶ *Grana Padano*: This cheese is as important as Parmesan and equally historic. The two are similar, differing only in the rules that govern their production. *Grana Padano* is made commercially in large cheese factories throughout the area to the north of the Po River, especially in the country around Piacenza, Milan, Cremona and Mantua. Production is possible all year long, and it sells at a lower price than Parmesan. The two cheeses are practically identical, however, and only by tasting them side by side is it possible to distinguish a special lightness and fragrance peculiar to the Parmesan. In the earliest known treatise on the dairy industry, *Summa Lacticiniorum* by Pantaleone da Confienza, a doctor who lived at the Court of the Duke of Savoy in the latter half of the fifteenth century,

Previous pages: Parmigiano (Parmesan) is the most famous of Italian cheeses. Once formed, the cheese is aged for anything between 18 and 36 months. Mainly a cheese for grating, it is also delicious served after dinner accompanied by a fine wine. APL/OLYMPIA

Opposite: Red-wine grapes from a vineyard at San Gimignano, Tuscany. Chianti is probably the most famous wine produced in the Tuscan countryside around Florence, Siena, Arezzo, Pisa and Pistoia.
JOHN CALLANAN

Grana cheese is described as a product of the Po area. Either Parmesan or Grana (which is also produced in limited quantities in the valleys among the foothills of the Alps around Trento, the Val di Non in particular) are used in almost all first courses in Italy, other than fish dishes. In the south, too, there are exceptions, where Pecorino or salted ricotta is used instead.

❦ *Gorgonzola*: Historical records mention Gorgonzola as far back as the ninth century. Produced in particular in the country around Novara, in Piedmont, Gorgonzola is a cow's milk cheese streaked with greenish mold, somewhat similar to French Roquefort and English Stilton, with a very strong odor. Two versions are available commercially, one very strong and the other a little less so. Gorgonzola is an important ingredient in a few typically Italian dishes — for example crumbled and melted to sauce a plate of *gnocchi* or used to enrich fresh or baked polenta.

❦ *Fontina*: This is another cheese whose production is protected by strict rules. It is an artisan cheese, made in huts high up in the mountains from the milk of cows grazing on Alpine pastures above 3,000 feet (1,000 meters) in altitude. This is the classic cheese used in Piedmontese fondue — very fatty (45 per cent fat content) and firm in texture. It is much used in recipes that require a final high-heat in the oven, such as *polenta pasticciata*. It comes in large round shapes of about 18 inches (45 centimeters).

❦ *Castelmagno*: This very rare and delicious cow's milk cheese takes its name from the town of Castelmagno, a community consisting of scattered houses 5,100 feet (1,700 meters) above sea level in the Western Alps between Italy and France, not far from Cuneo. It is made in summer, when the herds move up to the highest pastures that are rich in grass and mountain wildflowers. The cheeses are left to ripen all winter, covered in straw, and are ready for consumption the following season. *Castelmagno* is a soft, firm, white cheese streaked with green, as is Gorgonzola, but much lighter in taste.

❦ *Taleggio*: A classic cheese from the Bergamo area, *Taleggio* is made in Valsassina and the neighboring valleys among the mountains that separate the Po plains and the Valtellina, east of Lake Como. Made in the shape of a rectangle not more than 2 to 3 inches (6 or 7 centimeters) high,

it ripens in about 2 to 3 months. It is a soft cheese with a high fat content and a red crust. It is a superb, lightly salted table cheese. It is a tradition in Bergamo to eat *Taleggio* at the end of a meal, accompanied by preserved fruits.

❦ *Asiago*: This is a semi-fat cheese that takes its name from the tableland to the north of Vicenza, near Veneto. The mild and dry climate of this area is ideal for the production of this cheese as it requires constant attention and cannot be made industrially. *Asiago* has been produced since the Middle Ages but has only become known outside Veneto in the twentieth century. It is made from cow's milk and is ready for consumption after only six months of ripening. Those who prefer a stronger taste should select examples that have been aged two or three times longer. *Asiago* is primarily a table cheese, although it is used in cooking to finish baked polenta dishes.

❦ *Pecorino*: There are several different types of Pecorino, which as the name indicates is made from sheep's milk (*pecora* means sheep). Various regions produce it and safeguard the quality by means of co-operatives that guarantee its origin. Thus there is a Tuscan Pecorino, a Sardinian Pecorino, a Roman Pecorino, and so on. All are basically similar, each cheese weighing about 6½ pounds (3 kilograms), and they are ready to eat after 6 to 18 months' ageing. Sardinian Pecorino is also used for grating when it is very mature and sharp. On the border between Romagna and the Marches, inland from Rimini, a unique Pecorino known as *formaggio di fossa* is made, ripened in large underground pits that

1. Parmigiano; 2. Asiago;
3. & 6. Provolone;
4. scamorze; 5. caciotta;
7. Gorgonzola;
8. Siciliano al pepe

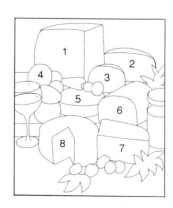

are filled to the top with straw and then hermetically sealed. In this way the cheese matures completely devoid of oxygen and acquires a very particular flavor. Worthy of separate mention are the Pecorinos produced in Sicily, where some varieties have black peppercorns or saffron added.

¶ *Scamorze*: These are small cheeses made from mixed cow's and goat's milk, typical of the mountain area of central Italy surrounding the city of L'Aquila. The villages here give their names to the different types of *scamorze*: Rivisondoli, Pescasseroli, Campotosto, Pescocostanzo and others. These cheeses are mature between three and six months.

¶ *Mozzarella*: This is the most famous Italian cheese after Parmesan, and certainly the most widespread of all fresh dairy products. Mozzarella was once restricted to the Naples area, but then its production spread throughout southern Italy, with local craftsmen producing a markedly superior product to the one achieved by the large-scale commercial cheesemakers. To find quality mozzarellas one must look in places like Aversa, Caserta, Capua, Salerno and Battipaglia. Especially sought after is the buffalo-milk mozzarella produced from buffaloes bred in the agricultural plains to the north and south of Naples. Magnificent mozzarellas and other cheeses meant to be eaten absolutely fresh are also produced in Apulia, the region with the greatest cheese choices. Anyone traveling to these parts has to taste the *Burrata*, an unforgettable soft cheese which must be eaten between 24 and 48 hours of being made.

¶ *Provolone*: There are several varieties of this hard, smooth cheese on the market, including a very good smoked version. Originally from the south of Italy, Provolone is now also produced in the northern country areas around Piacenza and Cremona. As well as being a table cheese it is often used in cooking, in layered fillings for macaroni pies, or broiled (grilled) in slices as a course by itself.

¶ *Caciocavallo*: This curious name does not mean the cheese is made from horse's milk, but relates to the fact that the cheeses are hung in pairs over a rod for the ageing period, hence "cheese on horseback." Caciocavallo has similar features to Provolone and is used in the same way.

¶ *Mascarpone*: A soft, creamy, almost sweet cheese, mascarpone has the consistency of very thick cream and does not keep well, which means it is generally used only in autumn and winter. With sugar and liqueur added, it becomes a light cream to serve with the Milanese *panettone*. Mixed with Gorgonzola, it makes a magnificent sauce for polenta, *gnocchi* or pasta.

¶ *Siciliano al pepe*: This cheese, also called *Pecorino Pepato* or *formaggio piacentino*, is made from sheep's milk to which the Sicilian cheesemakers at times add some goat's milk, to further enhance its characteristic flavor. The *Siciliano al pepe* comes in cylindrical shapes weighing from 2 to 55 or even 66 pounds (1 to 25–30 kilograms) each. The words *al pepe* (or *pepato*) in its name indicate that a generous quantity of *pepe* (pepper), in the form of whole black peppercorns, has been added during the preparation of the cheese, in order to contribute a pungent touch to the already sharp flavor of this delicacy. It was once commonly believed that *Siciliano al pepe* — consumed on its own as a table cheese or grated over some of the island's typical dishes — could act as a powerful aphrodisiac.

¶ *Caciotta*: The generic name *caciotta* (meaning "small cheese") is usually followed by another word indicating its origin. Normally *caciotta* is eaten when fresh: at this stage it combines a very pleasant and slightly "rubbery" texture with a flavor that is more delicate and mild than the one it will develop after a ripening period. In Lodi, the flourishing cheesemaking center near Milan, the *caciotta di Lodi* — made with cow's milk — weds a creamy texture to a mildly sour flavor. In other areas sea salt is added to the curdling milk to obtain *caciotta salata*. In Tuscany there are many varieties of *caciotta toscana*, produced by adding sheep's milk; the resultant cheeses have a firmer texture and a stronger flavor, further enhanced when the cheese matures. Goat's milk is used to produce tastier and sharper types of *caciotta*.

Opposite: Wine in Damigiane, Venice. Damigiane are big glass bottles (about 50 liters/11 gallons) with a straw covering. It is the common method of carrying and stocking the wine before bottling. RAY JOYCE

WINE

The first winemakers in history were the Egyptians, who cultivated wine in the delta of the Nile, crushed the grapes with their feet, strained the must and when it had fermented, stored it in terracotta jars. Subsequently the practice spread to Mesopotamia and later to Greece. Wine came to Italy relatively late. It was brought in by the Greeks when they colonized Sicily and spread from there throughout the peninsula.

❡ No other country in the world is as wine-rich as Italy. Elsewhere, in France and Spain for example, there are areas where wine is produced in quantity and others without a single bunch of grapes. In Italy every region has its wine. Some, like Piedmont, the Veneto and Tuscany, are great producers in terms of both quality and quantity; others are only medium producers, but there is always sufficient to ensure that each area has suitable wines to complement the local food. Often there are rare and genuine jewels. For a wine buff a trip around Italy can therefore be an exciting journey of discovery.

❡ In recent years Italy's wine production, with its age-old traditions, has seen substantial quality improvements, resulting from the adoption of the modern winemaking techniques and such ageing methods as transferring the wine to *barriques* or hogsheads, thus increasing the output considerably. Since a complete survey of Italian wines would require a volume in itself, we shall limit ourselves here to looking at the most important ones, divided according to region and the food they accompany.

PIEDMONT
Red wines
Barolo: Produced in thirteen areas of Piedmont including Barolo, La Morra, Verduno, Castiglione Falletto, Serralunga d'Alba, Monforte d'Alba and Novella, this wine is made from Nebbiolo grapes and is aged for at least three years, including two in oak casks. If it is more than four years old it has the right to the "reserve" label, and after five years it becomes "special reserve." A full-bodied, dry red with a velvety finish, it has an alcoholic

content of not less than 13 per cent, and is considered one of the great classic wines for drinking with big roasts and with game. The bottle should be opened at least six hours before drinking and kept at room temperature.

¶ *Barbaresco*: This wine takes its name from the town of Barbaresco, located near the city of Alba in Piedmont, in the center of the production area adjoining the one where Barolo is made. Like Barolo, it is made from Nebbiolo grapes. It has a shorter ageing period than its more aristocratic brother — a minimum of two years with one spent in oak casks. It is classed as "reserve" after three years and "special reserve" after four years, and has a minimum alcohol content of 12.5 per cent. This is a big red for drinking with game and roasts and with aged cheeses. It should be opened several hours before drinking.

¶ *Barbera*: Barbera is the name of a typically Italian species of vine, and there are various Barberas named after areas where they are produced. The best and most famous are those of Asti, Alba and Monferrato. The color is an intense ruby red and the bouquet intense and distinctly vinous, with an edge of bitterness in the taste. Alcohol content varies from 11.5 to 12 per cent, and average ageing time is two years. Barbera complements pork products, boiled meats, roasts, game and cheeses.

¶ *Dolcetto*: Like Barbera, the Dolcetto grape is cultivated in many wine producing areas, especially Piedmont (Acqui, Asti, Ovada), and the wines made from it acquire particular nuances according to local climatic and geological characteristics. A pleasant red wine to drink throughout the meal, Dolcetto goes particularly well with pork products, pasta (including filled pastas such as *agnolotti* or baked pasta pies), and white meats like lamb, kid, rabbit and chicken. It should be drunk young, one or two years old.

White wines

Moscato d'Asti Spumante: Made from Muscat grapes in a vast area of Piedmont covering the country around Asti, Cuneo and Alessandria, this straw-yellow wine has a persistent fine effervescence, a delicate bouquet and a sweet taste of considerable refinement. It is one of the famous Italian wines, served all over the world with cakes and desserts to end a meal.

LOMBARDY
Red wines

Franciacorta Rosso: Made from a combination of Cabernet Franc, Barbera, Nebbiolo and Merlot grapes, this wine comes from the Franciacorta area in the hills near Lake Iseo, between the cities of Bergamo and Brescia. Its color is a vivid red with violet tones, and its alcohol content is 11 per cent. Aged for at least a year, it is served with soups, pasta, risottos, meat and poultry dishes and cheeses.

¶ *Valcalepio Rosso*: This wine, made from a blend of Merlot and Cabernet Sauvignon grapes, and produced in the foothills of the Alps southeast of Bergamo, has an intense ruby red color with reflections of garnet. It should be aged for at least two years and is excellent with roasts and aged cheeses.

¶ *Oltrepo Pavese*: In the hills of provincial Pavia beyond the Po River some interesting reds are produced from Barbera, Bonarda and Crosatina grapes — in general, wines for drinking throughout the meal.

White wines

Franciacorta Pinot: This is an elegant wine obtained from Pinot Bianco grapes in the same area that produces Franciacorta Rosso. The same grape, either alone or blended with Pinot Noir and Chardonnay, provides the raw material for a particularly refined Spumante produced by fermentation in the bottle (*méthode champenoise*).

¶ *Lugana*: This is a fresh dry white which is made from Trebbiano grapes. It is pale gold in color and has a slight taste of saffron. It goes well with fish dishes.

VENETO, TRENTINO UPPER ADIGE, FRIULI VENEZIA GIULIA
Red wines

¶ *Bardolino*: This very famous wine from the country around Verona takes its name from a celebrated town on Lake Garda. There are two varieties, one light and rose-colored and the other a heavier sparkling ruby red wine with a minimum alcohol content of 10.5 per cent, for drinking young. A very pleasant wine to drink throughout the meal.

¶ *Cabernet*: There are many Cabernets, each

The annual grape harvest is the last flourish of summer — the culmination of the year's careful tending, watching and anticipation. It is the moment when you know how good next year's wine is going to be. APL/OLYMPIA/WALTER LEONARDI

linked to a restricted and protected production area, from the Colli Orientali of Friuli to Collio and Trentino. In a few cases the Cabernet grape is blended with a Sauvignon. Cabernet Franc is cultivated in Collio Goriziano. The wine is a strong ruby red with a minimum alcohol content of 12 per cent, and it is excellent with broiled (grilled) or roast meats, game and aged cheeses.

❡ *Merlot*: This wine is produced all through the wine-growing area of northeastern Italy, where the name is coupled with that of a particular area of production. Thus there are Merlot del Collio Goriziano, Merlot delle Grave del Friuli, Merlot del Trentino, Merlot del Piave and so on. This is a red wine suited to moderate ageing, alcohol content 11 per cent or slightly above, to be drunk with red and white meat.

❡ *Valpolicella*: This ruby red wine, produced over a very large area in the hills north of Verona, has a hint of almond fragrance. Like Bardolino, it goes well with everything, including white meats. The Valpolicella grapes are used in lightly dried

form to produce another illustrious wine, Rioto, in a slightly sweet dessert version, and another major version called Amarone for drinking with roasts and sharp cheeses.

White wines

Breganze Bianco: produced around Vicenza, near the village of Breganze, from Tocai grapes, this is a wine of great elegance, recommended for drinking with any fish dish.

❡ *Pinot Bianco*: From the Colli Berici in the Vicenza area to Trentino, from the Grave del Friuli to the Collio Goriziano, Pinot Bianco is one of the classic wines produced with excellent results, including a spumante version made by the *champenoise* method. The still wine goes with antipasto dishes, risottos, fresh seafood and fish dishes in general, while the spumante is a marvelous apéritif and may be drunk right through a light meal, especially where oysters or other shellfish are served as a starter.

❡ *Prosecco di Conegliano e Valdobbiadene*: This is a celebrated sparkling wine made from Prosecco grapes grown in the territory belonging to two towns to the north of Treviso. A limited production that is restricted to a small area of land and bears the name of the village of Cartizze is highly prized by connoisseurs. Prosecco is served cold and is perfect with seafood antipasto dishes, fish and shellfish.

❡ *Sauvignon*: This white wine with a soft fruity flavor, for drinking with fish, is produced in various areas and assumes the relative place name, as in the case of Tocai, Pinot and others.

❡ *Soave*: One of the most characteristic and best known of the Italian white wines, this one is produced outside Verona, around the village of Soave; it is straw-colored with greenish reflections and has a pleasant hint of bitterness in the taste. It is perfect with antipasto dishes, risottos and fish. Lightly dried grapes are used to make a Recioto di Soave, which in Verona is served with *pandoro* and yeast cakes in general.

❡ *Tocai*: This is the name of the grape cultivated all over northeastern Italy. There are many varieties of Tocai which take their names from the area where they are made: Tocai di Lison, Tocai del Piave, Tocai del Collio Goriziano, and so on. Their differences are related to the characteristics of the soil.

LIGURIA
White wines
Pigato: This is a very special white wine to go with fish, extremely elegant and much sought after, typical of the hilly interior of Liguria between Albenga and Imperia. Worth remembering are the Pigato from the Massaretti area near Albenga, and the one from Pieve di Teco.

❡ *Cinqueterre*: This wine comes from five villages (hence its name). It is a yellow-golden wine that has a slightly bitter taste. It is good served with gelato (ice cream).

TUSCANY
Red wines
Brunello di Montalcino: Produced in Montalcino outside Siena, this is a famous red wine of impressive lineage which benefits from long ageing. It must remain in wooden casks for at least four years.

❡ *Chianti*: This very famous name covers the wines produced in the Tuscan countryside around Florence, Siena, Arezzo, Pisa and Pistoia. A number of cooperatives exist to protect the geographic origins of the wines. Most famous of all is Chianti Classico, also known as Gallo Nero, followed by Chianti Putto. Made from a traditional blend of grapes, the wine has a ruby-red color that takes on orange reflections with age. When young, it can be drunk throughout a meal; when older, it goes with roasts and game.

CAMPANIA
Red wines
Taurasi: This is the finest southern wine to drink with roasts, and one of the best anywhere. It is made mainly at Atripalda, near Avellino, using Aglianico grapes grown in Taurasi and other neighboring villages.

White wines
Greco di Tufo: Also produced at Atripalda, this famous, elegant wine is for drinking with fish and cooked seafood in general.

SICILY
Red wines
Marsala: This exceptional wine, produced by the *solera* method used for sherry, is made around Marsala and Trapani on the west coast of Sicily. High in alcohol (17 per cent) it comes in a dry version that is superb as an apéritif and with *pâté de foie gras* or sharp aged cheeses, and a sweet one that is especially good with cookies and cakes.

SARDINIA
White wines
Vermentino: This is a distinctive, fragrant wine obtained from the grape of the same name, common to northern Sardinia and Liguria. There are two types, one made in Gallura and the other produced in larger quantities around Alghero. This is the preferred wine to drink with lobster and shellfish.

INDEX

ACKNOWLEDGMENTS

Weldon Russell Pty Ltd would like to thank the following people for their help with the production of this book:

Accoutrement Cook Shops; Appley Hoare Antiques; Barbeques Galore; The Bay Tree; Belinda's Corner Shop; Bohemia Crystal; Andrea Borghese for additional box text; Butler & Co.; Corso de Fiori; Country Floors; Country Road Homewares; Sandy De Beyer; Feature Cane; Paolo Guanori (Manager, Hotel Excelsior, Florence); Hale Imports Pty Ltd; IVV; Les Olivades; Oneida Silverware; The Parterre Garden; Fred Pazotti Pty Ltd; People's Behaviour; Royal Doulton Australia Pty Ltd; Villeroy and Boch (Australia) Pty Ltd; Waterford Wedgwood Australia Ltd; Woollahra Antiques Centre; Zyliss (Australia) Pty Ltd.

FOOD PHOTOGRAPHY

Carlo Cantini: pp. 24, 27, 30, 35, 46, 54, 69, 91, 96, 99, 102, 106, 108, 118–19, 134, 138, 146, 184–85, 186, 189, 199, 201, 202–203, 212–213, 237, 247.

Rowan Fotheringham (photographer) and Lucy Andrews (food stylist): page 164.

Rowan Fotheringham (photographer) and Carolyn Fienberg (food stylist): pp. title, 4–5, 23, 43, 44–45, 51, 56–57, 59, 61, 64–65, 67, 70–71, 77, 78, 81, 89, 93, 97, 100, 101, 105, 115, 116–117, 121, 122, 124–125, 126, 129, 130, 132, 133, 136, 139, 140, 141, 143, 147, 154, 156, 162–163, 166–167, 175, 177, 178, 179, 182, 187, 207, 210, 211, 229, 233, 240–241. Caroyln Fienberg's assistants: Donna Hay and Alex Slater.

Mike Hallson (photographer) and Jacki Passmore (food stylist): pp. 29, 36, 53.

André Martin (photographer) and Lucy Andrews (food stylist): pp. 26, 34, 37, 42, 49, 50, 52, 58, 62, 63, 68, 73, 74, 76, 79, 80, 83, 88, 90 (top and bottom), 94–95, 98, 103, 107, 109, 114, 145, 149, 158–59, 161, 169, 171, 172, 174, 176, 183, 188, 191, 195 (bottom), 198, 206, 209, 215, 217, 219, 225, 231, 235, 238. Lucy Andrews's assistants: Melanie Hickey and Tracey Rutherford.

Prima Press: pp. 20, 28, 32–33.

Gian Luigi Scarfiotti (photographer) and Fausto Monti (food stylist): pp. 6, 21, 75, 82, 157, 160, 165, 168, 173, 180, 190, 192, 194, 195 (top), 197, 226–227, 230, 232, 234, 239.

OVEN TEMPERATURE CONVERSIONS		
° Celsius	° Fahrenheit	Gas Mark
110°C	225°F	¼
130	250	½
140	275	1
150	300	2
170	325	3
180	350	4
190	375	5
200	400	6
220	425	7
230	450	8
240	475	9